Elementary Teachers Guide (for children ages 6-8)
Corresponds to the second year of a 3 year cycle of Sunday School lessons for Elementary Children.

TEACHER
Year 2

Published by:
Mesoamerica Region Discipleship Ministries
http://discipleship.mesoamericaregion.org/
www.SdmiResources.MesoamericaRegion.org

© 2018 - All rights reserved
All rights reserved

ISBN:978-1-63580-118-7

Category: Christian Education

Translated from Spanish to English by: Monte Cyr

Unless otherwise stated, all the Bible references are taken from the NIV version.

Reproduction of this material is permitted only for use in the local church.

Table of Contents

Helps for the Teacher — 4
  Lesson development — 4
  Suggestions for Bible Memorization — 5
  The Students, Their Behavior And The Teacher — 6
  Get to know the Elementary Student — 7

Christian education material for children — 8

Teaching Resources — 9

The importance of Students advancing in Sunday School — 11

Certificate of Sunday School promotion — 12

Unit I: WOMEN OF FAITH AND COURAGE — 13
  Lesson 1: Jochebed — 14
  Lesson 2: Debora Trusts in God — 17
  Lesson 3: Ruth is faithful — 20

Unit II: THE BIBLE TEACHES US HOW TO MAKE DECISIONS — 23
  Lesson 4: Solomon makes a wise decision — 24
  Lesson 5: Andrew decides to help Peter — 27
  Lesson 6: Mary and Martha decide to serve Jesus — 30
  Lesson 7: A wise steward makes a good decision — 32
  Lesson 8: Daniel Chooses healthy food — 34
  Lesson 9: A rich man makes a bad decision — 37

Unit III: THE HOLY LOVE OF GOD — 39
  Lesson 10: Wrong decisions — 40
  Lesson 11: Painful results — 43
  Lesson 12: Our God of love and mercy — 45
  Lesson 13: Our God of justice and grace — 47
  Lesson 14: Our God of forgiveness — 50

Unit IV: WE CELEBRATE HOLY WEEK — 53
  Lesson 15: We celebrate Jesus' triumphant entry! — 54
  Lesson 16: We celebrate Jesus' resurrection! — 56
  Lesson 17: The Emmaus Road — 59
  Lesson 18: Jesus is always with us! — 62

Unit V: THE CHURCH GROWS — 64
  Lesson 19: The Church starts to grow — 65
  Lesson 20: The Church needs helpers — 68
  Lesson 21: The Church is persecuted — 70
  Lesson 22: The Church shows God's love — 73

Unit VI: THE GREAT COMMISSION — **75**
- Lesson 23: The Great Commission — 76
- Lesson 24: Peter talks about Jesus to Cornelius — 78
- Lesson 25: The Church sends Paul and Barnabas — 81
- Lesson 26: Offerings for the mission — 83

Unit VII: GREAT STORIES OF GOD'S POWER — **85**
- Lesson 27: God is in control — 86
- Lesson 28: God rescues His people — 88
- Lesson 29: God honors Naaman's obedience — 91
- Lesson 30: God's invisible army — 94
- Lesson 31: God is patient and forgiving — 96
- Lesson 32: God is more powerful than the fiery furnace — 99

Unit VIII: JESUS TEACHES US TO PRAY — **102**
- Lesson 33: Jesus prays before deciding — 103
- Lesson 34: Jesus teaches his disciples to pray — 105
- Lesson 35: Jesus prays for others — 107
- Lesson 36: Jesus prays when he is sad — 110

Unit IX: THE BIBLE — **112**
- Lesson 37: The Bible is God's special book — 113
- Lesson 38: The Bible tells us about Jesus — 116
- Lesson 39: The Bible helps us do the right thing — 118
- Lesson 40: The Bible teaches us every day — 120

Unit X: THE POWER OF JESUS — **122**
- Lesson 41: Jesus heals the two blind men — 123
- Lesson 42: Jesus shows that he is the Son of God — 125
- Lesson 43: Jesus defeats temptation — 128
- Lesson 44: Jesus visits Zacchaeus — 131

Unit XI: A FAMILY CHOSEN BY GOD — **133**
- Lesson 45: God calls Abraham — 134
- Lesson 46: Abraham lets Lot choose first — 136
- Lesson 47: Abraham believes in God — 138
- Lesson 48: A wife for Isaac — 140
- Lesson 49: Isaac the peace keeper — 142

Unit XII: THE GOOD NEWS OF CHRISTMAS — **144**
- Lesson 50: Good News for Zechariah and Elizabeth — 145
- Lesson 51: Good News for Mary and Joseph — 148
- Lesson 52: Good News for the shepherds — 150
- Lesson 53: Good News for Simeon and Anna — 153

HELPS FOR THE TEACHER

I. GENERAL ASPECTS OF THE LESSON AND THE UNIT
INTRODUCTION TO EACH UNIT
In it you will find the biblical basis for the whole unit, the biblical references, the lesson purpose, the titles of the lessons and the reasons why the students need the teaching of the unit.

EACH LESSON CONTAINS:
Biblical References

Points out the biblical passage from which the lesson was taken. It can refer to one or more books or passages of the Bible. You must read the passage(s) and become familiar with them.

Lesson Objective

It clarifies where you should go with your students and what you should achieve through the teaching and learning process.

Memory Verse

It is considered more appropriate to use a single bible verse for the whole unit, with the purpose of emphasizing the central truth.

II. PREPARE YOURSELF TO TEACH!
PREPARE YOURSELF TO TEACH!
This second section presents a help for the biblical study passage, which will expand your knowledge on the subject. It also includes a biblical context and the way in which children of this age learn. For greater effectiveness, take into account the following:
- Pray and ask for God's direction.
- Read the Bible passage several times and write down in a notebook the central ideas you find.
- Consult other versions of the Bible, biblical commentaries, biblical dictionaries, etc.
- Compare your ideas with those presented in this book.
- Meditate on each of them, and reflect on how the passage applies to your own life and the lives of your students.

III. DEVELOPMENT OF THE LESSON
Here the different points of the lesson's development are identified. The Bible story must be presented with methods in which your students are actively participating. Be sure that the key points are clear in the minds of the children. You can practice the presentation of the theme in your home to be at ease in front of the students. Cheer up! The work is of the Lord, and you are an instrument in His hands to carry it out.

Bible story and Application for life
This is the moment for the student to reflect on his daily life. It is time to guide him to ask how his life is compared to what the Bible teaches. In general, these are activities with questions to answer in a personal way. Direct the child towards reflection and do not manipulate their answers, since these must be sincere and personal.

IV. ACTIVITIES
a. In this section you will find another series of reinforcement activities for the lesson, such as tasks on the activity sheets and games.
b. Memorization of the text, games.
c. To Finish: moments of prayer and reflection.

Suggestions:
- Keep in mind that it is best to prepare your lesson throughout the week, giving God's Holy Spirit opportunities to teach you, give you illustrations for the lesson, etc.
- Visit your students at least once every semester.
- Pray and communicate with your students through letters, texts, phone calls, invitations, etc. Be sure to quickly contact them/visit them if they miss a class.
- Send a note to the student and / or parents and mention special facts in the student's life, such as birthdays, special days, etc.

- Encourage your students through contests to motivate them to attend, learn, memorize verses, invite their friends, etc.
- Arrive early to be sure you have the room ready for the class.
- When preparing lessons, take into account the age, needs and problems of elementary kids.
- As the teacher, you are also a friend, counselor and Christian model worth imitating.

SUGGESTIONS FOR BIBLE MEMORIZATION

1. WHAT DOES THE VERSE SAY?

Have your students express what the verse says by using their senses.

See
- In the Bible.
- Visual Aids: on the chalk/white board, signs, posters, flashcards, etc.

Hear
- Read it out loud.
- Record it and play it back.

Speak
- Repeat it after listening to it.
- Read it together and individually.
- Sing it.

Touch
- Write the verse.
- Fill in the blank.
- Solve a crossword
- Use hand motions

2. WHAT DOES IT MEAN?

Explore the definitions.
- Let the kids express what they understand about each Bible verse.
- Explain words they don't understand.

Discuss the context.
- For more explanation, use Bible commentaries, dictionaries and other resources.
- Investigate the background of the verse.
- Who is speaking and to whom are they speaking?

Illustrate it.
- Show pictures/illustrations of the text.
- Create your own drawings.
- Use hand motions, sign language or act it out.

3. HOW DO I APPLY IT TO MY LIFE?

Discuss the following:
- The daily life application of this verse.
- In which circumstances will it be useful and what effect will it have on your life and others' lives.

Remember a Bible verse:
- When you are being tempted.
- When you are troubled.
- When you want to encourage others.

The Students, Their Behavior And The Teacher

1. **Understand Your Students and Allow For Normal Behavior.**
   - Children are active and curious.
   - They are not miniature adults: we must always differentiate between bad behavior and immaturity.

2. **Create An Atmosphere That Promotes Good Behavior.**
   - Let children know that you love them and appreciate them.
   - Show interest in what happens to them outside of class.
   - Be organized in how you handle the students.
   - Provide clear and consistent guidelines; let the children know what you expect of them.
   - Don't show favoritism.

3. **Acknowledge Your Position As A Teacher.**
   - Be in charge of the class.
   - Be a figure of authority that students can follow.
   - Become a friend to your students.
   - Explain to them what is expected of them and give them good examples.

4. **Use Methods That Involve the Children and Capture Their Interest.**
   - Be prepared and get to the classroom before any of the children.
   - Provide a variety of activities that are appropriate for your students' ages.
   - Use activities that capture their interest and ability.
   - Allow children to choose some of the activities.

5. **Focus on Positive Behavior.**
   - Limit the number of rules.
   - When you correct a child, discuss it with their parent, guardian, or the person responsible for them.

WHAT DO YOU DO WHEN A CHILD MISBEHAVES?

1. **Find the Cause of the Problem.**
   - Does the child have learning or medical problems that prevent their participation in class?
   - Does he try to control the class?
   - Is he academically talented and therefore bored with the class?
   - When you know the cause of the problem, you may be able to correct it after talking with the child's parents.

2. **Take Control of the Situation.**
   - Ignore behavior that doesn't interrupt the class.
   - Include the child in learning activities.
   - Let him see that you are observing his misconduct.
   - Approach the child in a loving manner.
   - Tell the child, quietly, what you want him to do.
   - Teach students the consequences of continued misconduct.

3. Talk to Parents or the Person Responsible for the Child.
- If you know that you will most likely have to talk to his parents or guardian, do it, don't delay.
- Start by telling the parents what you appreciate about their child.
- State the problem and ask for their ideas of how to resolve the problem..

GET TO KNOW THE ELEMENTARY STUDENT
- They are very active, and are fine-tuning their muscle coordination.
- Their ability to count, paint, paste, cut and fold are improving progressively.
- Their reasoning is based on previous experiences or interaction with concrete objects.
- They learn more by doing than by watching.
- They seek approval from adults and their peers.
- They value justice, and do not understand when the rules change.
- They have basic skills (reading, writing, organizing, classifying) developed enough to achieve objectives.
- They are learning the concepts of time, space and distance.
- Companionship is very important. At this age they care more about being accepted by their peers than by adults.
- They are learning to know the perspectives of other people and recognize that a problem can have several solutions.

Considering the characteristics of the development stage of your students, we include some tips to improve the dynamics of your class:
- Use visual aids, illustrations and varied examples to help them understand abstract ideas.
- Establish firm standards.
- Guide the discussions with questions that help them understand the concept, and use examples to illustrate it.
- Plan some activities to work in small groups.
- Ask students to give you ideas to plan projects to help members of the church and the community, and to participate in them. Emphasize the importance of missions work.
- Provide opportunities for them to discuss and think about moral issues. Present open ended stories for them to complete and make decisions.

Christian Education material for children

Mesoamerica Region Discipleship Ministries presents with satisfaction its complete collection of Christian education (Sunday School) books.

They were designed for teachers of children and for students from 4 to 11 years of age.

Children will learn the lessons of the Bible according to their age. And, by the end of their elementary school years, they will have gone through the challenging biblical stories, as well as various topics appropriate to each stage of their childhood and pre-adolescence.

This material was designed as different steps to achieve a holy life. It contains clear and possible goals.

The teacher's book will help equip those who have the beautiful task of leading children to connect with the message that will change their lives forever.

By promoting the child to the next year-according to his age-he will have studied only once each of the books. When he reaches 12 years of age - if he started with the first book - he will have studied the eight books of this valuable collection.

The books are designed to be used in Sunday school classes, happy hours, Saturday Bible schools, children's clubs, discipleship classes, and schools in general.

This series aims to:
a. Challenge the children to learn the Word of God.
b. Encourage them to grow in their Christian experience as children of God.
c. Guide them to accept Jesus as their savior and Lord.
d. Help them grow in their faith
e. Help them become part of the faith community, the church.

The following table will help you identify the corresponding book according to the age of the students:

- Preschoolers:4 and 5 years old (Year / book 1 and 2).
- Elementary:6, 7, 8 years of age (Year / book 1, 2 and 3).
- Words of Life (preadolescents):9, 10, 11 years of age (Year / book 1, 2 and 3).

Teaching Resources

Dear Teacher:

We have prepared a series of teaching resources that will improve the dynamic of your class. Each lesson has an activities section, please use the materials below to encourage your students to use their motor skills as well as help them gain a deeper understanding of the lesson. Prepare extra activities and crafts for the kids who visit your class.

RECIPES

Recipes for Play Dough or Molding Clay

Flour and Salt Dough
Ingredients:
2 or 3 Cups of Flour
¾ Cup Fine Salt
½ Cup Warm Water
Food Coloring

Instructions:
Mix the flour with the salt and add the warm water little by little as you stir. If you want it to be colorful, add drops of food coloring as it thickens. The consistency of the dough will depend on the amount of water you add. Store in a closed container in the fridge.

Cooked Dough
Ingredients:
2 Cups of Flour
1 Cup Salt
1 Tablespoon Vegetable Oil
2 Teaspoons
Food Coloring

Instructions:
Mix the dry ingredients and then add the water and the vegetable oil. Cook the mix over low heat until it thickens, stirring it constantly. Take it off the heat and let it cool. To make it the color you want, add drops of food coloring while you mix the dough. If kept in a closed container, it should last for over a month.

Mud Dough
Ingredients:
2 Cups of Dirt
2 Cups of Sand
½ Cup of Salt
Water

Instructions:
Mix the dirt, sand, and salt, and then add water a little at a time until you get a consistency that is good for molding.

Finger Paint
Ingredients:
1 ¼ Cup Corn Starch
½ Cup Powdered Soap
3 Cups Boiling Water
1 Tablespoon Glycerin
Food Coloring

Instructions:
Dissolve the starch in cold water. Pour it into the warm water slowly as you stir to avoid clumps. Add the soap and the glycerin. To add color, use food coloring. This recipe is not toxic. If stored in plastic cups, it should last several days.

White Glue
Ingredients:
4 Cups Water
1 Cup Wheat Flour
½ Cup Sugar
½ Cup Vinegar

Instructions:
Boil 3 cups of water. Meanwhile in a container, mix one cup of water and the flour, sugar, and vinegar. When the water starts to boil, add the mix and stir slowly over the heat. If there are clumps, stir it more. If it's too thick, add water. If it's too thin, boil it for longer. Store in a jar with a lid.

PAPER FOR CARDS AND CRAFTS
1. Soak 6 sheets of paper or pages from a magazine torn into small pieces in hot water.
2. Put it in the blender with half a cup of oatmeal or flowers or vegetables such as carrots or celery.
3. Strain the mixture and add 4 tablespoons of glycerin and 6 tablespoons white glue.
4. Spread the paste on a plastic sheet/tray with a rolling pin or stick until thin and even.
5. Let it dry in the sun for two days.
6. You can use this paper to make cards, bookmarks, letters, etc.

THE IMPORTANCE OF STUDENTS ADVANCING IN SUNDAY SCHOOL

Dear Leader and Sunday School Teacher;

As in school, children in our church Sunday Schools should be able to be promoted to a higher level of Sunday School. As a classroom teacher, it is very important that you be prepared to promote the students at the end of the church year or, at the end of the school year - whichever is easiest. To accomplish this, talk to the Sunday School Superintendent of your church or your pastor.

You can prepare in advance a "ceremony" and give a certificate (included in this book) to each child passing to the next class. The ceremony can be performed in the sanctuary for all the congregation to participate in. Invite parents and relatives of the children. This will be a good time for them to get to know and attend the rest of the service and hear the Word of God.

It is important to have teachers of the classes that the children are graduating from, as well as entering into as special participants in the ceremony. It will be a special time for them to say good bye to their present teacher with a hug, and for the teacher of the next class to welcome them to their new class with a hug. At the ceremony, you can present a card decorated with photos of the children that have been taken during the year. It can include some memories of the child's participation while he was in class, Special prayers they said, the date in which they gave their testimony, questions that they asked, and moments of joy experienced in the class. Prepare the child in advance, so they are not surprised in front of the entire congregation.

Talk to the Sunday School Superintendent so that at the ceremony the new Sunday School book for the following year can be given to the student(s).You can encourage the families of the church to give a book to each child (as if they were the godparents), especially the children whose parents do not attend church or are at an economic disadvantage. In every congregation there are adults whose children are already adults who would gladly participate by giving a book to a child who attends Sunday School.

It is understandable if, because of a lack of teachers, it is not possible to have classes for every age group. This however is a good reason to invite and bring more children to church, and also to prepare and train new teachers. In every congregation there are always teenagers that are eager to learn how to teach a class. Do not miss this opportunity!

We wish you the richest blessings in the challenges that the ministry of education presents to you and your congregation.

In Christ and His Ministry,

Discipleship Ministries

Sunday School Certificate

_____
(Child's Name)

Is Promoted to the Next Level *Sunday School Class*

Church:

Date:

"My son, pay attention to what I say…" Proverbs 4:20a

_____
Sunday School Superintendent

_____
Teacher

WOMEN OF FAITH AND COURAGE

Biblical References: Exodus 1:8-10, 22; 2:1-10; Judges 4, 5; Ruth 1-4.

Unit Memory Verse: *"My help comes from the Lord, the Maker of heaven and earth"* (Psalm 121:2).

UNIT OBJECTIVES
This unit will help the elementary students to:

- ❖ Know that God works through his faithful servants.
- ❖ Recognize that God intervenes when situations are out of control.
- ❖ Trust in the power of God, even when it is difficult to understand His will.

UNIT LESSONS
Lesson 1: Jochebed
Lesson 2: Deborah trusts in God
Lesson 3: Ruth is faithful

WHY ELEMENTARY STUDENTS NEED THE TEACHING OF THIS UNIT:

Elementary students are beginning to experience a certain degree of independence. They are growing up and have new experiences and responsibilities: they go to school, their parents allow them to walk or bike longer distances, spend more time with their friends without parental supervision, etc.

Despite this new freedom and independence, they need to feel security and stability. When they find themselves in difficult situations or in unfamiliar places, the world may seem too big and frightening. By exploring in this unit the story of these celebrated women of the Bible, your students will discover that God is powerful and, at the same time, a trustworthy friend.

No matter how difficult the situation they face, God has everything under His control.

Lesson 1
Jochebed

Biblical References: Exodus 1:8-10, 22; 2:1-10

Lesson Objective: That the students know that God has every situation under control, no matter how difficult it is.

Memory Verse: *"My help comes from the Lord, the Maker of heaven and earth"* (Psalm 121:2).

PREPARE YOURSELF TO TEACH!

Elementary students like to feel that everything is under control. At this stage of their development, emotional stability is very important. Therefore, knowing that God is in control in all circumstances will give them strength and tranquility.

Explain in a simple way what it means to trust in God. We can trust him because he is our friend and he wants to have a close relationship with us. Like Jochebed and Moses, the children of God face difficult situations and sometimes suffering. But it is important to know that God knows what is happening to us and has control over everything. Learning to trust in God is a big step in the spiritual growth of your students. Infuse in them the assurance that we have an almighty God on our side.

BIBLICAL COMMENTARY

The Israelites were in Egypt around 400 years. As the Hebrew people were increasing, the Egyptians decided to make them slaves. Also, fearing that they would rebel and try to seize the country, Pharaoh planned to control their increase by killing all the baby boys. So he ordered his officers to throw them into the Nile River.

At that time, Jochebed, a Levite woman, gave birth to her third child. Her daughter Miriam was then 10 or 11 years old, and Aaron was 3.

After hiding her baby for three months, Jochebed and her husband developed a plan to save the baby's life. She made a basket with rushes, and with great care sealed it with tar so that the water would not penetrate it. Then she put her son inside, took the basket to the Nile River and left it there.

Perhaps Jochebed knew that Pharaoh's daughter regularly went down to the river at that time and would find the baby. So it was. The princess found the basket and, although she knew that the child was a Hebrew, she felt sorry for him.

The story tells us that Miriam stayed close by, observing the scene, and did not hesitate to offer her mother's services as the baby's wet nurse. The princess would pay Jochebed to raise her own son!

As an adopted son of Pharaoh's family, Moses received the best education and military training of the time. He possessed power, fame and prestige. But before that, God gave Jochebed the opportunity to instill in Moses the traditions and religion of the Hebrew people.

Jochebed's role in instructing Moses in his childhood is fundamental to understanding the love he felt for his countrymen. Moses did not forget his Hebrew heritage, even though he was immersed in Egyptian culture.

Jochebed did not know what would happen to her baby when she left him by the banks of the Nile. She only knew that God would take care of him. And by faith she obeyed God, and trusted in His divine provision. The situation she was going through was beyond her control, but she was sure that God would keep His promises.

DEVELOPMENT OF THE LESSON

Choose some of the following activities to focus the attention of the students on the subject of study.

Introduction

Since this is the first lesson of the year, it is important that you relate to your students and make them feel welcome to the class. Give them time to get to know each other and become familiar with you. Explain the rules they must follow in the classroom, and pray together before the class begins.

Women of faith and courage

Look in magazines for pictures of women who perform different activities (work, cook, take care of their children, etc.). Stick them on a large piece of paper or cardboard.

Show the mural to the group, and ask for some volunteers to say what each illustration represents. Use this activity as a starting point to present the introduction to the unit. Tell them that during the next three lessons, they will study the story of three brave women of the Bible.

What is a hero?

For this activity you will need cardboard or card stock, scissors, colored markers and adhesive tape.

Before the class write the word HERO on the cardboard. Cut it out letter by letter, and hide the letters in different parts of the room. At this point of the lesson, ask your students to look for them. When you find them, ask them to put the word together, and then stick it in a visible place.

Ask them: *What is a hero?* (Someone who performs courageous acts to help people.)

Can you mention some? (If they mention science fiction or cartoon characters, clarify that although they are famous, they do not belong to the real world.)

Emphasize that heroes are real people, such as missionaries, firefighters, police officers, and especially, the characters in the Bible. Show them illustrations of biblical characters, or ask them to mention the heroes they remember, and write them down on the board.

Tell them: *All the biblical heroes we know had something in common: they trusted in the power of God. During these lessons we will study the story of three women who relied on God's care and protection.*

BIBLE STORY

Before the lesson, get a basket, a doll and a blanket or sheet to cover it. Encourage the children to hold and rock the baby. Ask them to treat it with love when it's their turn to take care of it.

Tell them that in the Bible story they will hear about a baby whose mother put him in a basket.

Remember that when you use illustrations to visualize the subject of the class, children focus their attention more easily. Get some pictures about the story, or draw them using drawings or clippings. You can also use the basket and the baby as illustrations while telling the story.

Jochebed saves her son

"What a beautiful baby!" said Jochebed softly when her third child was born. Jochebed and her husband were Hebrews and lived as slaves in Egypt. Since the Egyptian Pharaoh was not happy that there were so many Hebrews in his country, he had made them be slaves.

One day the evil Pharaoh thought, "There are still too many Hebrews." So he ordered his officers: "As soon as a Hebrew boy child is born, go through it in the Nile River to drown!"

After the baby was born, Jochebed said crying, "We must hide our baby. We can not allow the Egyptians to kill him."

Jochebed and her family hid the baby Moses for three months. But babies grow and, as time goes by, they get bigger and noisier. "What can we do to save our son?" they asked.

Jochebed thought and prayed.

One day she told her family, "I have a plan! Help me pick up papyrus canes to make a basket. Then we will cover it with tar so that the water does not enter it. The basket will be like a boat for our baby."

Everyone in the house helped. Miriam and her little brother of three years, Aaron, collected all the canes that their mother needed. Jochebed's husband got tar. Thus, she made a basket with the canes, and then she covered it well with the materials that her husband had obtained.

"Son, I must put you in the basket," said Jochebed in a soft voice as she put baby Moses inside.

"Miriam, come with me," she said to her daughter, and the two of them went silently to the river.

"Please, keep watch behind these plants," Jochebed said to Miriam as she very carefully put the basket in the river. How hard it must have been for her to leave the baby in the basket in the water! How brave she was to trust that God would take care of her baby!

"What do I do if someone approaches the river?" Miriam wondered after her mother left. She was watching the basket in which her little brother floated quietly in the river. "Little brother, please do not cry," the girl whispered.

"Oh no! Who's coming?" Miriam thought, listening to women talking and laughing. "It's the princess with her servants. Surely they have come to the river to bathe. What should I do?"

"What is that?" the princess asked, pointing to the basket. "Bring it to me," she ordered one of her servants.

"It's a baby!" she exclaimed as she opened the basket. "Look, it's a Hebrew child! Poor baby!" aid the princess as she rocked him in her arms. "I'll have him stay with me!"

Miriam knew what she had to do, so she ran quickly to the princess and said, "Would you like me to look for a Hebrew woman to take care of your baby?"

"Of course," said the princess.

Guess who Miriam found for her ... the baby's own mother ... Jochebed!

"Take care of this baby and I'll pay you," the princess told Jochebed.

Thus, the baby Moses could stay with his family for some years. They taught him about God and the traditions of his people.

"The time has come for our son to go to the palace to live with the princess," said Jochebed, while packing some belongings.

"I'll call him Moses, because I got him out of the water," said the princess. "He is my son and I will give him the best possible education."

Biblical review

Use the following questions to reinforce biblical learning and stimulate group participation. If you wish, give a prize to those who respond correctly.

- What brave act did Jochebed do? (She hid her baby in a basket and left it in the river).
- How would Jochebed have felt when she left the baby in the river? (Surely she did not want to leave him, fearing that something might happen to him.)
- In what way was God's power manifested when Jochebed was not in control of the situation? (God cared for the baby and allowed the princess to find him.)
- How can we know that God is in control of situations? (By remembering how God cared for and protected other people, like Jochebed, or our parents and grandparents.)

ACTIVITIES

The Jochebed basket

Distribute the student worksheets for lesson 1. Explain the instructions for the craft: Cut out the canes following the lines marked. Then, starting with the second cane, bend and cut one cane and not the next, so that there is a space between one cane and another. Fold the sheet along the dotted line. Roll the reeds around a pencil to give the figure greater dimension. It is important that you guide your students step by step during the development of this activity.

God is in control

Tell them go to the next page. Provide crayons or colored pencils.

Talk with the children about times when everything seems to be out of control in our lives. Remind them that despite the difficult circumstances, God is in control of everything.

Ask them to draw a picture that shows that even in a difficult situation, they can be brave, because God is with them. Ask some volunteers to explain what they drew. Remind them that we are not brave because of our character, but because we trust that God is sovereign and powerful in all circumstances.

Memorization

To teach the memorized text of this unit, write the words of Psalm 121:2 on a poster board or on the board. Read it together a couple of times. Then, erase a word and reread it; delete a second word and say it, and so on until the board is blank and the students can say the whole memory verse.

Hand out the Verse of the Month Club cards to take home and review the verse during the week.

To end

Encourage your students to attend class each week. Prepare a plan to reward or recognize children who, during a certain period, do not miss class and are punctual.

We also suggest that you have a clearly visible place to write down prayer requests and answers. Thus they will exercise the habit of prayer.

Ask your students if they have requests. Intercede for each one, so that they know that you care about them and entrust them into the hands of God.

Before saying goodbye, repeat the verse to memorize.

If possible, contact the parents of your students and request their information to create a class directory. This will be very useful during the year.

Lesson 2
Deborah Trusts in God

Biblical References: Judges 4—5
Lesson Objective: That the students learn to trust in God and obey Him even if it's difficult.
Memory Verse: *"My help comes from the Lord, the Maker of heaven and earth"* (Psalm 121:2).

PREPARE YOURSELF TO TEACH!

Most children of this age often worry. If they do not have a real problem, they worry about something that could happen: "What if a thief goes into my house? What if I fall in front of my friends and they laugh at me?"

The story of Deborah will help your students develop their trust in God. We should not be afraid, because God is in control of all situations. He does not ask us to be perfect, only that we have confidence and obey him.

Your students need to be constantly encouraged, reminded that God loves them. When they learn to put their trust in God, he helps them to be brave. They may not always feel prepared to face difficult situations, for Barak was also afraid to go to battle without Deborah. However, they can trust that God will help them and give them courage in all circumstances.

BIBLICAL COMMENTARY

Judges 4-5. The book of Judges tells us about the history of Israel, from the death of Joshua until before the reign of Saul.

During that time, the people of God were governed by judges. Debora, the fourth of the twelve judges mentioned in this book, stands out as the only prophetess to whom reference is made in the story.

The story we read in the book of Judges is cyclical, because events repeat themselves: Israel falls into idolatry and disobedience; God allows Israel to be attacked by neighboring nations; the people cry out for divine help; and God, in his mercy, helps the Israelites and rescues them.

The Canaanites had oppressed Israel for 20 years when God chose Deborah and Barak to fight against them. God chose those servants and gave victory to the Hebrews, humiliating Sisera and his army.

DEVELOPMENT OF THE LESSON

Use some of the suggested activities to enrich the learning process of your class.

Who is brave?

In advance, look for illustrations of biblical characters that your students know. While they are looking, ask them:

Which of these characters proved to be brave and why?

Listen to the answers. Then complement them by explaining that each of the characters was brave because he trusted God and obeyed Him. It is important that they learn to trust in the Lord, and not in their own abilities when facing difficult situations.

Who runs our church?

For this activity you will need white paper, and crayons or colored markers.

Hand out the materials and ask your class:

- What is a leader? (A person who is in charge and responsible for a group, someone who makes decisions, an example that others must follow, someone with authority and influence, etc.).

- Who is the leader of our church? (They may mention the pastor or the Sunday School teacher).

- Do you think that in our church there are leaders who are women? (Mention some of them.)

Ask your students to draw the women leaders of their local church, and in each drawing, write a phrase that mentions the name of the person and the role she plays.

As you work, remind them: *God uses all who are faithful and obey Him, no matter how big, strong or intelligent they may be. He does not care if they are men or women, boys or girls, what He really wants are willing hearts to serve Him even in the midst of difficulties.*

Although it is very difficult

Divide the class into two teams. Set up an "obstacle course" in your class room using chairs, tables and other objects at hand.

The two teams must go through the course, obeying the different instructions (for example: walk on tiptoe, jump forward, jump forward on one foot, etc.). Avoid asking them to do something that could cause injuries or put them in danger.

When they finish, ask them to sit down. Explain that it is often difficult to obey (for example: when we have to do something that we dislike or the circumstances are complicated).

Today's Bible story is about a person who obeyed and was brave in the midst of a very difficult situation.

BIBLE STORY

A special visit

Invite a woman from your congregation to visit your class and talk about her ministry and its functions. Explain to your guest that your class is studying the theme of "Women of faith and courage." Ask her to talk a little about her Christian experience. If you wish, provide the study material in advance and allow her to tell the story.

Deborah is brave

It had been many years since the day when Jochebed left the baby Moses inside a basket on the Nile River. Moses grew up and became a strong man, and helped the people of God to leave the land of Egypt. After Moses died, Joshua, his assistant, led the Israelites to Canaan, the land God had promised them.

The people of God had lived in Canaan for many years. For a time they obeyed God, and enjoyed prosperity in their new land. But unfortunately, later they began to disobey Him again and again. Finally, God decided to punish them. For this, he allowed the king of an enemy people to attack them.

Sisera, the captain of that king's army, had 900 iron chariots, nine hundred! The Israelites did not have iron or chariots. Sisera was cruel to the Israelites and treated them like slaves. Then once again, the Israelites cried out to God for help.

The Israelites went to speak with Deborah, a judge and prophetess, to intervene in this problem. Maybe she could help them deal with the situation. Deborah listened to the people and said, "Please, bring Barak."

When Barak arrived, Deborah said to him, "The Lord, the God of Israel, wants you to take 10,000 men to Mount Tabor. You must lead the army. I will get Sisera to go with his chariots and troops to the stream of Kishon. You and your 10 thousand men will fight against them."

But, Barak was afraid and said, "Deborah, I can not go alone. I need you to go with me."

"Very good," Debora said. "I will go with you, but this is not what God commanded, since you insist that I go with you, the glory of the battle will not be yours. The Lord will deliver Sisera into the hands of a woman."

Deborah and Barak gathered 10 thousand Israelites and went to Mount Tabor. When Sisera heard that they were going to that place, he gathered his 900 chariots and marched towards the stream of Kishon.

Then Deborah said to Barak, "Attack! Today the Lord has given Sisera into your hands. God goes before you."

Barak and his 10,000 men descended from the mountain to the army of Sisera. But do you know what happened? God took control of the situation. When the army of

Sisera began to attack, the 900 chariots had serious problems. God caused the valley of Kishon to be flooded, and the wagons were stuck in the mud!

When Sisera saw that the chariots could not advance, he got out of his chariot and ran as fast as he could. He was the only one of his entire army that could escape from Barak and the Israelite army.

Sisera ran to the tent of a woman named Jael and begged her, "Hide me!"

When Barak found Sisera in Jael's tent, he was dead.

That day God helped the Israelites win the battle against the Canaanites. The Israelites became an increasingly strong people.

ACTIVITIES

Deborah trusts in God

Distribute the student worksheets, colored paper, scissors and glue.

Before class, cut out triangles of brown paper, which will represent the mountains. You can also cut strips of blue paper to simulate the sky.

Ask the children to cut out the figures on the worksheet and paste them on a sheet or card, as if it were a stage. Then, give them time to decorate using colored paper or some other material within reach, such as colored pencils or crayons.

As they work, review the Bible story with them. Encourage them to be brave, even in difficult situations.

Memorization

On paper cards, write the words of Psalm 121:2, placing a word on each card. Repeat the verse together twice. Then, mix up the cards and give the opportunity for your students to take turns putting the words in the right order. Repeat the verse each time they order it correctly.

Keep the cards in a plastic bag for use in the next class.

To end

Thank your students for their attendance and announce something about the next lesson to spark interest in them.

Emphasize that we can trust in the power of God in difficult times. Finish with a prayer, thanking God that He helps us to be brave, even when we feel afraid.

Lesson 3
Ruth is Faithful

Biblical References: Ruth 1—4
Lesson Objective: That the students know that God wants to bless others through them.
Memory Verse: *"My help comes from the Lord, the Maker of heaven and earth"* (Psalm 121:2).

PREPARE YOURSELF TO TEACH!

Most elementary students trust easily and have no problem believing the words of others. They trust their parents, teachers and friends. They probably do not fully understand what it means to have "faith", but they know what loyalty and dedication are. This lesson will help them understand that God is faithful, that is, dedicated, constant and loyal. In addition, they will begin to understand how they can be faithful, loyal and dedicated to God, their parents and their friends.

BIBLICAL COMMENTARY

Ruth 1-4. The book of Ruth can be read in three different ways. First, as a masterpiece of Hebrew literature that contains some of the most beautiful passages of the Bible. Second, as a beautiful example of the way God uses those who choose to be faithful to him. Third, as a demonstration of God's faithfulness and care for those who suffer and need.

Ruth and Naomi were two brave women who depended on the care and provision of God in times of greatest need. Ruth was a Moabitess, and was married to a Jewish man who served God. When her husband died, she decided not to return to her village or serve false gods. Rather, she decided to take care of her mother-in-law, moving to a strange country for her.

Ruth is a clear example of the way in which God accepts, protects and provides for those who place their faith in Him.

DEVELOPMENT OF THE LESSON

Use some of the following activities to enrich the development of the lesson.

What will happen to me in the future?

For this activity you will need white paper or pieces of cardboard, glue, crayons or colored markers, and magazines or used newspapers.

Distribute the work materials, and ask your students what they would like to be when they grow up. Ask them to draw or cut out illustrations that express their dreams for the future.

Discuss what they need to do to prepare for these jobs. Explain that they can now strive to do their best at school and take care of their bodies to grow up healthy and strong.

Give them time to show their drawings. Tell them: God cares for all people, and often wants to bless others through us. He is responsible for choosing people to help Him meet the needs of others.

Allow them to mention some ways in which they can perform this task (for example: through prayer, offerings, visits to the sick, gathering food, etc.).

Trust and obedience

For this activity you will need a cloth to cover the eyes of your students and a chair.

Ask a volunteer to come forward, and cover their eyes. Tell him that you will help him through the room from side to side, and then guide him back to his chair.

Take the child's hand and guide him around the room. Then choose other child and do the same. Explain that trust is knowing that God will help us move forward, even when we can not see the way. Having faith in God is an act of trust.

BIBLE STORY

Make simple puppets representing Naomi, Ruth and Boaz to illustrate the Bible story. Make them using socks or paper bags, and decorate them with buttons, pieces of cloth, etc. If you wish, prepare a scene with cardboard boxes, which you can also use in other classes. Ask an adult to help you manage one of the characters.

Ruth, a faithful woman

Long ago, when the people of God were ruled by judges and not by kings, there was hunger in the land of Israel. The people did not have enough food. For that reason, Elimelek, his wife Naomi and their two sons went to live in a distant place called Moab.

After some time, Elimelek died. His sons grew up and married Moabite women, Ruth and Orpah. Ten years later, Naomi's sons also died.

Naomi was very sad. She was alone in a foreign country, far from home.

Then she said to Ruth and Orpah:

"I will return to my land. I have heard that God blessed Israel and now there is food there."

"We'll go with you," her daughters-in-law answered.

"My children," said Naomi, "go back to live with your families. You were very good with my sons and with me. May God have compassion on you and give you other husbands."

Naomi approached to kiss them before leaving, and they began to cry from sadness because they did not want her to go.

But Naomi insisted that they return to Moab, so Orpah kissed her goodbye and took the road back to her land.

"Look Ruth," Naomi said, "Orpah will return to her village with her family. Go with her."

"No, I will not go," Ruth replied.

"But I do not have other sons with whom you can get married, daughter."

"It does not matter, I will not leave you. Wherever you go, I'll go with you. Your people will be my people and your God, my God."

When Naomi saw that Ruth was not going to change her mind, she stopped insisting.

The two women set out on the road to Israel, and arrived in Bethlehem just as the harvest began.

When the reapers cut the grain and picked it up, a little grain always fell to the ground. God had commanded the Israelites to leave the fallen grain on the ground so that the poor people could pick it up and have food. Since Ruth was poor, she went behind the reapers, collecting the grain that fell from them.

Ruth was very hardworking and did not stop to rest. She knew that if she did not work, Naomi and she would not have anything to eat.

While Ruth worked non-stop, Boaz, the owner of the fields, was supervising the harvest.

"Who is that woman?" Boaz asked the manager of the reapers.

"Her name is Ruth. She came from Moab with Naomi," the manager replied. "She has worked tirelessly all day."

Boaz went to where Ruth was working and said, "Do not work in any other field, because someone could hurt you. It is better to work in my fields. Here you will be safe."

"You are very kind!" said Ruth. "Why are you so kind to me, being a foreigner?"

"Because I've heard you're very good to Naomi," Boaz replied.

When Ruth returned home that night, she told Naomi about the grain she had collected and the kindness of the owner of the fields.

"Boaz is a relative of my husband," said Naomi. "I'm glad that he treated you well. So do not be afraid to work in his fields, he will protect you."

As time passed, Boaz fell in love with Ruth. They got married and had a baby they called Obed.

When Obed grew up, he had children and then many grandchildren. One of those grandchildren was named David, who killed a giant named Goliath. David was a descendant of Ruth and Boaz.

Many, many years later, another baby was born who was also a descendant of Ruth and Boaz. That baby was also born in Bethlehem and they laid him in a manger.

God rewarded Ruth's faithfulness and faith, allowing her to be part of the family of King David, but above all of the Lord Jesus.

ACTIVITIES

Ruth is faithful. God is faithful.

Hand out the figures for this lesson found in the Cutout Section (pg. 127) and the student worksheet for Lesson 3 and provide scissors for the children. Follow the instructions to set the stage.

Ask for some volunteers to tell the first part of the story, using the figures of Ruth, Orpah and Naomi. Emphasize Ruth's fidelity to Naomi when she decided to travel with her to Bethlehem.

Turn the stage around so that it is on the side where it says "God is faithful". Choose some children to narrate the second part of the story, using the figures of Ruth, Naomi and Boaz.

Emphasize that God was faithful to Naomi and Ruth, providing them with food and work. He also prepared a husband for Ruth and allowed them to have a beautiful baby.

Encourage them to use this activity to tell their family members what they learned during class.

Monthly review

As the unit's last lesson, we suggest that you briefly review the three lessons learned this month.

Use a fun method to ask these questions to your students. Do a round and pass an object from hand to hand, while listening to some melody. When the music stops, the child with the object in hand will answer the question. Feel free to add more questions, depending on the number of participants.

- Who hid her baby from the Pharaoh's officers? (Jochebed)
- According to Pharaoh's order, what should they do to the Hebrew babies? (Throw them in the Nile River to die).
- Who cared for Jochebed's baby when he was in the river? (God).
- Who helped make the basket and watched the baby while he was floating on the Nile River? (Miriam)
- Who found the baby and adopted him? (The daughter of Pharaoh).
- What was Debora? (Judge and prophetess).
- Who did Deborah tell to gather an army of 10,000 men? (Barak).
- What did the army of Sisera have that made them feel very powerful? (900 iron chariots)
- How did God help the army of Israel to overcome the army of Sisera? (He flooded the valley so that the iron chariots could not advance in the mud.)
- What is the memory verse for this month (*"My help comes from the Lord, the Maker of heaven and earth"* (Psalm 121:2).
- Who said, "I will not leave you. Wherever you are, I will go. Your people will be my people and your God, my God?" (Ruth)
- To whom did Ruth demonstrate her fidelity? (To her mother-in-law Naomi.)
- By doing what did Ruth live on when she arrived in Bethlehem? (She worked picking up grain in the field.)
- Who did Ruth marry? (Boaz)
- Name one of the two famous people who were part of the family of Boaz and Ruth. (King David or Jesus)

Memorization

For this week we suggest you use the cards that the last class prepared. Divide the class in small groups or in pairs. Give them time to order the cards on the table. Say the verse together to memorize, and re-mix the cards. The team that takes less time to order the cards will be the winner.

To end

Distribute the work your students have done during these three lessons, and encourage them to be brave and trust in God's care.

Form a circle, and intercede for each of them. It is important that even if it takes more time, mention the name of each child when praying. In that way they will feel appreciated and valued, not only by you but also by God. After thanking them for their attendance and faithfulness during these first lessons, invite them to the next class, in which they will study the importance of making decisions.

Ask them to write down all the important decisions they make during the week, to tell in the next class.

THE BIBLE TEACHES US HOW TO MAKE DECISIONS

Biblical References: 1 Kings 3:4-15; 4:29-34; John 1:35-42; Luke 10:38-42; Matthew 25:14-30; Daniel 1:3-20; Luke 12:13-24.

Unit Memory Verse: *"But seek first his kingdom and his righteousness, and all these things will be given to you as well"* (Matthew 6:33

UNIT OBJECTIVES

This unit will help your students to:

- ❖ Understand that the decisions they make are important.
- ❖ Want to make decisions that honor God.
- ❖ Make decisions based on Biblical principles.

LESSON UNIT A

Lesson 4: Solomon makes a wise decision
Lesson 5: Andrew decides to help Peter
Lesson 6: Mary and Martha decide to serve Jesus
Lesson 7: A wise steward makes a good decision
Lesson 8: Daniel chooses healthy food
Lesson 9: A rich man makes a bad decision

WHY ELEMENTARY STUDENTS NEED THE TEACHING OF THIS UNIT:

Elementary students are beginning to be more independent. They have started their school life and feel "bigger". It is normal that many of them do not want to be compared with young children.

They explore around without fear, and are able to make decisions for themselves. With the level of independence they have achieved, they must also accept the responsibility of making the right decisions. Therefore, they need a guide that helps them make decisions that honor God.

The lessons in this unit will provide biblical principles that will help elementary students make wise decisions.

Provide opportunities for them to exercise their ability to decide. Provide a safe environment in the classroom, where your students explore and have new learning experiences. Observe the decisions they make during class time, and praise them when they choose something that glorifies God.

Lesson 4

Solomon makes a wise decision

Biblical References: 1 Kings 3:4-15; 4:29-34

Lesson Objective: That the students learn that God helps them make wise decisions.

Memory Verse: *But seek first his kingdom and his righteousness, and all these things will be given to you as well* (Matthew 6:33).

PREPARE YOURSELF TO TEACH!

Daily life is full of choices. Even young children face a series of new decisions every day that they must make. Some are simple; others will affect the rest of their life.

Elementary-aged children must learn to use good criteria to make wise decisions, but above all, they need to learn that God is willing to help them make the right choice. It is important that they know that their decisions not only affect them, but also the community, and above all, their relationship with God. This lesson provides you with a great opportunity to guide your students, teaching them to seek divine direction before making decisions for themselves.

BIBLICAL COMMENTARY

This biblical passage tells us about Solomon's leadership, but it also shows us God's kind character. We read that God made an unmerited offer to Solomon. It also reminds us that God wants us to follow him wholeheartedly, that he is pleased when we make good decisions and that, if it is his will, he can bless his children with wisdom, prosperity and a long life.

History tells us that Solomon went to Gibeon, a place that was 17 kilometers from Jerusalem. That is where the ancient tabernacle was. At that time, it was a meeting point for the Hebrews; the temple had not yet been built.

Solomon was a young man in his 20's when he became king. Obviously, he had no experience to govern or lead a nation. When the Lord appeared to him in a dream, perhaps the task of reigning worried the young king.

At the offer of God, Solomon's response shows that he wanted to please the Lord and that he had a great sense of responsibility. This young man knew that only with the help of God could he carry out the great task that lay before him.

Solomon's request pleased God because he was not selfish. It showed that Solomon cared about the welfare of others. Then, God not only granted his wish, but blessed him with well-being, prosperity and health.

1 Kings 4:29-34. This passage shows the great wisdom of Solomon, who had attained fame beyond the borders of Israel. The list of his writings is impressive. And when we combine the great architectural projects with his commercial achievements, we see that God fulfilled the promise he had made to Solomon. Undoubtedly, this king enjoyed wealth and honor all his life.

DEVELOPMENT OF THE LESSON

Use some of the following activities to enrich the learning of your class.

Who decides?

This activity will help your students see how other people's decisions can influence them.

Fold three sheets of paper in half. Glue the sides to form envelopes. On the first envelope write: "ME ONLY"; in the second: "ME WITH THE HELP OF AN ADULT"; and in the third: "AN ADULT".

Then, hang the envelopes on the board or on the wall. On paper strips, write each of the following statements:

- The games that I have fun with.
- Who I can befriend?
- The music I listen to.
- The clothes I wear.
- The food I eat.
- The places where I play.
- The shows I watch on television.
- The job I'll have when I grow up.
- Who I am going to marry?
- Where I will live.

Add other phrases, if desired. Then, ask each student to choose a strip. After everyone has read the phrase on the strip they chose, give them time to tell who should make that decision. Then they should put the strip in the correct envelope. Some decisions can lend themselves to comments. Encourage the participation of the group, and guide them to a constructive debate.

Discuss with them about how external influences affect their decisions, and vice versa.

Proverbs

For this lesson we suggest that in advance, you write some of Solomon's proverbs (for example, Proverbs 16:6) on poster board, and show them as you tell the story. You can also ask the students to keep their Bibles open to the book of Proverbs.

Bright ideas

For this activity we suggest you use cardboard or poster board to prepare the figure of a light bulb for each of your students.

Read the following sentences out loud. When your students believe that it is a wise decision, they should raise their light bulbs. Discuss whether the decision is wise or not. Some answers may vary, depending on the situation, place or climate. Emphasize that some decisions may be appropriate in certain situations, but inadequate when circumstances change.

1. Fly a kite.
2. Raise your voice to your parents.
3. Attend church on Sundays.
4. Ride a bike.
5. Take your friend's book.
6. Camping in an outdoor tent.
7. Listen carefully to the teacher.
8. Participate in a field day.
9. Be kind to others.
10. Go to the beach.

Save the figures from the bulbs for use next week.

BIBLE STORY

Tell the story using your own words and modulating the tone of your voice to give it more realism. Another option is to invite someone to help you read and act out the part of Solomon.

Solomon is wise in deciding

"I have taken a long journey to get to Gibeon to worship God," thought Solomon. "I am very tired and I need to rest to recover my strength."

As soon as Solomon went to bed, he fell asleep immediately and began to dream.

In the middle of his dream, God appeared to him and said, "Ask me what you want and I will give it to you."

"Lord," answered Solomon, "you were very good to my father David. Now you have allowed me to be king of this great nation. But I am very young and I do not know how to be a good king. I'm not wise enough. Give your servant wisdom to govern your people. Help me know what is good and what is bad."

"You have asked for something very good," said God. You could have asked for long life or wealth. But, since you have asked for wisdom to govern the people, I will give you what you want. There will be no one wiser than you. And since your request was unselfish, I will give you much more; I will give you many riches and glory. In addition, if you follow my ways and obey me, as your father David did, I will also give you a long life."

Solomon woke up and realized that it had been a dream. But God fulfilled his promise and endowed Solomon with great wisdom. And he was known throughout the world as the wisest king in history.

Solomon wrote and collected wise sayings throughout his life, some of which are written in the Bible in the book of Proverbs.

Solomon's decision

Distribute the student worksheets and pencils. Explain to the children that they must choose the correct word to complete each sentence. Tell them to use the letters in the colored boxes from their first three answers to complete the last sentence.

Remind them that Solomon made the right decision by asking God for wisdom to lead the people.

When they finish the activity, go to the next page. Allow time for them to cut out the figures from the bottom. Tell them to paste them in the appropriate blank spaces. As they work, explain why it is important to seek help in making wise decisions, and where they can find it:

- Bible. If in making decisions we follow biblical principles, we are sure that God will be pleased with our choice. The Bible is full of good advice that helps us make wise decisions.
- Prayer. Through prayer we ask God to help us decide.
- Jesus. He is always willing to help us when we must make decisions. He is wise and knows what is best for us.
- Parents. They love us and want us to make the best decisions.
- Pastor. He/She cares about our spiritual well-being and is willing to help us make decisions that please God.

Talk with the children about the impact of their decisions. Remind them that Solomon's decision in his youth impacted the rest of his life and that of his people.

Memorization

Write the memory verse on a piece of poster board and place it in a visible place in the room.

Ask the girls to come forward and read it; Then ask the boys to do it. Then choose different groups (for example: all those who have black shoes, everyone who has clothes of the same color, etc.). Continue the game with different variants, until the verse has been read at least five times.

Finally, ask some volunteers to say it by heart.

Hand out the verse cards of the month so they can take them home and review the verse with their parents.

To end

Sing a song, and come together to pray. Ask the Lord to help everyone make wise decisions during the week, and intercede for each other.

Before saying goodbye, ask everyone to help you clean the room and put away the materials they used.

Lesson 5
Andrew decides to help Peter

Biblical References: John 1:35-42

Lesson Objective: That the students learn that they can influence other people to make good decisions.

Memory Verse: *"But seek first his kingdom and his righteousness, and all these things will be given to you as well."* (Matthew 6:33)

PREPARE YOURSELF TO TEACH!

All people are likely to be influenced, whether by friends, family, media or ideologies, among many others. Children this age are especially influenceable. For that reason they need help to recognize and evaluate the influences that surround them.

For example, it is good that they learn to appreciate the influence of their parents, the Bible and their Christian friends. On the other hand, they must avoid the negative influences that come from the television, their non-Christian friends, and the anti-Christian culture in which we live.

When elementary students learn to identify good influences, it is easier for them to make correct decisions.

BIBLICAL COMMENTARY

John 1:35-42. The ministry of John the Baptist was to prepare the hearts of the people to listen to the message of the Messiah. His testimony, "Behold the Lamb of God!" was enough for two of his disciples (Andrew and John) to follow Jesus. Andrew decided to follow Jesus and influence his brother Simon, declaring to him, "We have found the Messiah!"

Andrew's influence on his brother Simon began to produce a profound change in the life of this disciple.

When Jesus saw Simon, he said, "You are Simon, son of Jonah; you shall be called Cephas - that is, Peter" (v. 42). The Beacon Bible Commentary notes: "Jesus saw Peter not only as he was, but as he could be through the transforming grace of God." Jesus knew that God could transform Simon into Cephas (or "Peter" in Greek), which translated is "rock".

DEVELOPMENT OF THE LESSON

Choose some of the suggested activities to facilitate the learning process of your students.

Bright ideas

Distribute the figures of the light bulbs they used the previous week. Ask your students, as you read the following statements, to raise their lights when they think it is a wise decision. Talk about the reason why each decision mentioned is or is not wise. Make additional clarifications if necessary.

- Invite your neighbor to Sunday School. (It is wise because we must influence others to come to church.)
- Be nice when playing with your brothers and sisters. (It's wise because it pleases Jesus and your parents.)
- Join your classmates in making a joke about the teacher. (It's not wise, we should not let our friends influence us to do wrong.)
- Help your parents clean the house. (It's wise, it's an excellent decision to be helpful.)
- Join your friends in making fun of a kid at school. (It is not wise to follow the influence of others to treat people badly.)
- Talk during the worship service. (It is not wise, because in that way one does not worship God or pay attention to service.)
- Be kind to your neighbor. (It is wise because we follow the example of Jesus.)
- Teach your younger sibling to treat animals well. (It's wise because Jesus likes us to help others behave well.)

What does influence mean?

Write the word "INFLUENCE" on a card, and the following definition on another: "The power to get someone to do what you want."

Then, cut up the cards as if they were pieces of a puzzle.

Divide the class into two groups. Give each group the pieces that make up the word or the definition. Ask them to put the puzzles together, and then read what they formed out loud. Give them time to think about what it means as an introduction to the Bible story.

BIBLE STORY

Mysterious characters - I

For this activity we suggest that you write the names ANDREW and PETER on a card. Cut out each letter separately, and store it in a basket or bag.

Bring your students together to hear the Bible story, and tell them: *In today's story, one man made a decision that influenced the life of another. I'm going to show you the letters that make up the names of these characters (show each letter). Do you know who it is? Listen carefully to identify the two characters of today.*

The disciples follow Jesus

"Look, there it is!" said John the Baptist. "He is the Lamb of God of whom I spoke."

John was very excited! He had told Andrew and his friend about Jesus. Now suddenly, Jesus was there, in front of them.

"Let's go with him!" Andrew told his friend.

Andrew and his friend followed Jesus.

After a while, Jesus turned around and saw them.

"What do you want?" Jesus asked them.

"Teacher, please tell us where you live," they said.

"Follow me and I will show you," Jesus answered.

Andrew and his friend went with Jesus to the place where he was staying. There they spent the rest of the day talking.

When the two men left, Andrew was very excited.

"He really is the Christ, the Messiah!" exclaimed Andrew. "I have to find my brother Simon to tell him this good news."

Andrew quickly ran to his boat, which was on the Sea of Galilee. Since they were fishermen, Simon was busy preparing the nets for another day of work.

When Andrew saw him, he said, "Simon, I have very good news. We met the Christ, the Messiah!"

"What are you talking about?" Simon asked. "Are you sure?"

"It's true!" said Andrew. "I saw him; his name is Jesus. Come with me. I will take you to where he is and you will see that he is the Messiah."

Simon ran after Andrew to find that man his brother was talking about. Finally, they arrived at the place where Jesus was staying.

Andrew took Simon to Jesus. Upon seeing him, Jesus said to him, "Your name is Simon, but from now on you will be called Peter." And, from that day on, Peter and Jesus were good friends.

Mysterious characters - II

Place the letters of the two names on a table or on the floor. Ask for help from several volunteers to carry out this activity.

Each one must go through and try to put together the names of the two disciples as quickly as possible. Whoever does it in the shortest time will be the winner.

Andrew's decision helps Peter

Hand out the student worksheets for lesson 5. Provide scissors and glue. Instruct them to cut out the boxes at the bottom with the figures and paste them in the blanks, following the sequence of the story. As they work, review the story, and ask questions about the Bible story to reinforce learning.

Then, go to the next page and read each of the sentences together. Discuss which situations represent good or bad influences.

Instruct them to circle the pictures that represent positive influences, and to mark with an X those that represent negative influences.

What kind of influence do you exert?

Read the following situations to your students. Talk about the ability we have to influence others positively or negatively, and what God wants us to do as Christians.

Miriam went shopping with her mom and younger brother. Suddenly, she saw a beautiful doll in the toy store and, although she had several dolls at home, she wanted that one. Miriam asked her mother to buy it, but her mother said no. Then Miriam started screaming and crying. Miriam's younger brother observed everything his sister did. What kind of influence is Miriam having on her little brother?

On many occasions, Samuel has invited his best friend David to church, but he never came. One day David invited Samuel to go to a lake to spend the weekend. Samuel thanked him for the invitation, but told him that he could not miss church on Sunday, because he liked to go to his Sunday School class. On Sunday, when Samuel was ready to go to church, David decided to go with him. What kind of influence did Samuel have on David?

Memorization

To study the verse of the unit, cut strips of poster board, and on each strip write some words of the verse to memorize. Tape them on the wall or on the blackboard, so that, after repeating the verse several times, you can put them in different order so that your students can point out the correct order.

To end

Form some groups or ask for volunteers to put away the materials they used in class and pick up trash.

Then, sing songs of praise.

Conclude by guiding them in prayer, asking God to help all of you exert a good influence wherever you are.

Say goodbye, and do not forget to invite them to the next class.

notes

Lesson 6

Mary and Martha decide to serve Jesus

Biblical References: Luke 10:38-42

Lesson Objective: That the students understand that at times they must decide the best among various options.

Memory Verse: *"But seek first his kingdom and his righteousness, and all these things will be given to you as well."* (Matthew 6:33)

PREPARE YOURSELF TO TEACH!

Elementary students are in the process of developing skills and recognizing their individual interests. They need to understand that God gave them their abilities as a gift. However, they are responsible for making good use of those gifts and talents.

It is possible that many elementary students need guidance to recognize their talents. Once identified, they can discover the joy of using their time and abilities to please and serve God.

BIBLICAL COMMENTARY

Luke 10:38-42. The two women in this story had different abilities, and decided to use their time in different ways. Martha was the hostess. The preparation of the food and its service were motivated by her hospitality and love. But she took care of that more than she should.

On the other hand, Mary chose to sit at the feet of Jesus and listen carefully. She was more concerned about learning from the Master than about serving the food.

Martha was distracted by all the preparations she thought necessary for the Lord's visit. When she complained to Jesus about her sister's lack of help, he reminded her with great love that she should prioritize the most important issues. Jesus recognized that Martha wanted to help him, but he helped her see that she was allowing the superficial to hinder the spiritual. By prioritizing other matters, her communion with the Lord was hindered.

Commentator Bruce Larson says: "History really is about our goals in life. What occupies most of our time? Martha was focused on her own goal. She was so busy trying to be an excellent hostess, that she did not have time to be with the Lord. We can say that everything we have - time, life, money, etc., is from the Lord. But do we dedicate time? Maybe we are very busy doing good deeds, but we forget that the most important thing is our relationship with him."

As we study this lesson, let's make Jesus our priority. We will discover that he is the key to everything.

DEVELOPMENT OF THE LESSON

What kind of influence?

This activity will help your students identify two kinds of influences.

Before class, cut out squares of green and red paper, one of each color for each student.

Distribute the squares to the class, and read the following statements out loud. Ask the children to raise their red square if the statement talks about bad influences, and the green square if it is about good influences.

- Mark cleaned his room when his mother asked him to. Then, he helped his younger sister pick up her toys.
- Natalia saw a television program in which a child spoke to her parents in a disrespectful way, so she decided to do the same when her parents ordered her to do something.
- John, when leaving school, had to go straight to his house but his friends invited him to go to the park. He thought he could play for a while and go home before his parents arrived, so no one would notice.
- Liliana taught her little sister to sing the song "Jesus loves me".
- Irma invited her best friend to come spend the night at her house on Saturday. On Sunday morning, Irma's mother woke them up early to go to Sunday School. Irma asked, "Do we have to go to Sunday School today? We wanted to play in the park."
- Edward saw that his friend was bothering a younger child in the park. So he went over to tell him that if he wanted to have friends, he should be kind to others.

God's gifts

For this activity you will need an instrument or music box, a paint brush, a ball and a book.

Place the objects on a table, and tell your students: *God gave us all special gifts that are called gifts or talents* (show the objects). Talk to them about the gifts that each object represents, and how or where we can put them into use. Write on the board the gifts and talents they mention (for example: service, talents for music, sports, crafts, etc.).

Tell them that in today's story we will learn more about that topic.

What can I do?
Bring the children together and ask them: *What kind of skills or talents do you have?* As they respond, write on the board the name of the student and the talent they mentioned. Make sure everyone participates in that activity. If necessary, help those who have difficulty recognizing their talents.

BIBLE STORY
We suggest you invite two young women from your congregation to represent Martha and Mary. Get two tunics or fabrics to make the staging more real. Ask them to tell the Bible story from each character's point of view, and let each one tell how she expressed her love for Jesus.

Mary and Martha decide to serve Jesus
"Look, there's Bethany," said one of the disciples. That's where Martha and her family live. Maybe we could rest awhile at their house.

"That is a good idea!" affirmed Jesus.

They arrived at Martha's house.

"Jesus!" Marta exclaimed as she opened the door. "What a nice surprise! Please come in."

Marta called her sister. "Mary, come quickly! Jesus and his friends are here!"

"Surely they will be very tired," said Marta. "Sit down and rest. I'll prepare something for you to eat."

Marta hurried and went to plan what she was going to cook. "I have to make a very special meal for Jesus," she said to himself, and thought about what she would need to feed everyone.

Then, she worked hard preparing the food and cleaning the house. She was worried because she wanted to serve them very well.

While Marta prepared the food, Jesus sat down to talk with his disciples. Mary, Marta's sister, sat at the feet of Jesus to listen to what he was saying.

After a while, Marta came to where everyone was and saw that Mary was sitting, listening to the words of Jesus. She was so busy working, so she got very angry because her sister wasn't helping her."

"Jesus, Mary has left me alone doing the work. Please, tell her to help me!" said Martha.

"Martha, Martha," Jesus answered. "You are very worried and busy with the small things. Only one thing is necessary and important, and Mary has discovered it. She chose the most important thing, and nobody can take it away."

The most important
Briefly review the Bible story, and ask your class: *What was the most important thing that Mary chose?* (Spend time with Jesus).

Emphasize that there is time to do work for Jesus, and time to be alone with Him. It is important to use our talents to serve the Lord, but they should never replace our time of prayer and communion with Him.

ACTIVITIES

Decide to use your gifts
Pass out the worksheets for this lesson. Based on the Bible story, ask your students to circle the phrases that represent the way Martha and Mary decided to serve Jesus. Then, give them time to color the drawing, and follow the instructions to complete the activity on the back of the page.

As they work, emphasize the importance of recognizing and putting our talents and abilities at God's service.

Let's use our gifts!
This activity will help them put their gifts into practice and use their talents.

Give a specific job to each member of your class, based on their talent or ability. For example: those who have the gift of service, will pick up the offering and organize the materials when the class ends. On the other hand, those who have the ability to do manual work will help the children and the teacher when necessary. Others can lead the singing time, or receive the visitors that arrive to the class and attend to them.

No matter what task you assign to each child, remind them that all the work we do for God is important and valuable.

Memorization
Ask your group to sit in a circle, and you stand in the center. Lightly throw a light ball to them. The child who catches it should stand up and say the memory verse.

Repeat the exercise so that all your students participate. Help the little ones or those who have difficulty with memorization.

To end
Sing a song that deals with the subject of the lesson. Remind the class that God gave them gifts and talents that will help them serve Him better.

Pray giving thanks to God for the gifts you all have received, and ask Him to help you use them for His service.

Lesson 7

The wise steward makes a good decision

Biblical References: Matthew 25:14-30

Lesson Objective: That the students learn to use their talents and abilities to serve God.

Memory Verse: *"But seek first his kingdom and his righteousness, and all these things will be given to you as well."* (Matthew 6:33)

PREPARE YOURSELF TO TEACH!

The majority of your students are beginning to have more responsibilities in their homes. They are also learning to take care of their belongings, and discovering their abilities and limitations.

Children must recognize that God is the owner of everything and the giver of all gifts. They are simply stewards of what He gave them and, as such, they must learn to be faithful to God.

BIBLICAL COMMENTARY

Matthew 25:14-30. This is the second in a series of three parables about God's judgment. This means that, as Christians, we must prepare ourselves to give an account of our actions on that glorious day.

In biblical times, the steward was a high-ranking servant, or a slave who had proven to be a responsible person. His responsibility consisted of managing the assets of his master's house. The steward was not the owner of the money, but was entrusted to take care of it. The steward was expected to be a faithful administrator and to handle with wisdom all that pertained to the master's house. The faithful servant was given greater responsibility because he earned the trust of his master. The greater the responsibility, the more he had to administer. The punishment for the unfaithful servant was severe.

In the parable, the first two servants were rewarded for their faithful work with words of praise and a beautiful invitation: "Come and enter into the joy of your Lord." In this statement, apart from the rich man who arranges the accounts with his employees, we see the reward for the faithful servants, whom Jesus invites to accompany him to his table in the kingdom of heaven. It is very significant that the two servants were rewarded for being "good and faithful", and not for being "capable and ingenious".

God wants us to put our gifts at his service and to fulfill his will.

DEVELOPMENT OF THE LESSON

Choose some of the following activities for your students to achieve more meaningful learning about the subject of study.

My responsibilities

Give your students paper and crayons or colored pencils. Ask them to draw jobs they need to do daily at home (e.g., make their bed, pick up their toys, wash the dishes, etc.). Discuss the different tasks for which they are responsible, and the way they carry them out. When they finish the drawing, ask them to write "MY RESPONSIBILITIES" at the top of the page. Once the activity is finished, hang all the works on the wall to make a mural.

Use your skills

Ask your students to sit in a circle. Have a musical instrument or a song at hand.

Play the music while your students pass a small ball from hand to hand. Stop the music after a while. When the music stops, the student with the ball must stand up and say how and where he can use his talents to serve God. Continue playing until everyone has participated.

What is a steward?

Write the word "STEWARD" on a piece of cardboard or poster board. Show it to your students and ask them what the word means.

After listening to their opinions, explain that a steward is a person who administers the belongings of another.

Then, tell them: We are stewards of what God gave us. For that reason, we are responsible for taking care of everything that he entrusts to us.

Open your Bible to 1 Corinthians 4:2 and read aloud: "Now it is required that those who have been given a trust must prove faithful."

Tell them: God has trusted us to take care of his creation. This verse tells us that we must be faithful stewards of God. Jesus told a parable about some stewards (administrators). A parable is a pretend story that teaches us a lesson. Listen carefully to what Jesus wanted to teach us through this story.

BIBLE STORY

To enrich the learning, we suggest that you prepare visual aids to illustrate the lesson. Prepare graphics that represent servants and talents. If you wish, use the example of the illustrations in the student worksheet.

The wise servants

Crowds followed Jesus everywhere he went. Everyone wanted to hear his teachings.

Jesus often told stories to help them understand what he wanted them to know.

"Who is a faithful and wise servant?" asked Jesus. And he told them this story:

The kingdom of heaven is like a man who had to make a long journey. He called his servants and handing them his money, he asked them to take care of his possessions during his absence. One servant was given five sacks, and each sack had a large amount of money. To another servant he gave two sacks, and to the third one he handed him one. He entrusted his money to each servant according to the abilities of each, and then the man went on a trip.

The servant who received the most money went to work immediately. He took the five bags, invested the money, and earned five more bags. The servant who had two sacks did the same and earned two more. But the man who received a single sack dug a hole in the ground and hid the money for fear that it would be stolen.

The homeowner was on a trip for a long time. When he finally returned, he called his stewards to review the accounts. The man who had received five sacks gave ten to his lord. "You gave me five bags. I have earned five more," he said with satisfaction.

The servant with the two bags of money approached his master and said, "Sir, you gave me two sacks of money. I've earned two more."

His master replied, "Well done, good and faithful servants! You have been faithful with the little I gave you; Now I will give you more responsibility. Let's celebrate!"

Then, the man who had received the one sack of money approached his master and said, "Sir, I know it is difficult to please you; that's why I was afraid and hid your money in the ground. Here is the sack of money that belongs to you."

His master replied, "You bad and lazy servant! You should have kept my money in the bank; at least that way I would have earned interest! Take the money and give it to the one who has ten bags. And the useless servant, throw him out," ordered the master.

ACTIVITIES

Who was wise?

Hand out the student worksheet. Ask the children to complete the figures, adding the bags of money that the servants brought to their master (boss). Give them time to draw the expressions on the faces of the servants when they were in front of their master.

Use these questions to help them reflect on the meaning of the story:

How do you think the servants felt when they were in front of their master? What lesson did Jesus want to teach when he told this parable?

Then, go to the next page of the worksheet. Ask the kids to draw a star on the figures that represent children who wisely use what they have.

Talk about the meaning of each drawing, and what makes children good or bad stewards.

Faithful stewards

For this activity you will need cardboard, tape, paper strips and colored pencils.

On the top of the card write: "Faithful stewards." Distribute the strips of paper and the colored pencils, and have the children write a phrase that indicates how they can be good stewards (for example: taking care of my toys, cleaning my room, feeding my pets, watering the plants, etc.).

Then, each one should put a piece of adhesive tape on his strip and stick it on the cardboard. When all have done so, place the cardboard on the door of the room or in some hall of the church so that the members of the congregation can see the work your students did.

Memorization

Divide the class into two groups. Ask one group to say the first sentence of the memory verse, while the other group repeats the second part. Then, let both groups say it together.

Exchange the phrases of the two groups to study the full text. Repeat the exercise several times, and then choose some to say it alone.

Hand out the Club cards of the verse of the month to take them home and review the verse of this unit.

To end

Before leaving, give time for everyone to cooperate in the cleanup, and the organize the room and materials.

Then, sing some songs, and lead them in a prayer, asking the Lord to help them be faithful stewards of what He gave them.

Lesson 8
Daniel chooses healthy food

Biblical References: Daniel 1:3-20

Lesson Objective: That the students learn to honor God by taking care of the body He gave them.

Memory Verse: *"But seek first his kingdom and his righteousness, and all these things will be given to you as well."* (Matthew 6:33)

PREPARE YOURSELF TO TEACH!

Most schools begin to teach health issues to first and second grade children. Others have already learned good health habits at home. Good health is truly a reward, and for believers, it is even more so, since we want to honor God in all the decisions we make, wherever we are, whatever we're doing. Even simple decisions, such as what we will eat or drink, become matters of faith.

Although we do not know in detail why Daniel and his three friends refused to eat the king's food and wine, we know that they were considered a threat to their faith. Daniel 1:8 tells us, "But Daniel resolved not to defile himself with the royal food and wine, and he asked the chief official for permission not to defile himself this way."

This lesson will help elementary students understand that by caring for their bodies and deciding not to contaminate themselves with what could harm them, they are honoring God.

Most children are impulsive when choosing what they want to eat. Excessive advertising stimulates their egocentricity, causing them to say, "Let's eat what we like!" This lesson will teach them that God is the owner of their bodies. They can honor God by making decisions that reflect a good stewardship of their body.

BIBLICAL COMMENTARY

Daniel 1:3-20. Daniel and his friends were taken captive to Babylon. Because they were descendants of royal lineage, well educated and wise, they were chosen from many young people to work to serve the Babylonian king in a special way.

In addition, their Hebrew names were changed to Babylonian names. That was very significant, since the Hebrews took special care in choosing names for their children. The Hebrew names honored the one true God and gave testimony of him. Instead, the new names honored pagan gods that the Babylonian people worshiped.

The passage does not explain why these young people did not want the royal food. But it is evident that they rejected it motivated by their firm beliefs, because eating the royal food would have contaminated their bodies. It was a great challenge for these young Hebrews, since, for the descendants of Abraham, participating in food offered to idols meant breaking their communion with the one true God. After all, the law of God was violated by participating in the worship of false gods.

Faced with this challenge, Daniel and his friends spoke with two officers to ask them to give them only vegetables and water, instead of the royal food. The first petition was denied outright. The officer explained to Daniel that if they did not look as healthy as the other young men, he would be executed for disobeying the king's orders and changing their food.

Daniel, convinced that his decision pleased God, did not give up, and insisted once more. This time he spoke with the guard who took care of them, proposing that he allow them to go through a trial period. Verse 15 shows us the result they got:

"At the end of the ten days they looked healthier and better nourished than any of the young men who ate the royal food" (Daniel 1:15). At the end of the trial time, the guard saw that he had nothing to worry about, and allowed them to continue with their special diet.

Through this story, we learn that we must honor God by taking care of the body he gave us, because it is a temple of the Holy Spirit.

DEVELOPMENT OF THE LESSON

Choose some of the following activities to activate group dynamics and promote better learning.

My favorite foods

For this lesson you will need magazines, paper, scissors, glue and colored pencils.

Distribute the materials to your students. Then, ask them to write: "My favorite foods" at the top of the page. Then, give them a few minutes to look for illustrations in magazines of their favorite foods. Ask them to cut and paste them on the paper. If you do not have magazines, tell them to draw their favorite foods.

When they are finished, explain that they will use these in the next activity.

Healthy food

During the week, prepare illustrations of healthy and unhealthy foods. Use the advertising of stores or supermarkets, or look in magazines. You can also bring some food boxes or empty containers to the class.

Divide a white card into two columns. Over one column place the title: HEALTHY FOOD, and over the other: UNHEALTHY FOOD.

Stick the cardboard on the wall, and have adhesive tape on hand. Ask your students to choose one of the boxes or containers, or one of the cutouts that you brought, and glue it in the corresponding column. When they are finished, ask them to compare healthy foods with those they pasted or drew on their papers.

Talk to them about the importance of good nutrition. Then, tell them that today they will study about a young man that pleased God by taking care of his body. .

BIBLE STORY

Mysterious character

Give the following clues to your students so they can guess which biblical character is in today's story:

- I am a man of the Old Testament.
- I prayed three times a day.
- They threw me into the lions' den.

Who I am?

Tell them: Our Bible story today tells us about a decision Daniel made when he was young. Listen carefully to find out what happened.

Daniel chooses healthy foods

"Bring some young Israelites to serve me in the palace," ordered Nebuchadnezzar, the king of Babylon.

The king's chief officer listened carefully to the instructions:

"Choose strong, healthy and good-looking boys," said the king. "They must be smart and have the ability to learn quickly. They must eat the food from my own kitchen" the king ordered. "I want them to be strong and healthy so they can serve me better."

Daniel and three of his friends -Hananiah, Mishael and Azariah- were part of the group that the Babylonian soldiers had chosen.

The chief officer gave the young Hebrews Babylonian names. Daniel was called Belteshazzar; Hananiah became Shadrach, and Mishael became Meshach; and Azariah was called Abednego.

But when the king's food was served to them, Daniel told the officer, "I cannot eat the king's food. God warned my people that we could not eat certain foods. I have to obey God's commandments."

"But I cannot disobey the king's orders," the officer said. "If you do not eat what the king ordered, you will become weak and thin, and the other boys will be stronger. The king will think that I am not doing my duty, he will be furious, and maybe even order me to be killed!"

Then Daniel spoke with the guard who watched them, "Please," Daniel asked. "Give us a test. For ten days, give us only vegetables and water. After that time, you can compare us with the other boys who eat the king's food. Then you will decide who looks healthier and stronger."

The guard agreed to give the test.

After ten days he took Daniel, Hananiah,

Mishael and Azariah to where the other boys were.

The guard could not believe what he saw! Daniel and his friends looked much healthier and stronger than the other young people.

"The king will be happy when he sees how well you look," the guard said. "From now on, you can choose the foods you want to eat."

God blessed Daniel and his friends by giving them knowledge and intelligence.

When the training time ended, King Nebuchadnezzar ordered the chief officer to bring the young men before him. After asking them some questions, the king realized that Daniel and his friends were ten times stronger and smarter than all the other people of the kingdom who were at his service.

Biblical review

Telling the Bible story in your own words will reinforce the learning of this lesson to your students. Use the following questions to direct the review:

- What decision did Daniel and his friends make?
- Why did Daniel not want to eat the king's food?
- Why did the king's officer not want to let Daniel and his friends eat vegetables and drink water?
- What happened when Daniel convinced the guard to allow them to eat vegetables and drink water for ten days?

Listen to the answers, and supplement the information as necessary.

As a conclusion, tell them: *Daniel and his friends decided to please God through this decision. God blessed them, giving them better health and greater strength and intelligence than others.*

As Daniel did, we can honor God when we decide to keep our bodies healthy.

ACTIVITIES

God wants me to take care of my body

Hand out the student worksheet, and read the instructions for your students to do the suggested activities.

Allow time for them, in the blank space on the second page of Lesson 8, to draw or write a list of good decisions that can help them take care of themselves during the week.

Time to eat healthy foods

If time and resources allow, bring vegetables or fruits (carrot sticks, oranges or apples) and glasses of water to share with your students.

Explain the benefits that our body receives by eating vegetables and fruits.

Tell them: God made fruits and vegetables because they are good for us. They have vitamins that help us grow healthy and strong. We must also drink at least 5 glasses of water a day, because it keeps us hydrated, and helps our kidneys and other organs function properly.

Memorization

To review the memory verse, ask your students to form a circle. A volunteer must stand in the center of the circle blindfolded. Give a bell to one of the children in the circle. He/she should pass it to the next child, who passes it to the next, and so on.

The blindfolded child should say "Stop" whenever he wants, and the one with the bell should repeat the verse. The child in the center then tries to guess who said the verse.

Then, blindfold the eyes to the child who said the verse and he/she then goes to the center of the circle and repeat the exercise.

Let the group help those who still do not know the verse.

To end

Encourage your students to make the decision to take care of their health and strive to honor God in that way. Pray before saying goodbye, thanking God for creating us and sustaining us.

Invite them to the next class, which will be the last of this series of lessons about decisions.

Lesson 9

A rich man makes a bad decision

Biblical References: Luke 12:13-24
Lesson Objective: That the desire of the students is to love God and learn how to share.
Memory Verse: *"But seek first his kingdom and his righteousness, and all these things will be given to you as well."* (Matthew 6:33)

PREPARE YOURSELF TO TEACH!

Nowadays, the media and society pressure children to want all sorts of things. Some think that they must have toys, clothes and everything that is "fashionable."

In some places, if children do not have the right image, they are often isolated or ridiculed by others.

This world is too materialistic. What is valued is not the person, but what he has. And elementary students are not immune to that kind of influence. They want to be accepted and often relate acceptance to material possessions. They need guidance to eliminate the false idea of what provides happiness.

By studying the parable of the rich fool, your students will understand that people should not be "possessed" by their goods. That will help them develop a healthy attitude towards their belongings. They need to learn that their relationship with God is more important than what they have or wear.

BIBLICAL COMMENTARY

Luke 12:13-24. In general, the parables of Jesus responded to circumstances that were experienced at that time. Jesus told them to teach a great truth or an eternal principle.

The parable of Luke 12:13-21 was the answer to a request that had been made of him. Someone in the crowd asked him to convince his brother to share the inheritance he had received with him. Jesus' answer, after refusing to be part of the conflict, is one of the greatest principles of the Christian life: "The life of man does not consist in the abundance of the things he possesses."

Contrary to what is believed, possessions do not produce a life of joy and happiness. When we analyze the lives of many of those who are rich and live in prosperity, we realize that material goods are the most important thing for them. However, their lives are full of anxiety and discontent, not happiness. Most of those who possess great material wealth never know how wonderful it is to have Jesus in their hearts. In addition, they do not experience deep treasures such as love, peace, a clear conscience, hope and the promise of eternal life.

This parable speaks of a man whose harvest had been so plentiful that he did not know what to do with it all. God had given him the land, the light of the sun and the rain to bless him. But the man's error was to make bad decisions, as much in the storage of all his harvest as in his administration. Building larger barns was not wrong; however, his motivation was wrong. He wanted to store everything for himself.

Having spiritual wealth is the most valuable thing in life. That means having faith in God, yearning to please Him, and showing love and compassion towards others. We can trust in God and be assured that he will always provide us with what we need!

Commentator Charles L. Childers mentions: "There is nothing more foolish than living for time and forgetting eternity, or living for oneself and forgetting God."

After this parable comes a teaching of Jesus to his disciples. The focus changes from ambition to anxiety. Ambition makes us want more; anxiety makes us worry about not having enough. Wealth represents a danger for those who possess it and for those who wish to possess it. In this lesson, God teaches us to depend on him and get rid of materialism.

Verses 22-24 confirm that God cares for us and that we should not worry about tomorrow, but depend on his mercy every day.

DEVELOPMENT OF THE LESSON

Use some of the following activities to enrich biblical learning and stimulate your students' participation.

The most valuable

Draw, or get from magazines, illustrations of objects that are valuable to society: cars, houses, money, clothes, electronic games, jewelry, etc.

Before your students arrive, hide the pictures in the room.

Ask your students to look for them, and after they find them, give them time to describe the objects.

Discuss the value of such possessions, and explain that during the lesson they will talk about what is most valuable.

BIBLE STORY

A rich man makes a bad decision

"Master," said one of the crowd, "tell my brother to divide the land and the money that our parents left us, and give me the part that belongs to me."

"Who has put me as a judge over you to decide those things?" Jesus answered. "Be careful not to become greedy people! Nor should you desire everything that you do not possess. It is not important how much money or how many possessions you have. Life does not consist in that. Let me tell you a story," said Jesus.

There was once a rich man who had a beautiful estate. There he cultivated different kinds of grains. His harvests had been plentiful and he had no place to store it all.

The rich man began to think, "What should I do? I no longer have room to store all of my harvest." Finally he exclaimed, "I know! I will tear down my old barns and build bigger ones to keep all the grain I have. Then I can sit down to rest," said the man. "I will have a lot of stored grain and enough wealth for many years. Then I will not worry anymore; I will just enjoy life. I will be able to eat and drink as much as I want. I'll have all the fun I want and enjoy instead of working all the time."

Jesus let people meditate on that story for a moment. Then he continued, "But God said to the rich man, 'Foolish man! Tonight you will die, and who will keep all that you have saved for yourself?'"

That is what happens with people who invest all their time and energy trying to obtain possessions. They do not devote time to love and serve God, much less to their neighbor. It really is not important what you eat or what you wear. Life is worth much more than that. If God cares for birds and flowers, he will surely take care of us.

ACTIVITIES

The most valuable thing to me

To reinforce learning, ask your students to draw, in light of what they learned today, what they consider most important. As they work, observe their drawings, and emphasize the importance of valuing things according to God's perspective.

Then, ask everyone to come forward and give a brief explanation of what they drew and why.

The rich man

For this activity you will need paper fasteners and scissors.

Ask a volunteer to help you distribute the student worksheets. Give them time to cut out the two circles on the sheet. Then, join them in the center with the paper fastener. Make sure that the circle with the drawings is below the yellow circle.

Encourage this kids to use their craft to tell their family what they learned in class.

Memorization

Since this is the last class of the unit, prepare simple prizes for those who have learned the memory verse. Remind them to use their Club verses of the month cards to review the unit's verse in their homes.

To end

Distribute the crafts done during this unit. Organize groups of volunteers to clean the room and put away the materials they used.

Then, thank them for attending class and invite them to the next unit that will begin next week.

Pray with them, thanking God for the blessings received, and ask Him to help all of you make wise and useful decisions.

If the Holy Spirit tells you to, guide your students to apologize for the bad decisions they have made.

Tell them that the most important decision someone can make in their life is to accept Christ in their hearts.

Year 2 Introduction – Unit III

THE HOLY LOVE OF GOD

Biblical References: Genesis 2:16—3:24; 4:1-16; 6:5—9:17; 18:16—19:29; Leviticus 4; Hebrews 10:1-14.

Unit Memory Verse: *"For all have sinned and fall short of the glory of God, and all are justified freely by his grace through the redemption that came by Christ Jesus"* (Romans 3:23-24).

UNIT OBJECTIVES
This unit will help the students to:

- Know that sin separates people from God.
- Understand that, even when we disobey, God continues loving us.
- Compare the consequences of disobedience with those of obedience.
- Ask for forgiveness from God and accept Jesus as their Savior and Lord.

LESSON UNIT A
Lesson 10: Wrong decisions
Lesson 11: Painful results
Lesson 12: Our God of love and mercy
Lesson 13: Our God of justice and grace
Lesson 14: Our God of forgiveness

WHY ELEMENTARY STUDENTS NEED THE TEACHING OF THIS UNIT:

This unit provides the opportunity to relate the learning of the previous unit. Elementary students often decide if something is good or bad depending on the consequences it will have. However, their reasoning is limited and they do not reflect on the consequences that will occur in the long term.

This unit will help them understand why it is important to allow God to guide them in their decisions.

Elementary students are able to understand that the decision to disobey God is a sin. In a world so confused about what is good or bad, it is important to help them understand what sin is and to accept responsibility for their negative actions. Maybe "sin" is a new term for some of them. However, they are aware that people can do "bad things" or "hurt someone." They also know that some behaviors are "acceptable," and others "unacceptable."

By studying the biblical stories of this unit, they will learn what sin is and its consequences, as well as God's solution to that problem.

They will discover that sin is all that one thinks, does or feels that separates them from God.

Once your students understand the problem, they will be ready to hear that God has a solution to remove sin from the hearts of people, because we trust in a holy and loving God.

Lesson 10
Wrong decisions

Biblical References: Genesis 2:16—3:24

Lesson Objective: That the students understand that disobedience of God is sin and separates us from Him.

Memory Verse: *"For all have sinned and fall short of the glory of God, and all are justified freely by his grace through the redemption that came by Christ Jesus"* (Romans 3:23-24).

PREPARE YOURSELF TO TEACH!

Elementary students identify easily with the temptation to eat the forbidden fruit, just like Eve. The fruit looked nice and the tempter made the woman believe that eating the fruit would make her wise. Regrettably, Eve decided to believe Satan's promise instead of believing God. She ignored the Lord and his warning. Therefore, her relationship with God changed. She had disobeyed, defying the authority of God.

Your students must learn that God has the right to guide our lives, for he is our Creator. When, instead of trusting him, we ignore his direction and disobey him, we break our relationship with him. In that way, we let something different occupy the place that belongs to God. That is sin.

Separation is the consequence of a broken relationship. This lesson gives us an example of the separation that sin produces. Your students can feel the distance from God when they disobey Him. However, there is hope because God is merciful and does not treat us as we deserve. He devised a plan to restore His relationship with us.

BIBLICAL COMMENTARY

Genesis 2:16-3:24. In this passage, sin and its consequences are mentioned for the first time. God gave Adam and Eve the Garden of Eden to take care of and enjoy. God lived there with them, and they enjoyed a beautiful love relationship. However, there was only one requirement: "You are free to eat from any tree in the garden; but you must not eat from the tree of the knowledge of good and evil, for when you eat from it you will certainly die" (Genesis 2:16-17).

Commentator Stuart Briscoe points out that God's commandment was not a burden for Adam and Eve. Rather, it was a reminder that God created the human being to depend on him.

Sin consists of committing a conscious act of disobedience against God. It is rebellion against the absolute authority of God. Adam and Eve despised the Lord's prohibition and decided to take their own path.

The essence of the first sin of humanity was disobedience to God, not eating the forbidden fruit. The consequences of their actions were spiritual and physical. In the spiritual, they were separated from God, and they suffered this consequence immediately. The physical consequences - pain, suffering and death - came later.

Although the consequences of sin were final, God had mercy on them. When Adam and Eve were expelled from the garden, they had to work to survive, but the resources that God had created were still available to them. Giving birth to children was painful for Eve, but she would still have the blessing of giving life to another human being.

DEVELOPMENT OF THE LESSON

Choose some of the following activities to make the study of the biblical truth more understandable and enjoyable.

What should I choose?

Write the names of your students on strips of white card. Use large letters so you can color them.

Put colored pencils or crayons on the table and ask them to choose the one they like best to color the letters of their name.

When they finish, ask them: Was it easy or difficult for you to choose a color? (Allow them to respond.) Introduce the topic of the class, saying: *Sometimes we must make simple decisions; other times, more complicated. For example, we must choose between being good and obedient, or the opposite. God wants us to obey Him. In today's Bible Story, we will learn about an important decision that Adam and Eve made.*

The consequences of sin

During the week, draw or look in magazines or newspapers for some illustrations that represent the consequences of disobedience (for example: broken cars, incarcerated people, people smoking or drinking, etc.). Be careful to choose images that are appropriate for the age of your students.

Place the images on the board. Discuss with the children what might have happened to get to that situation (for example: the car overturned because the driver disobeyed the speed limit; the man is incarcerated because he violated the law; the person is sick because he decided to smoke, although he knew it was bad for his body, etc.).

Ask them to give examples of what happens in their daily lives when they disobey their parents or teachers. Use those comments as an introduction to the Bible Story.

BIBLE STORY

Enriching the Bible Story with illustrations will help you better capture the attention of your students. Also, modulate your voice and make the class interactive, allowing the children to participate by giving their opinions; in this way the narration will be enriched.

Wrong decisions

In the beginning, God created a wonderful world and filled it with beautiful plants and animals. Afterwards, he created man and woman. He decided to make them different from all other creatures, and gave them the privilege of making decisions.

"You can eat the fruit of all the trees in the garden; but you must not eat from the tree of the knowledge of good and evil, because if you eat it, you will die," God said to Adam and Eve.

One day Eve walked through the garden. Suddenly, she heard a strange voice calling her, "Woman!"

"What is that? Who is calling me?" Eve asked herself. She looked around and saw a snake in a tree.

The serpent came and said, "So God has told you not to eat the fruit of any tree in the garden?"

"We can eat the fruit of all the trees in the garden, except God told us, 'Do not eat the fruit of the tree that is in the middle of the garden, and neither should you touch it, or you will die,'" said Eve.

"I assure you that you will not die!" said the snake. God knows that the day you eat the fruit of that tree you will see what you have never seen. You will be able to know what is good and what is bad; then you will be like God."

Eve knew that she had to get away from the snake, but decided to stay and contemplate the appetizing fruit. "The fruit looks tasty; besides, it's so pretty. The serpent says that God is wrong and that if I eat it I will not die. God should allow us to eat this fruit," thought Eva. Then she decided, "I'm sure this fruit will make me as wise as God! I will do what I want. I'll eat the fruit!"

So Eve took the fruit and bit into it. "The snake was right, this fruit is delicious!" Eve thought.

Then, she offered it to her husband, and he also decided to eat the forbidden fruit.

Suddenly, Adam and Eve felt different, but that did not make them feel happy. On the contrary, they felt guilty and ashamed.

"God is coming! What will we do now?" they asked each other.

"Let's hide," said Adam.

"Adam and Eve, where are you?" God called out.

"When we heard you were coming through the garden, I was scared because I'm naked, that's why I hid myself," replied Adam.

"Did you eat from the tree that I prohibited you from eating from?" God asked them.

Adam and Eve had never before been afraid of God.

"Eve gave me the fruit to eat," Adam replied fearfully.

"What have you done?" God asked Eve.

"The snake said it would be good for me. It lied to me and I ate," Eve answered with great fear.

"Why didn't you trust me? Now you will have to suffer the consequences of your bad decision," said God. "I warned you that if you ate it you would die. But first you will have to work hard to get your food. Having babies will be painful, and you will no longer be able to live in this garden."

Everything had changed for Adam and Eve. And every day they thought sadly, "Why did we make that bad decision and disobey God?"

ACTIVITIES

The first sin

Pass out the worksheet for this lesson. Ask the students to fold the page along the dotted lines and review the Bible story. While they are doing that, ask them the following questions as a review:

- Why was it bad to eat that fruit?
- How did Adam and Eve feel after they had disobeyed?
- What did God do about their disobedience?
- Was it the serpent's fault that Adam and Eve disobeyed?
- What did the serpent tell them to deceive them?

Then, have them go to the next page and tell them: *Here we see symbols that warn us about dangers. Look carefully at the pictures on the top, and circle those that are most familiar to you. Some only inform us. But others are warnings and protect us from danger. When we decide to obey those warnings we remain safe.*

Then ask them to look at the bottom of the page and circle the ways we receive warnings from God to protect us from danger. Explain: *God wants us to be safe from sin and its consequences. That is why he has given us his Word, and wise people who guide us to make good decisions that please God.*

Mural

For this activity you will need a large card, strips of colored paper, scissors and tape.

On the top of the card write the title of the unit: THE HOLY LOVE OF GOD. And in the lower part write down the memory verse (Romans 3:23-24).

In the middle space, stick the paper strips vertically, leaving about 3 cm. between one and the other. There must be a strip of paper for each member of the class. If the group is large, make two murals or use a larger piece of paper.

Each week the children must add a figure from the Cut-out Section from the student book pg. 137 to their strip.

Pass out figure 1 (yellow oval) and have them write their name on it. Explain that they should continue to add figures to the mural throughout the unit, so they should be faithful in attending to complete the project. Give time for everyone to paste the figure of the day.

Memorization

Use the mural to review the verse. Ask that three or four volunteers read it using different voice modulations, for example: in a low voice, with a low voice, with a high voice, etc. Then ask those who already know it by heart to say it without reading it.

To end

Talk with your students about the importance of applying what they learn in class to their daily lives. Ask them to stay alert this week to everything that encourages them to disobey God, and pray for God to strengthen them.

Form a circle, and pray for each of your students. Also intercede for sick family members and for children who missed class.

Lesson 11
Painful results

Biblical References: Genesis 4:1-16

Lesson Objective: That the students learn that ignoring God's warnings brings painful consequences.

Memory Verse: *"For all have sinned and fall short of the glory of God, and all are justified freely by his grace through the redemption that came by Christ Jesus"* (Romans 3:23-24).

PREPARE YOURSELF TO TEACH!

Many elementary students know that making decisions always has consequences. However, there are consequences that are difficult to face (for example: emotional wounds, restriction of privileges, distrust, broken relationships and punishments).

Cain suffered painful consequences due to his bad decision. Even so, he experienced the mercy of God. Help your students understand that the decision to sin has painful consequences, but God is merciful. He always treats us better than we deserve.

BIBLICAL COMMENTARY

Cain, the main character of this passage, treated his brother Abel with cruelty and injustice. Then, like his parents (Gen. 3), he tried to avoid the consequences of his action.

God gave justice to Cain, but with mercy. We read that he did not kill Cain to pay for his guilt. Rather, he implemented measures to protect his life, making sure that no one mistreated him, even though he had killed his brother.

Help your students understand that God does not tolerate sin, but loves the sinner. Although he treated Cain harshly, he also showed his mercy. It is an example of how we should treat others. Cain not only acted badly against Abel, but also against his family, and especially against God.

Remind them that God is the Creator of life and the only one who has the right to take it. Cain claimed the power to take the life of his brother; that is why he had to face the consequences of his sin. But God, who is great in mercy, took care of his life.

Help your class understand that every decision has consequences. Therefore, they should ask God to help them make the best decisions. It is also necessary to know that the consequences of sin are irreversible, but God's grace and forgiveness are greater.

DEVELOPMENT OF THE LESSON

Mural

Pass out Figure 2, which says WARNING, from the Cut-out Section of the student worksheets (pg. 137) and have the kids paste it on the appropriate strip of the class mural. As they work, review what they learned last week and relate it to the new topic. Tell them that today's story is about a warning we must learn. If you have visitors, help them add their strip to the mural.

What would happen if...?

Pass out the student worksheets for Lesson 11. Ask the students to draw what would happen if they ignored those warnings. Then, give them time to show their drawings and ask them: *Why do you think there are warnings? Warnings are not posted to ruin our fun, but to keep us safe from danger. God warned us to stay away from sin.*

Ask them: *What do you think happens when we ignore God's warnings? Allow them to respond, and emphasize what happened to Adam and Eve when they ignored God and ate the forbidden fruit.*

BIBLE STORY

The disobedience of Cain

Life was difficult for Adam and Eve outside of the beautiful garden that God had made for them. But one day God sent them something that made them feel happy again.

"God has blessed me by giving me this son," said Eve. They called their first son Cain. Then they had another baby, which they named Abel.

The brothers grew up, and Abel decided to be a shepherd of sheep, while Cain was devoted to agriculture.

The two boys worked with effort and dedication.

One day they decided to offer an offering of gratitude to God.

Cain offered part of his harvest, while Abel chose a sheep from his flock.

"Abel," said God, "I accept your offering. But I can not accept yours, Cain."

Upon hearing those words, Cain became very angry and jealous of his brother.

"Why are you angry?" God asked Cain. "If you do the right thing, I will accept your offering. But if you do not, you will be sinning. Sin wants to rule your life, but if you decide to trust me you will be strong to resist sin."

Cain decided not to listen to God's warning. On the contrary, his jealousy grew more and more.

One day Cain said to his brother, "Abel, let's go to the country for a walk."

When they were in the field, Cain attacked his brother and killed him.

Soon after, God asked Cain, "Where is your brother Abel?"

"I do not know," said Cain, "I do not have to take care of him."

Then God said to him, "What have you done? You can not hide anything from me. You killed your brother, and therefore you will never have good harvests again. You will live on the move, always traveling from one place to another."

"That is too much!" Cain replied. "My punishment is terrible, and anyone who finds me will want to kill me."

"No," replied the Lord. "I will put a mark on you, as a sign that no one can kill you. If someone kills you I will punish them seven times more than you."

ACTIVITIES

How does sin harm us?

Allow time for the children to help Cain find the right path on the worksheet. There are different options to start, but only one will take them to the end. However, as in the biblical story, Cain will not be able to get to his house or to where his family is. His sin led him to wander from one place to the other.

As they work, stress to your students the terrible consequences of Cain's sin.

Water and oil

Use these elements to illustrate to your students that God is holy and that he is separate from sin. Get a glass jar with a lid. Fill it halfway with water, and add a few drops of red vegetable dye to make it easier to observe. Fill the rest of the bottle with oil and cover it well.

Tell your students: Our God is holy and does not tolerate sin. Sin is disobeying God, and separates us from him.

Ask some volunteers to shake the container to try to mix the two liquids. Tell them to watch how they separate.

Explain that in the same way, sin separates us from God. The holiness of God and the life of sin cannot be mixed. That is why it is important that we repent and seek God.

Memorization

In advance cut out several large circles of cardboard. Write in each of them one or several words of the memory verse. Hide them around the room before your students arrive. Then, ask them to look for them and put them in order according to the original text. Repeat it together several times.

Save the circles for use next week.

To end

Encourage your students to obey God's warnings and stay away from sin. Ask them to stay alert and avoid getting close to what could separate them from God.

Intercede for your students. When you pray for them, it helps them feel appreciated and valued as part of the church family.

Lesson 12
Our God of love and mercy

Biblical References: Genesis 6:5—9:17
Lesson Objective: That the students are thankful to God for his mercy, and wish to obey Him.
Memory Verse: *"For all have sinned and fall short of the glory of God, and all are justified freely by his grace through the redemption that came by Christ Jesus"* (Romans 3:23-24).

PREPARE YOURSELF TO TEACH!

The story of Noah has a special teaching for every child. For those who think that sin is not evil until they see the consequences, the story of the flood shows the seriousness of sin. This story talks about the justice of God, but also shows his great love and mercy. By God's command, Noah was to warn people about the consequences of their sin; however, they did not want to listen. God showed his love by saving Noah and his family with the ark.

Many times the child is expected to obey simply because he must do so. Understanding what the reasons are for doing something is better than obeying just because someone orders it. Help them understand that God loves them and wants them to obey Him.

BIBLICAL COMMENTARY

Genesis 6:5-9:17. The emphasis of this story is not placed on a person, the flood, or the animals, but on the mercy of God and his plans for a new beginning of his creation.

Genesis 6:6 shows the intense anguish of God to see that the heart of man was inclined only to evil. He was not angry, but sad and repentant. "And the LORD repented that he had made man on the earth, and it grieved him in his heart."

Unfortunately, the human heart continued to lean towards evil, but the flood caused an irreversible decision in God. After that, he made a pact with his creation: that he would not destroy it again with water. Our God was committed to having a love relationship with his creation from the beginning, but that commitment intensified. For the first time God felt pain and suffered for man's betrayal. But once again we see that his love is so great that he did not completely exterminate mankind, but gave him a new opportunity.

DEVELOPMENT OF THE LESSON

Choose some of the following activities to complement the development of the class.

Repeat the phrase!

Have the students sit in a circle, and tell them: *God made a perfect world where everything that was there was good. Imagine what a perfect world would be like. I'm going to start. "In a perfect world, there should be ..." (much love). Complete the sentence with a phrase or a word.* The child next to you should repeat the sentence as you said it and add another idea (for example: In a perfect world there should be a lot of love and no hate).

Continue the game around the circle, allowing time for each student to repeat the phrase and add the words they want. When someone can not remember the whole sentence, stop the game and start over.

Tell them: *When God created the world, He made everything perfect. What happened that changed everything?*

Allow them time to respond, and remind them that sin came through the disobedience of Adam and Eve.

Mural

Pass out figure 3 of the cut-out section, where the ark with the word PROMISE is seen (pg 137), and have the kids paste it on the corresponding strip on the class mural. Take this time to review with them what they have learned in the previous lessons, and briefly introduce today's topic.

BIBLE STORY

Gather your students to hear the Bible story, and tell them: *After the first sin of Adam and Eve, their children and grandchildren continued to disobey God. Today we are going to learn about a man named Noah and what he did.*

Try to use some visual materials when teaching the story. If you do not have printed illustrations, draw an ark on a card.

Then, get drawings or photographs of animals and use them as visual aids to illustrate the story.

Noah obeys God

After God created Adam and Eve, the number of people was increasing. They all lived in the beautiful world that God had created.

However as time passed, people forgot God and began to do evil. They no longer heard the voice of the Lord, and disobeyed Him; they did things that they knew were not the right ones. That hurt the heart of God and made him feel very sad, so much so that he wished he had not created mankind.

But among so many bad people, there was a man who loved the Lord and had obeyed him all his life. His name was Noah.

One day God told him, "You are the only person of this time who lives according to my will. The others are bad and disobedient. That is why I am going to send a great flood to cleanse the earth of all evil. Build an ark of the measures that I will give you. In it, you and all your family will be safe. You must also put in it a pair of each species of animals. In this way they will be protected from the water."

Noah worked day and night to build the ark. When he had finished it, he put food and everything needed in it.

After all the animal pairs were inside the ark, Noah and his family took their belongings and entered there as well. Then, God closed the door of the ark and it started to rain. It rained for 40 days and 40 nights. When at last it stopped raining, the whole earth was covered with water. Noah could only see water everywhere. The only ones left alive were those on the ark.

After many days, the water level began to fall, leaving the ark on top of a mountain. Forty days passed and Noah sent a raven outside. But not finding a dry place, it returned to the ark. After a few days, he sent out a dove, which also returned to the ark. Noah waited another seven days. When he sent the pigeon again, it returned with an olive branch in its beak. That meant that the earth was beginning to produce again.

Seven days passed and Noah sent the pigeon again, but this time it did not return because it had found dry land to live on.

When the water finally dried up, Noah, his family and the animals left the ark. God put a beautiful rainbow in the sky as a reminder of his promise that he would never again send another flood to destroy the earth. Noah built an altar of stones and thanked God for having saved him from the flood.

ACTIVITIES

Hidden words

Hand out the student worksheet and ask that your students look for the seven words hidden in the drawing of Lesson 12 (love, obedience, goodness, hatred, sin, evil, faithfulness). Help those who have reading difficulties identify the letters.

Talk to them about the difference between Noah and the other people. Ask them to look in their Bible for Genesis 6:8-9 and emphasize the characteristics that Noah had.

Have them go to the next page, and give them time to color the marked spaces to find the hidden message.

Handwork

Provide each student with half a paper plate, and provide the time needed to decorate it with pencils or colored crayons, as if it were heaven. Prepare several strips of paper of different colors to stick on the plates forming a rainbow. Glue the strips following the outline of the plate; let the edges protrude so that, when the plate is shaken, the movement of the strips makes the work look attractive.

As they work, emphasize that the rainbow reminds us that we have a God of love and mercy.

Memorization

Divide your class into two teams, and put on the table the circles you prepared last week. Mix them, and ask that each team try to put the memory verse in order in the shortest possible time. Every time a team finishes, everyone should repeat the text aloud.

Then ask that some volunteers stick the circles on the wall to keep them in a visible place for the rest of the unit.

To end

Conclude the class by thanking God for the love and mercy He has for His children. Remind your students that God cared for Noah because he was obedient.

Encourage them to bring guests to the next class, and say goodbye in praise of God.

Lesson 13
Our God of Justice and Grace

Biblical References: Genesis 18:16—19:29

Lesson Objective: That the students understand that God is just, and that disobedience brings serious consequences.

Memory Verse: *"For all have sinned and fall short of the glory of God, and all are justified freely by his grace through the redemption that came by Christ Jesus"* (Romans 3:23-24).

PREPARE YOURSELF TO TEACH!

Impartiality is important for elementary aged children, because it provides order and a sense of fairness, that is, everyone receives the same treatment. Children complain immediately if they believe a situation is unfair. This lesson will help them trust that God is just.

Either way, justice demands judgment towards evil. In the story of Sodom and Gomorrah, God showed his great mercy even to the wicked, when he pledged to forgive the city if there were 20 righteous people there. In spite of everything, the cities were sinful and that demanded judgment.

In truth, God is just, but life is not. Bad decisions, ambition and sin make our society full of injustices. The righteous often suffer as much as the unjust.

Although God spared the lives of Lot and his family, they also suffered. Lot lost his wife, his friends and his possessions.

God is just and merciful. He is merciful with everything and, in many cases, saves the righteous from great difficulties. However, God will finally judge and punish the evil ones.

In this story we see that the judgment and grace of God act together. The trial is obvious in the destruction of cities that were in complete chaos. People had rejected God, and their behavior was characterized by violence, perversion and total lack of control.

Abraham's faith marks a huge contrast between him and the people of those cities. Abraham and Lot were faithful to God and interceded for their neighbors. Abraham interceded for the cities, and Lot interceded for the angels who visited him.

This story helps us see how God deals with humanity, showing his grace and mercy to all. He did not destroy the cities immediately; He did it when the outcry against Sodom and Gomorrah increased and their sin became extremely severe.

The justice of God demands a response. Those who continue to reject God will suffer the consequences of their sins. But, we can be sure that God will save the righteous.

DEVELOPMENT OF THE LESSON

Use some of the following didactic suggestions to make the development of the lesson more interesting and effective.

Review game

This activity will help your students remember what they learned in the previous lessons, and it will serve as an introduction to this week's topic.

Prepare nine boxes or containers of the same size, in which a small ball fits. Arrange them three by three, and connect them with duct tape, so that they are all attached. Then, number them from 1 to 9.

A student will throw the ball into one of the containers and, according to the number in which it falls, will answer the corresponding question:

1. Mention something you remember about the first time someone disobeyed God.
2. What is sin?
3. Who sinned?
4. What did Cain do?

5. What happened to Cain after he sinned?
6. How did God have mercy on Cain?
7. How did God feel when he saw all the bad things that people were doing in the time of Noah?
8. What is the love of God like?
9. How can people approach God?

Mural

Hand out Figure 4, which says "Watch Out," from the Cutout Section of the student book (pg. 137), and have your class paste it on the appropriate strip in the classroom mural.

Ask them to look at the figure as you tell them: God sent these visitors with a special mission. By listening to the biblical story we will learn more about what they did when visiting two large cities.

What does it mean to be fair?

Write the word JUSTICE on the board or on a card. Ask your students to say what that word means, and write the answers on the board.

Then, explain to them that being fair means giving each one what they deserve; To not show favoritism; act correctly.

Use this activity as an introduction to the Bible Story.

BIBLE STORY

Keep your Bible open in the Bible passage so your students know that what they will learn comes from the Word of God. If you wish, ask that some volunteers read the passage before beginning the narration.

Rescued from Sodom

"Welcome!" said Abraham to the foreigners who came to his tent. He did not receive many visitors in the hot land where he lived. "Please, come and rest a moment, and stay for lunch with us."

The strangers accepted the invitation. However, they were not ordinary travelers. They were messengers of God!

"Within a year or so, you will have the son God promised you," they told Abraham. But that good news was not the only news that the messengers brought. They were going towards two cities where there was a lot of evil. Abraham walked with them for a while when they continued on their way.

God thought, "Do I tell Abraham what I'm going to do?" Then he said through the angels, "The sin of Sodom and Gomorrah is so terrible that I will destroy those cities and all the people who live there."

Abraham was very worried. His nephew Lot lived in one of those cities. When the messengers continued their journey to Sodom, Abraham prayed, "God, will you kill the good ones along with the bad ones? If there are 50 good and righteous people in Sodom, will you kill them all? Will you not save the city for the love of the 50 righteous? I know you would not treat the good the same as the bad. You are merciful and forgiving! I ask you not to do it! But I know you: the Judge of the whole universe will do what is right."

"If I find 50 righteous people in the whole city, I will not destroy it," answered God.

"And if there were only 45 righteous people, will you destroy the whole city because of those other five bad people?" Abraham asked.

"If there are 45 righteous, I will not destroy it," said God.

"Do not get angry now, my Lord, but maybe there are only 30 good people," Abraham continued.

"I will not destroy it if I find 30 good people," God answered once more.

"What if there were 20?" Abraham asked again.

"For those 20 people I will not destroy it," God answered.

"I will ask for the last time. What would happen if there were only 10 good people in Sodom?" Abraham asked.

"For love of the 10 righteous, I will not destroy it," concluded God.

Finally, the angels arrived in Sodom. When they reached the city gate, they saw Lot there and approached him. When Lot saw them, he got up and bowed before them.

"I beg you to stay at my house tonight," said Lot.

"No, we'll camp on the street," the visitors replied.

"Stay at my home," insisted Lot.

In the end they accepted.

The visitors were sad to see what was happening in the city. The perversion and sin of the city was terrible! There were not 10 people in the whole city who loved or obeyed God!

"Do you have more family in this city?" the visitors asked Lot. "Get them out of here because we will destroy this place. The clamor against the people of Sodom and Gomorrah is so great that God has sent us to destroy it."

Very quickly Lot went to look for the men his daughters intended to marry and when he found them, he said to them, "Come on, let's get out of this city because God is going to destroy it."

But they thought it was a joke.

At dawn, the angels told Lot, "Get up, and take your wife and your daughters so they do not die when the city is destroyed!"

"I'll go get them," Lot said.

Since Lot and his family took a long time, the angels took them by the hands and took them out of the city.

"Save yourselves!" the visitors told them, "and do not look back."

So Lot and his family ran to save their lives. But Lot's wife looked back, and at that moment she became a statue of salt.

Very early the next day, Abraham got up and went to the place where he had prayed to God. From there he looked toward Sodom and Gomorrah and all the plain, and saw that from all that land arose smoke coming from the burning cities as from a furnace.

God destroyed those wicked cities, but He remembered Abraham's prayer and rescued his nephew Lot.

ACTIVITIES

The rescue

Distribute the student worksheets, scissors and glue.

Hand out the figures of Abraham and the city from the Cut-Out section of the student book (pg. 139) and follow the instructions to make the booklet.

Help those who have difficulties understanding the directions or with cutting.

Take time to walk through the Bible story, using the booklets they have just completed.

Memorization

Ask your students to close their eyes as you write the memory verse on the board. Then, ask them to open their eyes and read the verse several times.

Ask them to close their eyes again, and delete a keyword. Then have them read it again, adding the missing word. Continue until all the text is deleted.

To end

Cultivate in your students the discipline of prayer, interceding during each class for each of them and their families. If possible, write the petitions on a poster board and stick it in the classroom. In this way they will remember them, and each time God responds, they can put a star next to the petition.

Pray giving thanks to God for his mercy and justice.

Encourage them to attend the next class of this unit next week.

Lesson 14

Our God of forgiveness

Biblical References: Leviticus 4; Hebrews 10:1-14

Lesson Objective: That the students know that God has provided a way for the forgiveness of our sins.

Memory Verse: *"For all have sinned and fall short of the glory of God, and all are justified freely by his grace through the redemption that came by Christ Jesus"* (Romans 3:23-24).

PREPARE YOURSELF TO TEACH!

The tragedy of sin is that it separates people from God. Your students learned about the origin of sin in the first lesson of the unit. In the subsequent lessons they studied the consequences of sin, and how God responds in a just and merciful way. This lesson reaffirms the theme of God's mercy. They will learn that he created a sacrificial system to solve the problem of sin and, finally, he gave his only begotten Son so that all who believe have eternal life.

Most of your students have a tender conscience. They feel their own guilt when they do wrong, and they know that sin separates them from God. Use this lesson to bring them closer to God and to discover that he offers forgiveness and has provided a way for us to receive salvation.

BIBLICAL COMMENTARY

Leviticus 4. The covenant established in Exodus shows a call to the people of God to be a holy nation (Exodus 19:6). Leviticus was like a manual explaining to the people of God how they should worship Him. Confession, repentance, and sacrifices to receive forgiveness were essential in worship. Chapter 4 deals with the offering to obtain forgiveness (for unintentional sins). It is evident that every deliberate sin excluded the sinner from the holy nation. The punishment for the rebellion was death (see Exodus 21:12-17).

The sin offering shows that it is possible for the holy people of God to violate some of their laws unconsciously or unintentionally. The people of God were to seek atonement for their sins as soon as they realized it.

In this type of offering, the worshiper admitted that he had done evil before God, and presented the animal for sacrifice. As part of the ritual, he had to place his hands on the animal. This was a way of identifying with the animal that would be sacrificed. Through this, the sinner offered his life to God.

In this system, a sacrifice was made on behalf of the person, and the priest was the mediator. It is difficult for us now to understand how the sacrificed animal took the place of the sinner. However, the first believers could understand it when Jesus Christ died on the cross for the sinner. They understood that Jesus had taken their place because of their sin.

Today, sins that are not intentional are easily overlooked as "mistakes." God liberates his people from unintentional sin, but the sinner must acknowledge his sin and repent heartily before God.

Hebrews 10:1-14. The problem was that sacrifices became a routine and lost their meaning. The prophets repeatedly denounced this fact, describing the sacrifices as "empty". Sacrifices that did not change the sinner were not true.

The writer of the book to the Hebrews focused on explaining that Christ fulfilled the sacrificial system once and for all. The Lord Jesus Christ was the Lamb of sacrifice, and at the same time, the High Priest. Christ is now the mediator between us and the Father.

DEVELOPMENT OF THE LESSON

Choose some of the following activities to enrich the development of the lesson.

Mural

Pass out Picture 5 from the Cut-out section (p. 137) and ask your students to add it to the appropriate strip on the class mural. For a general review of this unit, ask volunteers to share what each one of the mural figures means.

Place the finished mural in a visible place so that everyone will know what the class studied.

The cross

Before class, draw a cross for each child and cut them out. During the class, distribute the crosses to each student and have them decorate them using different materials (paper, colored pencils, sand, paints, etc.).

As they work, tell them: Do you know why there are crosses in many churches? Listen to their answers and, based on them, ask them: Why do you think Jesus died on the cross?

Use the answers your students give to begin the development of the biblical story.

BIBLE STORY

Water and oil

Use the "Water and oil" activity suggested in the previous lesson to represent the separation between God and sin.

After several volunteers have tried to mix the liquids, explain that just as with water and oil, our God who is holy does not mix with sin. However, God does not want us to be separated from him because he loves us and has provided a way to forgive our sins.

The sacrifices of Israel

One day, when Moses was on a mountain, God told him, "Moses, tell the Israelites that although I am the sole owner of the whole earth, I chose them to be my special people. They will be for me a kingdom of priests and a holy nation. If the people obey me, they will be my special treasure."

Moses came down from the mountain quickly. He wanted to tell the people what God had told him. After he had done so, they responded, "We will do all that God has said."

To remind people that they were His chosen people, God gave them the Ten Commandments. These laws helped them know what was right and what was wrong. God told Moses to build a special tent, which they would call a tabernacle, so that people would remember that God was always with them.

God expected his people to obey him. But he knew that sometimes they would break his commandments. That is why he made a way in which he could forgive people for their sins.

So he said to Moses, "When people disobey any of my commandments, they will have to offer a sacrifice. Tell them they should choose their best animal, whether it's an ox, goat or lamb. It must be a perfect animal, without spots, wounds or diseases. And then they must take their animal to the tabernacle. When they are there, they should put their hands on the animal to show that they are sorry for what they did. Then, the priests will take the animal and sacrifice it as I have indicated."

God gave very clear instructions about how they should prepare and offer animals as sacrifices. Day after day, year after year, they followed the instructions that God had given them. They chose animals and sacrificed them, as an offering of repentance for their sins.

Some were very sorry for the wrong they had done. But others were not. They made sacrifices only because everyone else did. The prophets knew that some sacrifices that people made did not show their repentance.

"God is not satisfied with your sacrifices," said the prophet Jeremiah. "God told us how to offer them. He wants you to love him and obey him."

Although God's plan for sacrifices was good, many people offered burnt offerings only out of habit, but in their hearts there was no repentance or love of God.

However, God had a better plan for the forgiveness of sins for our good. He sent his Son Jesus to die on the cross for the sins of the whole world. God allowed Jesus to be sacrificed so that our sins would be forgiven without offering more animal sacrifices. Also, when people trust in Jesus as Savior and Lord, the Holy Spirit comes to dwell in their hearts and changes them so they can love God more.

ACTIVITIES

Two types of sacrifice

Hand out the student worksheets. Ask the children to cut out the figure from Lesson 14, following the solid dark lines. Instruct them to bend it by the dotted lines so that when they open the card, they see the figure of the cross. (See illustration on worksheet.) Ask a volunteer to read the phrase that says: "In the Old Testament, when people sinned they sacrificed animals."

Explain that the picture shows an altar, like the ones in the tabernacle. The altar was the special place where priests burned the sacrificed animals.

Then, ask everyone to read together the phrase that says: "We no longer have to sacrifice animals. Jesus made forgiveness possible by dying on the cross for us."

Talk about the differences that exist between those sacrifices. Explain that the two types of sacrifices were provided by God for the forgiveness of sins. Both must be perfect for God to accept them. However, animal sacrifices had to be made again and again. But when Christ died, he did it once for all people. The sacrificed animals could not change the hearts of people, but Jesus has the power to change us and transform us into his image.

Evangelistic invitation

If the Holy Spirit guides you, encourage your students to make a personal decision to follow Christ and repent of their sins. Use your Bible and the passages suggested in the student worksheets to guide them to accept salvation.

To be a child of God you must:
- Recognize that you have sinned. (Romans 3:23)
- Believe that Jesus died for you. (Rom. 5:8)
- Repent of your sins. (Romans 6:23)
- Ask God to forgive you. (1 John 1:9)
- Now you are a child of God. (1 John 1:12)

Use this simple prayer to help those who have trouble praying:

Dear God, I recognize that I have sinned and I repent for all the wrong I did. I ask you to forgive me. I believe that Jesus died for me and I receive Him as my Savior and Lord. Help me to obey and love you every day. Thank you for forgiving me and allowing me to be your son. Amen.

It is important that you set aside a special time to talk with each of your students before or after inviting them to receive Christ in their lives. Help them understand that this is a personal and decisive decision for the rest of their lives.

Memorization

Write the words of Romans 3:23-24 on different cards or sheets. Glue them with tape on a table or on the board, so that it is easy to take them off and put them back on. Read the verse several times. Ask a volunteer to move the cards and another to put them in order again. Do this exercise several times, and repeat the verse each time the cards are in order.

To end

Get together to pray and give thanks to God for having provided a way for our salvation. Sing a song of praise, and congratulate those who have accepted Christ.

It is important that you keep track of these students to help them grow in the Christian faith. We suggest that you also talk with their parents, and let them know the decision their child made, and make a plan for discipling the child. Remember that in the first years of the spiritual formation of your students, your task as a teacher of Christian education is fundamental.

Year 2 — Introduction – Unit IV

WE CELEBRATE HOLY WEEK

Biblical References: Matthew 21:1-11; Luke 19:28-38; John 20:1-18; Luke 24:13-35; Acts 1:1-11.

Unit Memory Verse: *If you declare with your mouth, "Jesus is Lord," and believe in your heart that God raised him from the dead, you will be saved (Romans 10:9).*

UNIT OBJECTIVES

This unit will help the students to:

- Worship God for what he did through Jesus Christ.
- Believe that Jesus lives.
- Know that Jesus went to heaven and will return to get us.

LESSON UNIT A

Lesson 15: We celebrate Jesus' triumphant entry!

Lesson 16: We celebrate Jesus' resurrection!

Lesson 17: The Emmaus Road

Lesson 18: Jesus is always with us!

WHY ELEMENTARY STUDENTS NEED THE TEACHING OF THIS UNIT:

Society and the media have diverted children's attention from the true meaning of Holy Week. Many secular symbols continue to captivate elementary students, who are not properly prepared for this solemn celebration.

The focus of this unit is on the celebration of the resurrection of Jesus. Your students will be excited to know who Jesus is and what he did for them.

During these lessons, you will have the opportunity to pass on to the children the plan of salvation, and guide them to a deep relationship with Jesus Christ. Pray for the guidance of the Holy Spirit as you prepare these lessons. Remember that, through your teaching, God can transform not only the lives of your students, but also those of their parents. Take this opportunity to tell others what Christ did for you!

Lesson 15
We celebrate Jesus' triumphant entry

Biblical References: Matthew 21:1-11; Luke 19:28-38

Lesson Objective: That the students worship God for sending Jesus as our Saviour.

Memory Verse: *If you declare with your mouth, "Jesus is Lord," and believe in your heart that God raised him from the dead, you will be saved (Romans 10:9).*

PREPARE YOURSELF TO TEACH!

Why do elementary students praise God? Maybe because you do it, or because they observe that everyone in the church does it. But they may not really understand what praise means.

Remember that they tend to imitate the actions of others even if they do not know their meaning. Therefore, in this lesson, teach your students the importance and meaning of praise.

They must learn that we praise someone when we recognize that they did something extraordinary. It is an expression of recognition. Therefore, praising with one's heart cannot be a secondary feeling.

On the first Palm Sunday, the crowd worshiped God for the miracles they had seen Jesus do. They also praised him because they thought he would free them from Roman rule and establish Israel as an independent nation. However, realizing that this was not Jesus' mission, their praises became complaints.

As you study these lessons, help your students discover what Jesus did for them to give them salvation and eternal life.

BIBLICAL COMMENTARY

Matthew 21:1-11. The triumphal entry into Jerusalem was the end of a busy day for Jesus and his disciples. Jesus had been teaching and healing the sick, and the miracles had attracted a large following. When Jesus entered Jerusalem, the hopes regarding the Messiah who would come to set them free were at their highest level.

Jesus came to the holy city as an uncommon king. He did not arrive in a beautiful carriage or on a war horse. On the contrary, he arrived riding on a donkey and his clothing was not that of a king. There were no royal decorations on the mountain or on the road; however, the people laid down their coats and palm leaves. Jesus was humble and his mission was peaceful. He offered himself as someone who would conquer, not with weapons but with love. The people on the road shouted, "Hosanna!" Which means: "Save us, Lord!" They did not know that he would bring true salvation. However, he would not do so by causing suffering to his enemies, but by enduring suffering and humiliation.

As Zechariah prophesied: "Behold, your king will come to you, righteous and savior, humble, and riding on an ass" (Zechariah 9:9), the Lord Jesus did not come to Jerusalem to conquer a throne or an empire, but to conquer their hearts.

The city shuddered, but it was not saved. The salvation they expected was political and material. The salvation that Jesus offered them was spiritual. Therefore, the same people who at that moment shouted "hosanna," hours later shouted "crucify him."

This lesson will provide you with the opportunity to teach your students that Jesus wants to occupy the throne of their hearts.

DEVELOPMENT OF THE LESSON

Palms of praise

Make paper palm leaves with your students, or get real palm leaves. To make them, you will need palm stencils to draw them on green paper, or you can also make them on white paper and provide green pencils for children to color. Then, ask them to cut them out.

Tell them: *Today is Palm Sunday, and I will tell you a very special story. These are palm branches. When Jesus entered Jerusalem, the people waved palm branches like these and shouted: "Hosanna, Hosanna!" They were very excited and happy because they were praising Jesus. You can also wave your palm branch and shout "Hosanna!" to Jesus.*

What is praise?

Have your students sit in a circle, and ask them: *Do you know what "praise" means?* After listening to their responses, explain: *Praise is our response to someone who did something extraordinary. Praise is an expression of love and admiration towards someone special.*

God is the only one worthy of our praise. What are some reasons why it is good to worship the Lord. Write them on the board (for example: because he created everything that exists, because it is good, because he takes care of us, etc.).

BIBLE STORY

Praise the Lord!

Sing a song of praise while they wave their palm branches and march around the room. Ask the children to sit down to listen to the story.

Instruct them to put their palm branches on their legs and, during the story, each time they hear the word "hosanna," shake them.

Before starting the story, show the Bible and tell them: *This is the Bible, the Word of God. We learn to know God better by listening to the stories in this precious book.*

Holy Week is a very beautiful and special time in which we celebrate the surrender of Jesus, the Son of God. In today's story we will learn what happened before the first Holy Week, when the children sang and praised Jesus.

The triumphal entry

"Tell us the story of Easter again," the children asked their father.

"A long time ago, our people were slaves in Egypt," began the father. "God told Moses to guide us to our land, but Pharaoh did not allow us to leave. Finally, the angel of death passed through Egypt. All the firstborn of the Egyptian families died. Then Pharaoh released us."

"When will the Romans let us be free?" asked the children.

"Someday a King Messiah will come and deliver us," said the father. "The Messiah will deliver us from the Romans."

The people of Jerusalem were enthusiastic. Thousands of Jews had gathered there to celebrate the feast of the Passover. Jesus and his disciples were also heading to Jerusalem for the celebration.

"Go to the next town," Jesus said to two of his disciples. "Upon entering, you will find a tied up donkey that was never ridden. Untie it and bring it."

Jesus needed the donkey for a special reason. A long time ago, the prophet Zechariah had said that the king of Jerusalem would arrive peacefully, riding on an donkey. As Jesus had told them, the disciples found the donkey. Then they put their cloaks on him and took him away. Then, they helped Jesus get on and they took the road to Jerusalem.

When they saw Jesus approaching, some people spread their coats on the road. Soon the crowd became aware of the presence of the Lord.

"Is not he the man who has done so many miracles?" they asked each other.

"Yes it's him! Look, he's coming to Jerusalem! Do you think he is the promised Messiah?"

Immediately the people began to praise God with joy for all the miracles they had seen, "Hosanna! Blessed is he who comes in the name of the Lord! Peace in heaven and glory in the highest! Hosanna!"

Many went to cut palm branches, and put them along the way. And, as Jesus passed, many exclaimed, "Hosanna, Hosanna!"

ACTIVITIES

Hosanna!

Ask the children to look at their worksheet for Lesson 15, and cut out the bottom strip. Tell them to fold the sheet next to the dotted lines.

Then, double the figure of Jesus where the dotted lines indicate and glue/tape the bottom together. Move the figure through the crowd, to review the story of Palm Sunday.

Praise mural

During the week, prepare illustrations about different ways that children can praise God in their daily lives. Include scenes of children who help their parents, pray, sing praises, read the Bible, etc. Show them to the class and tell them that they can praise God in different ways. Ask them to stick the illustrations on the wall or somewhere that you indicate.

Memorization

Ask your students to look up the memory verse (Romans 10:9) and read it out loud. After repeating it several times (by rows, by groups, only boys, only girls, etc.), ask some volunteers to say it by heart. Hand out the Month's Verse Club cards for review at home. Ask parents to study with their children during the week.

To end

Make sure children take home their work, and thank them for attending the class. Announce something about the next lesson, trying to make a connection and awakening the interest so that they do not miss.

Form two circles, and assign a prayer leader for each.

At the end, lead them in a united prayer. Do not forget to include the petitions, and encourage your students to praise God every day.

Lesson 16
We celebrate Jesus' resurrection

Biblical References: John 20:1-18

Lesson Objective: That the students learn that Jesus Christ was raised from the dead.

Memory Verse: *If you declare with your mouth, "Jesus is Lord," and believe in your heart that God raised him from the dead, you will be saved* (Romans 10:9).

PREPARE YOURSELF TO TEACH!

In many places, the celebration of Holy Week has lost its true meaning. Advertising, the media and consumerism divert children's attention, causing them to easily forget that it is about commemorating the sacrifice of Jesus and his resurrection.

Through the resurrection we better understand the great love that Christ showed in dying for us on the cross.

At the same time, God demonstrated his power in the resurrection. Both events proclaim the message of hope, love and salvation. Any other type of celebration is insignificant when compared to the great gift of God.

Be sensitive to the reactions of your students when they hear the story of the resurrection. The fact that Christ was resurrected will bring hope to their hearts and a new perspective on life. The message of Christ's death and resurrection will help them to understand more deeply God's love for them and for others.

BIBLICAL COMMENTARY

John 20:1-18. Jesus' enemies were satisfied, because they had planned to kill him many months ago. They had finally witnessed his execution on a Roman cross.

For many people, it meant the end. Some went crestfallen to their houses, while others walked away thinking that they had fulfilled their mission to kill Jesus.

Mary Magdalene came down from Golgotha with a broken heart. Jesus had forgiven her so much, and she had believed that he was the Christ, the Son of God. Maybe Mary's hopes had died with her Master.

All the Gospels present the story of the resurrection of Jesus. Each emphasizes different details; However, here we can see that John remained firm in emphasizing faith.

In chapter 19, John points out that they quickly buried Jesus' body because the Sabbath was about to begin.

He also says that the tomb was in a garden, near Golgotha, and that Joseph and Nicodemus placed Jesus in the tomb after preparing his body with 100 pounds of spices.

On the third day, when it was still dark, Mary went to the tomb. When she arrived, she saw the stone removed and Jesus' body was not there. She assumed immediately that someone had stolen the body of her Master, and ran to warn Peter and John, "They have taken the Lord from the tomb and we do not know where they have put it." Maybe she wondered who had done it, or if Jesus' enemies were behind it all.

Peter and John ran to the grave. There they found the linens and the shroud. Then they returned to the other disciples to tell them what had happened.

It is interesting that John writes that the "other disciple" believed when he saw the empty tomb. It has been thought that John believed that Jesus had risen and not that someone had stolen his body.

Apparently, Mary did not think the same way because she was crying outside the grave. But when she looked inside, she saw two angels who asked her, "Woman, why are you crying?" She replied, "Because they have taken my Lord and I do not know where they have placed him."

Mary, blinded by her great sadness, did not recognize that it was Jesus himself who was with her. Then he called her by her name. In that instant, she recognized her beloved Master.

The resurrection was the final confirmation that Jesus was the Christ, the Son of the living God, who was resurrected and lives forever.

DEVELOPMENT OF THE LESSON

Choose some of these activities to help your students better understand the topic of study.

The crucifixion

For this activity you will need some things related to the crucifixion (a crown of thorns, nails, a cross), or use illustrations on the subject. Supervise sharp objects with extreme attention to avoid accidents.

Tell them: *Many religious leaders wanted to kill Jesus because his teachings were different from theirs. Some feared that Jesus would initiate a rebellion against the Roman Empire. That's why they arrested him and nailed him to a cross to kill him.*

Why do you think they treated the Son of God that way? Listen to their responses, and remind them of the importance of what they learned in lesson 14 about forgiveness through the sacrifice of Jesus.

Handwork

For this activity you will need crosses made of cardboard or poster board, glue, and clean, dried, crushed egg shells.

Ask the children to put glue on the cross and then sprinkle the shells on them. Place the finished work on a table so that the glue dries and the shells adhere completely.

Talk about the meaning of the cross and what it represents for Christians.

BIBLE STORY

Mary's happiness

"Poor Jesus," Mary thought as she walked towards the garden.

It was so early that the sun had not yet come out. "I miss him so much! The least we can do is bury him in an appropriate way. We did not have much time to finish everything before the Sabbath."

Mary could not believe what had happened. She had placed all her hopes on Jesus, however, he had died and he would no longer be with them.

When she continued walking through the garden, she saw something that filled her with amazement.

"It can not be!" exclaimed Mary. "Someone moved the stone. Someone has taken Jesus' body! Where is my Lord? I must go and tell Peter!"

When Peter and John heard what Mary told them, they ran to the garden. Their hearts were pounding, and they were confused.

John was the first to arrive. He approached and looked inside the cave, but only saw the cloak in which Jesus had been wrapped.

"Mary was right," he thought. "Jesus is not here."

As soon as Peter arrived, he entered the tomb and began searching everywhere, but he did not find Jesus.

"John, come here!" shouted Peter. "Look, the linens are here! But where is the Master's body?"

The two disciples returned to tell the others what they had seen. However, Mary stayed there. "My Lord is gone," she said crying.

Then she looked again into the grave and, to her surprise, the tomb was no longer empty. There were two angels in shining white robes!

"Woman, why are you crying?" the angels asked her.

"It is that they have taken my Lord and I do not know where they have put him," said Mary sadly.

When Mary was about to leave, suddenly, she saw a man in the garden.

"Woman," he said, "why are you crying? Who are you looking for?"

"Surely he's the gardener," Mary thought. "Maybe he took Jesus to another grave."

"Sir, did you take Jesus' body elsewhere? Do you know where it is? Please tell me where you put it and I'll go find it," Mary said.

"Mary!" said the man.

When Mary looked at him attentively, a deep happiness filled her heart and she exclaimed, "Teacher!"

That man was not the gardener. It was Jesus! He was there, talking to her in the garden. Jesus was alive!

"Do not touch me yet, Mary," Jesus said tenderly. "I have not returned to my Father yet. Go and tell our friends that I will go up to where they are."

Mary ran down the road to tell the others the good news.

"I have seen the Lord!" she exclaimed excitedly. "I have seen him, he has risen!"

ACTIVITIES

Jesus lives!

Distribute the worksheets, and ask your students: *How do you think Mary felt when she realized that the person she saw in the garden was Jesus?* (Happy, excited).

What did Mary do when Jesus left? (She went and told the others what she had seen.)

Now we will do something to help us tell others about the exciting story of the resurrection.

Ask them to color the picture that appears at the end of Lesson 16. Then, fold the sheet along the dotted lines to form a booklet.

Encourage them to use the work they did to tell the story of Jesus' resurrection to their friends and family.

The stone

Prepare old newspapers in advance. Give two sheets to each child. Ask them to wrinkle them into a ball. Tape around it to prevent it from falling apart.

Tell them that the ball represents the stone that was placed at the entrance to the tomb, and that it was removed when Jesus was resurrected.

Instruct them to stand at one end of the room, and when you say, "Jesus rose!", they must make the balls roll, pushing them with their feet to the other end. Then, let them return to the starting point.

Vary the dynamics of the game, giving different instructions (for example: push the ball with your hand, with your eyes closed, with your nose, move it on one foot, etc.).

Memorization

Line your students up in a row. Tell them that when you say "up," they should stretch as much as they can, like trying to touch the ceiling, and say the memory verse loudly. And when you say "down," they should duck and repeat the memory verse in a low voice.

Repeat the game several times to reinforce memorization.

To end

Encourage your class to say their prayer requests. Ask if a volunteer wants to pray aloud. This will increase their confidence to pray in public.

Conclude by thanking God for the resurrection of his Son Jesus.

Invite them to the next class, and do not forget to visit those who are sick or missed class.

Lesson 17
The Emmaus Road

Biblical References: Luke 24:13-35

Lesson Objective: That the students know that Jesus helps us know him better.

Memory Verse: *If you declare with your mouth, "Jesus is Lord," and believe in your heart that God raised him from the dead, you will be saved. (Romans 10:9)*

PREPARE YOURSELF TO TEACH!

Last week your class learned that God raised Jesus from the dead. This week they will learn that he showed that he was alive, appearing to his followers. These apparitions strengthened the faith of the first Christians. In the same way, knowing that Jesus lives will strengthen the faith of your students.

Today Jesus continues to reveal himself to his disciples and does so through the teachings of the Bible.

Prepare your heart to tell this important biblical truth to your students. Remember that your task as a teacher of Christian education is to reflect the image of Christ to the children you teach.

BIBLICAL COMMENTARY

Luke 24:13-35. It was the afternoon of the resurrection day when Jesus appeared to two of his followers while they were going to Emmaus. Why did Jesus decide to reveal himself first to these two followers, and not to his intimate group of disciples?

In last week's lesson we saw that Jesus appeared to Mary Magdalene. In today's story, he appeared to Cleopas and his companion, whose name we do not know. Although we do not know exactly why Jesus decided to appear to these two men, we might think he wanted to disprove the rumor that the priests were spreading. Realizing that Jesus' resurrection was real, the priests paid the soldiers to say that the disciples had stolen Jesus' body.

Some disciples responded with skepticism when listening to the testimonies about the Resurrection of the Master. It was not until Jesus appeared to them that they believed and rejoiced greatly.

Like the crowd present at Jesus' triumphant entry, Cleopas and his companion expected Jesus to free the Israelites from the Roman Empire. Without really knowing who they were talking to, they opened their hearts and expressed their sadness when they saw that Jesus had been crucified, frustrating their hopes for freedom.

And, as happened with Mary Magdalene in the tomb, the walkers to Emmaus did not recognize Jesus because their sight was blinded.

According to verse 31, after Jesus took the bread and blessed it, their eyes were opened and they recognized the Master. We see clearly that Jesus was in control of the situation and that it was revealed to them in the time he had prepared.

The Bible tells us that, as they walked, Jesus began to declare to them everything the Scriptures said about him, beginning with Moses and continuing with the prophets.

We can be sure that Jesus continues to reveal himself to us through his Word every time we seek him from the heart.

When Jesus disappeared from their sight, Cleopas and his companion immediately returned to Jerusalem, as they said to each other: "Did not our heart burn in us, while he spoke to us on the road and when he opened the Scriptures for us?"

When they arrived, they found the eleven gathered, surprised with the news that the Lord had revealed himself to some. Immediately, Cleopas told how the Lord had revealed himself to them. This served so that his disciples believed that Jesus was no longer among the dead, but had risen, as he had promised.

Jesus continues to reveal himself to the world through his church, and it is important that we teach our children to tell the wonderful news that "Jesus lives, and lives forever."

DEVELOPMENT OF THE LESSON

Choose some of these activities to encourage the participation of your students and focus on the subject of study.

Surprise guest

Invite an adult that many of your students know. Ask him to wear a costume, and let his students try to guess who he is.

Ask the mystery guest to break a piece of bread and give a piece to each child.

After a while, remove the disguise and say who it is.

Explain to the children: *In today's story some walkers did not recognize a very important person. Let's see if you discover who it is.*

The road to Emmaus

Get a map of the Holy Land, or use some of the Bible maps to show the children. Indicate the location of the cities of Jerusalem and Emmaus, more than 11 km away from each other. For children to have a reference about the distance the disciples walked, make a comparison with known places that are at that distance from your church. Explain that the Bible story is about two disciples who walked that distance to get to the city of Emmaus, but something very special happened to them on the way.

News! News!

For this activity you will need newspapers or magazines or tablet with internet access. Show one of the items to your students and ask them what their usefulness is. Taking their responses into account, explain: *These are news media through which news is disseminated. When something extraordinary or very important happens, many people find out reading it in the newspaper, magazine, or online.*

In today's story something very important happened, but it did not spread through one of these. Listen carefully to know who it was who told the Good News.

BIBLE STORY

On the road to Emmaus

"Did you hear why Mary was so excited this morning?" Cleopas asked.

"Yes," said his friend. "Can you believe what she said? She says she saw angels!"

"She also said that Jesus is alive," Cleopas said. "That would be wonderful, but I can't believe it's true."

"Exactly. We saw with our own eyes how Jesus died on the cross. He died, so he won't be with us anymore. Now what will we do?"

While traveling from Jerusalem to Emmaus, a third traveler joined them.

"Hello," the mysterious stranger greeted them. "What are you talking about with such interest?"

"Are you the only one in Jerusalem who hasn't heard about everything that happened these days?" Cleopas answered.

"What happened?" the stranger asked.

"What they did to Jesus, the prophet of Nazareth."

"He was a powerful prophet! Everyone listened to him."

"All, except the Jewish priests and our rulers," Cleopas said. "Three days ago he was executed on a cross."

"It was terrible!" lamented Cleopas' friend. "We thought that he would make Israel a great nation again, but now he is dead."

"We were talking about a friend who told us that she had had a vision of angels. She also said she saw Jesus alive! We're very confused and don't know what to believe."

(Pause the narration, ask the children how they think the two travelers felt, ask them to guess who the mysterious stranger might be.)

"Don't you remember what the Scriptures say?" the stranger asked. "Didn't the Promised One of God have to suffer first, and then enter into his glory?"

Cleopas and his friend listened attentively while the mysterious traveler spoke to them of the Scriptures.

When they were near the city of Emmaus, the unknown traveler pretended to go further, but they told him, "Please, stay with us. It's late."

"Thank you very much," the stranger replied. "That's a good idea."

The three entered the city. When dinner was ready, they sat at the table. Then, the stranger took a piece of bread, gave thanks for it, broke it and gave a little to the two men. It was at that moment when the disciples could recognize him, but he disappeared.

"It was Jesus! Didn't we feel something special when he told us about the Scriptures?" said Cleopas and his friend.

At that moment they decided to return to Jerusalem to tell others what had happened to them.

The eleven apostles and many of Jesus' other followers were gathered together, telling the stories of people who had seen Jesus.

"It's true!" said some of the disciples. "The Lord is risen! Peter and some others saw him!"

Suddenly, the door opened. Cleopas and his friend came running in.

"We just saw Jesus!" they announced almost breathlessly. "He's alive!"

ACTIVITIES

Jesus is the son of God

Hand out the student worksheets for Lesson 17. Ask the children to cut out the strip at the bottom of the page. Then, have them cut out the box and instructions (make sure they keep the part of the instructions for use in the next activity).

Help them paste the box on the line marked in the illustration. Show them how they should lift the box to see the face of the disciples when they recognized Jesus.

Let's tell the good news!

Ask the class: *How did Jesus reveal himself to travelers on the road to Emmaus?*

Perhaps they'll answer that Jesus came and walked with them. Although this is true, remind them that: *Jesus revealed himself to them through the Scriptures. He used the Old Testament to help them understand who he was and what his mission was on earth.*

Ask: *How is Jesus revealed now?* (Through the Bible, the Word of God. Also through the community of believers, the church and prayer.)

Ask them to go to the second page of their worksheet and read the part that says, "Go and tell the Good News to others." Follow the instructions to complete the activity.

Help your students think of people they could tell about the Good News of Jesus' resurrection.

Memorization

Have the class hold hands and form a circle. Then while walking in a circle, they are to repeat the memory verse together a couple of times. When you tell them to stop, one of the children should say the verse alone. Then, have everyone start walking in a circle again and repeat it together, following the same instructions. The game ends when everyone has participated.

To end

Thank God for allowing us to know his Son Jesus. Sing songs of praise before saying goodbye.

Make sure that the children take home their handicrafts and personal belongings. Say goodbye with affection, and encourage them to attend the next class on time.

Lesson 18

Jesus is always with us!

Biblical References: Acts 1:1-11

Lesson Objective: That the students know that they must be prepared for Jesus' return.

Memory Verse: *If you declare with your mouth, "Jesus is Lord," and believe in your heart that God raised him from the dead, you will be saved. (Romans 10:9)*

PREPARE YOURSELF TO TEACH!

The resurrection of Jesus is not just an event that happened in the past. He was not just a good man who lived a long time ago. Our risen Lord is alive today and will return to earth. When? Nobody knows, except God. However, the church has always waited for the return of Christ. This instills value in believers and gives meaning to the mission of the church.

It is common that when hearing about these events, children may feel some fear, but we must remind them that they should not fear the return of the Lord. Children should expect it with the same excitement and exhilaration with which the faithful Jews awaited his first arrival.

This lesson forms a bridge between Easter Sunday and the beginning of the church and its mission. Jesus ascended to the Father, but before leaving he left his followers a job to do. When he returns, will he find that we are faithful in fulfilling his work?

BIBLICAL COMMENTARY

Acts 1:1-11. In this passage Luke reviews what he had discussed in his Gospel. Here he confirms that Jesus was indeed alive, that he appeared to his apostles for 40 days, and that he spoke to them about the kingdom of God.

One of the greatest proofs that Jesus was resurrected is that the disciples would not have begun the work of the church had they been demoralized, defeated and disorganized. Because of Jesus' resurrection, they had hope, conviction, and total dedication to the mission entrusted to them.

In verse 4, Jesus gives the last instructions to his disciples, telling them not to leave Jerusalem, but to await the promise of the Father. It is unquestionable that without the direction and power of the Holy Spirit, they would not have been able to carry out the mission that lay ahead.

Having given this commandment, Jesus ascended to heaven, a cloud received him, and his disciples did not see him anymore. At that moment, two angels in white garments appeared before them and said, "Men of Galilee, why do you stand here looking into the sky? This same Jesus, who has been taken from you into heaven, will come back in the same way you have seen him go into heaven" (Acts 1:11).

The promise that the disciples received is for us too. It is true that the Holy Spirit descended on the day of Pentecost on the disciples, but he can still do so on our lives today. Sometimes we think that these issues are difficult for children to understand. Let us pray that the Holy Spirit speaks to their hearts so that they understand that he wants to fill our lives with his presence and power, and we can share the message of salvation to those around us.

Let us also emphasize that, as the times show, the coming of Jesus is near. Invite your students to consecrate their lives to Jesus and to always be ready for his coming.

DEVELOPMENT OF THE LESSON

How is the sky?

Provide various materials for your students to make drawings of the sky, according to the way they imagine what is and what is in it. As they work, praise their drawings and encourage them to use their imagination.

Special guest

Invite a mission leader from your congregation to talk about a missionary for whom the church is praying, or for whom they have info. Then ask the class: *What do you think missionaries do? Why do you think our church supports them and prays for them?*

They may respond that the missionaries help people and speak to the people of God.

Listen to their answers and tell them: *As you listen to today's lesson, try to discover the most important reason why our church supports missionaries.*

BIBLE STORY

Since the book of Acts is a letter, we suggest that to tell the story, copy it on paper and put it inside an envelope. Tell the children that you are going to read them a letter that Luke sent, and start the story.

Remember to read slowly and with pauses. Explain the words that are difficult for your class to understand.

Jesus is with us

Dear Theophilus, you do honor your name. It must be nice to have a name that means "someone who loves God."

Well, I have much more to tell you.

Do you remember that in my first letter I wrote to you about Jesus? There I told you who he was, what he did and what he taught. I told you everything, from his birth until he ascended to heaven.

Now I have much more to tell you. The events were many. Where do I start? I know, I will continue from where I finished the previous time.

As I told you, it is true that Jesus suffered and died. But God raised him from the dead. At first we doubted that it was true, but Jesus appeared to us and we saw him several times during 40 days. He gave us many proofs of his resurrection, and he convinced us all.

He continued to speak to us about the kingdom of God.

Once, when he was eating with us, he told us, "Do not leave Jerusalem. Stay there to wait for the gift that my Father promised you, of which you have heard me speak." That caught our attention. "Present! What gift?"

Jesus continued to tell us about the baptism with the Holy Spirit, but we did not understand that it was the gift. We kept thinking that Jesus would have a throne and be crowned as king of Israel.

When we saw Jesus for the last time, we asked him, "Lord, will you now restore the kingdom of Israel?"

It was a bit embarrassing to keep asking the same question and always receiving the same answer. Jesus told us that we could not know when he would do it. That meant: "No", or at least, "not yet."

We were on a mountain, talking with Jesus and trying to learn more about the gift of God and his kingdom. Then, Jesus said something we will never forget: "You will receive power when the Holy Spirit has come upon you, and you will be my witnesses in Jerusalem, in all Judea, in Samaria, and to the ends of the earth."

We were still trying to understand what he had told us when suddenly, Jesus began to rise from the ground. We all followed him with our eyes as far as we could, but then a cloud covered him and we could not see him anymore. Then, we saw two men dressed in white.

They asked us. "Why are you looking at heaven?" And, before we could answer, they added, "This same Jesus, who has been taken from you to heaven, will come as you have seen him go to heaven."

So we did what Jesus told us. We returned to Jerusalem to wait. We did not know that only 10 days later we would receive the best gift of our entire lives!

ACTIVITIES

Jesus ascended to heaven

Distribute the student worksheets and the strip with the Jesus figure from the Cut-out Section (pg. 140). Help them make the cuts at the marked black lines on the worksheet, and fold the sheet in half. Show them how to insert the drawing strip through the openings.

Move the strip from top to bottom to represent the ascension of Jesus.

Then, go to the next page to continue with the activity.

Remind your class that Jesus will return to earth and will do so as He went to heaven. We call this the "second coming of Christ."

Ready!

Tell your students: *Before Jesus ascended to heaven, he asked his disciples to do something. What were they to do?* (Wait for the Holy Spirit and be his witnesses.)

What should we do while we wait for the second coming of Christ? (Be his witnesses.)

Talk about what it means to be a witness for Christ. One way to do this is to talk about Jesus, or to live in such a way that people see that Jesus has changed our life.

Prepare a mural about what it means to be a witness for Christ, and place it in a visible place in the church.

Memorization

Since this is the unit's last lesson, prepare simple prizes for those who have memorized the verse. Give time for everyone to individually say the verse and tell others what they studied during these lessons.

To end

If time and space allow, present an exhibition of the work your students did during this unit. In this way, you will recognize the work of the children, and the parents will be able to identify with what their children studied. If parents attend that are not regular members of the congregation, attend to them with courtesy, and talk with them about the plan of salvation if the situation warrants it.

Year 2 — Introduction - Unit V

THE CHURCH GROWS

Biblical References: Acts 2:1-41; 6:1-7; 6:8—8:3; 9:36-42.

Unit Memory Verse: *Go into all the world and preach the gospel to all creation* (Mark 16:15).

UNIT OBJECTIVES

This unit will help the students:

- ❖ Know that the church grows through its members believing in the message of salvation and passing it on to others.
- ❖ Understand that the church works to supply it's owns needs and to help the needy.
- ❖ Actively participate in the church's ministries.

LESSON UNIT A

Lesson 19:   The Church starts to grow
Lesson 20:   The Church needs helpers
Lesson 21:   The Church is persecuted
Lesson 22:   The Church shows God's love

WHY ELEMENTARY STUDENTS NEED THE TEACHING OF THIS UNIT:

Elementary students are just beginning to understand that the Christian world is bigger than their local church. This unit presents the early church, its development and growth.

It is important that they know what it means to be part of the church. Help them understand that being part of the church is more than attending Sunday school or weekly services.

Through this unit, your students will better understand what the church is, its mission, the Christian fellowship and the blessing of belonging to the great family of Christ, and in that way appreciate it more.

Lesson 19
The Church starts to grow

Biblical References: Acts 2:1-41
Lesson Objective: That the students know that the Holy Spirit helps the Church grow.
Memory Verse: *Go into all the world and preach the gospel to all creation* (Mark 16:15).

PREPARE YOURSELF TO TEACH!

Elementary students understand the concept of growth because they are growing rapidly. It is common for them to notice changes in their bodies, and that the clothes that they wear get too small at any moment.

What many of them may not understand is the way in which the church grows. Some may relate it to a contest to see who invites the most friends to the class. These activities contribute to the numerical growth of a church and sometimes the spiritual results are lasting. But, the key to the growth of the church is the work of the Holy Spirit.

Understanding how the Holy Spirit helps in the growth of the church will not be an easy concept to assimilate for your students. However, they can begin to understand the following ideas:

- The Holy Spirit gives courage and power to Christians to talk to others about Jesus.
- The Holy Spirit helps people who are not Christians to understand the Good News and wish to be part of God's family.

Few elementary-aged children are prepared to be filled with the Holy Spirit, but they must learn that he can work through children to achieve God's purposes.

Through this lesson they will better understand the work of the Holy Spirit, and desire to be part of God's work on earth.

BIBLICAL COMMENTARY

Acts 2:1-41. It was the dawn of the day of Pentecost, which was celebrated 50 days after the Passover. The disciples were together, just as Jesus had commanded them. However, that day began in an unusual way: "Suddenly a sound like the blowing of a violent wind came from heaven and filled the whole house where they were sitting." (v. 2).

The Holy Spirit descended with power and filled the house where they were gathered. Instantly, their lives were completely transformed and consecrated. All were filled with the power of the Spirit of God! The Bible explains that tongues of fire appeared and settled on each one of the disciples. And they began to proclaim the good news of salvation in other languages.

After these demonstrations, Peter preached a powerful message and 3,000 people converted to Jesus. For many, this message marks the beginning of the church of Jesus Christ; but this would not have been possible if Peter had not received the fullness of the Holy Spirit.

Remember that Peter denied Jesus three times; he also tried to persuade him not to go to the cross. But now Peter had stood boldly to preach the message of salvation. Without a doubt, he could not have done it if he had not experienced that transformation in his life.

It is wonderful to see that the Holy Spirit not only acted in the apostles, but in those who heard the message. They "were sorry of heart, and said to Peter and the other apostles: Men and brethren, what shall we do?" (V. 37). It was only through the intervention of the Holy Spirit that the church began to grow so explosively.

The Holy Spirit today continues to work in the church, making it grow so that many will not be lost, but will come to repent of their sins. The church does not grow through strategies or evangelism plans. It only does so through the Holy Spirit who operates in the life of the believer and the unconverted.

Help your students seek the filling of the Holy Spirit at this early age. Do not believe that God cannot use them because they are children. Many families convert to the Lord because the children start going to church, and then they bring their parents and siblings. Pray for your students. They can be instruments of God through the Holy Spirit.

DEVELOPMENT OF THE LESSON

Use some of the following activities to focus your students' attention on the topic of study.

Our church

Prepare a large piece of poster board, crayons and other materials to decorate the drawing.

Place the materials on a table, and have your students draw a picture of their church. If there are many children in your class, divide them into small groups and ask each group to make a different drawing.

As they work, talk with them about the people who make up the church: the pastor, Sunday School teachers, children, youth, etc. Tell them that each person is important for the growth of the congregation, but that in today's class they will learn about someone who brings blessing and growth to churches.

How does the church grow?

Prepare several posters that show the stages of growth (for example: of a plant, an animal and a person).

Draw a vertical line to divide the poster into two sections. On one side draw a small plant; on the other, a tree. Ask the children what the plant needed to grow. Listen to their answers. Ask them the same question regarding the other examples.

Tell them: *We have seen that plants, animals and people need certain things that help them grow. In the same way, the church of Jesus needs very special help for its growth. Listen to the story carefully to know what it's about.*

BIBLE STORY

The church begins to grow

"Dear friend!" exclaimed a young man, "what a joy it is to see you! How I wish you could come this year!"

"Shalom," replied the friend, "peace be with you and your family. I just arrived from Rome to celebrate the feast of Pentecost. The trip is long, but I did not want to miss the celebration. Let's go eat something and, meanwhile, we'll talk about the old days."

Throughout the city of Jerusalem, voices and laughter of old friends who were reunited could be heard.

Many people had traveled hundreds of kilometers from other places to attend the Pentecost celebration. For many Jews, this was the favorite celebration of the whole year.

It had been only ten days since Jesus had ascended to heaven. Do you remember what he told his disciples to do? (Wait in Jerusalem until God sends them the promise of the Holy Spirit to empower them.)

Now, on the day of Pentecost, 120 followers of Jesus were gathered. In that group were Peter and the other disciples, and many other people who loved Jesus. Suddenly, they heard something.

"Listen!" one of the believers exclaimed. "Listen to that wind!"

Suddenly, the wind began to blow even stronger, and something special happened. Flames of fire that looked like tongues descended from heaven, and a bright light filled the room. The believers saw that the tongues of fire remained on them, but did not hurt them. Then, all who were there were filled with the Holy Spirit. Their hearts were filled with love and joy.

From that moment on, Jesus' followers wanted all people to feel that joy and love. Through the power of the Holy Spirit, they began to speak in other languages, as the Spirit empowered them. Filled with emotion, they rushed out of the house, praising God. They were no longer afraid to talk about Jesus. The Holy Spirit gave them the power and courage to speak.

The people who had come to celebrate Pentecost heard the noise and commotion, so they approached with curiosity. And seeing they were amazed because, even though they came from many different countries, they all understood what the disciples were saying."

"What is happening?" they asked each other. "These men are from Galilee, but they are speaking in our languages. What does that mean?"

Then Peter stood up for all to see, and began to preach:

"Jews and all who live in Jerusalem, let me explain what is happening. Listen carefully to what I have to tell you. Long ago God promised to send the Holy Spirit. The prophet Joel told us about that promise. And today God has fulfilled his promise, and the Holy Spirit has come."

Then, Peter spoke to them about Jesus: "God sent Jesus of Nazareth to us. He was a very special man. He did many miracles to prove that God had sent him. Everyone knows it because it happened here, among you. Even so, you allowed perverse men to kill him on a cross. Those bad men believed that they had killed Jesus, but that had been God's plan for a long time. He knew all of that would happen. However, God resurrected Jesus, and we witnessed that amazing event. Do you understand me? Jesus of Nazareth, the man they nailed to the cross, is our Lord and Savior."

When the people heard that, the Holy Spirit helped them recognize that they had disobeyed God, and they repented of their sins.

"Brothers, what should we do?" they asked with sadness and concern.

"Each of you must repent and be baptized in the name of Jesus Christ so that your sins are forgiven, and you will receive the gift of the Holy Spirit," Peter told them.

That day, 3,000 people believed in Jesus Christ. Through the power of the Holy Spirit, they asked God to forgive them for being disobedient. And the Holy Spirit came into their lives. Then the church began to grow, just as God had planned.

ACTIVITIES

Biblical review

Write the following questions in advance on strips of paper, and put them in a basket or bag. Then, have several children pull out a strip, read the question out loud and respond. If someone has difficulties, let the group help.

If you wish, add more questions, according to the number of people attending your class.

- What were the 120 followers of Jesus doing on the day of Pentecost? (They waited for the promise of the Holy Spirit.)
- What did the disciples see coming down from heaven? (Tongues like fire.)
- What happened to the disciples when they heard the wind and saw the fire? (They were filled with the Holy Spirit.)
- How did they feel after receiving the Holy Spirit? (Joyful, full of power and courage to talk about the Good News of Jesus).
- What did they do after receiving the Holy Spirit? (They spoke in other languages.)
- Who preached to the crowd in Jerusalem? (Peter)
- What did the people do when they heard Peter's message? (They repented of their sins and were baptized.)
- How many people believed in Jesus that day? (3000)

The Holy Spirit helps the church grow

Hand out the student worksheets, and allow time for the students to draw some ways in which the Holy Spirit helps the church grow. If they have difficulty doing so, give them some ideas or discuss the subject.

Ask them to observe the differences between the early churches and the current churches. Remind them that, although the situation and time are different, we have the same mission: to make disciples in all nations.

Memorization

Use the second page of the student worksheets for the children to review the memory verse. Ask them to look for Mark 16:15 in their Bibles, and fill in the blanks.

Hand out the Verse of the Month Club cards for them to take home and study the verse during the week.

To end

Form teams of children to help you clean the room and put away the materials before you say goodbye.

Get together to pray, thanking God for sending the Holy Spirit on the Day of Pentecost. Intercede for each other, and remember also the sick and needy.

Lesson 20

The Church needs helpers

Biblical References: Acts 6:1-7

Lesson Objective: That the students learn to work in the Church to serve others.

Memory Verse: *Go into all the world and preach the gospel to all creation* (Mark 16:15).

PREPARE YOURSELF TO TEACH!

Who do your students think of when they talk about "working in the church"? The pastor? The teachers? They may think they are not old enough to take responsibility in the church. Or maybe they think it's the church that should do something for them. Although adults have greater responsibilities, children must understand that the church grows when its members work together to solve problems and help others. During this stage, elementary students want to help in what they can. Generally, they are helpful and cooperative. Take this opportunity to assign tasks they can do, and recognize their efforts.

This is the best age to teach your students that God is pleased when we do his work, and to motivate them to serve in their local church.

BIBLICAL COMMENTARY

Acts 6:1-7. In this biblical passage we see that the early church grew by leaps and bounds, and that caused a serious dispute. Many had stopped attending the synagogue and gathered around the houses to praise God.

One of the activities of the synagogue was to meet the needs of the poor, and Christians continued that practice in the house churches. However, the task was not easy. The leaders realized that caring for the poor was an important and full-time ministry.

Although the apostles tried to participate in everything, they needed help to make the church work well. Therefore, they asked for the guidance of the Holy Spirit to find suitable people to carry out this task.

The brothers of the early church knew that it was necessary to collaborate and preach the gospel to attract more people to salvation. And there were seven men willing to accept the call, and to fulfill the mission of taking care of their neighbor and "feeding the hungry."

Use this lesson to teach your students that it is important to participate in the work of the church and care for one another.

DEVELOPMENT OF THE LESSON

Choose some of these activities to complement the biblical learning of your students.

Thanks for your job

Ask your students to make cards or write thank-you letters for those who work in church ministries (the pastor, teachers, ushers, deacons, etc.). It would be better for each child to write to a different person.

We suggest you use the recipe to make recycled paper that is included at the beginning of the book.

Ask them: *What are some of the jobs that people in our church do?* (Allow them to respond and you complement the information.)

Who is in charge of doing those jobs? (Allow time for them to respond; they may express that they do not know who performs the different ministries.)

When finished, make sure all cards reach their recipient.

What is my work?

Have your students sit in a circle, and together make a list of the jobs they can do in the church. Write the answers on the board or on a poster board. Afterwards, each one must choose a job and commit to do it during the next week. (Remember that the work should be appropriate for the age of your students, for example: sort classroom materials, pick up trash, clean tables, organize Bibles, help collect the offering, welcome visitors, help the teacher, etc.)

BIBLE STORY

If possible, invite a young man to dress up as a character from biblical times and tell the story. Tell your students that today's guest represents a member of the early church and will tell them a very interesting story.

The church needs assistants

"Peter, James, Matthew, we need to talk with you. You are forgetting to take care of our widows when you distribute the daily food."

The apostles listened attentively to what they were telling them. They were Greeks who had come to Jerusalem from a distant place. When they heard the good news about Jesus, they had become Christians. The church was growing rapidly, but now these Greek brothers had a problem.

"Your custom of giving food to widows and orphans is very good," the Greek believers said, "but they are not fair. Most of the food is given to the Hebrew widows, but Greek widows and orphans do not receive enough."

"If that is what is happening, it is not fair," the apostles answered. "Let's gather all the Christians to talk about this problem."

"That sounds good to us," the others replied.

In that meeting, the apostles reported on the complaint that the Greeks had presented.

"There is a problem," said the apostles. "It would not be right for us to stop preaching, because that is the ministry that Jesus left us. But the widows and orphans need food, so we thought of a plan that we are sure will work. We are going to pray and then we will choose seven men, full of the Holy Spirit and wisdom. We will give them the task of caring for the sick, feeding the hungry, and taking care of the widows and orphans. Thus we apostles can devote ourselves to prayer, teaching and preaching the Word of God."

"It's a great idea!" expressed the others. "Who will we choose?"

"What do you think of Stephen?" someone suggested. "He is a man full of faith and the Holy Spirit."

"We recommend Philip," said others. "He is also a Christian filled with the Holy Spirit."

In this way, they chose Stephen, Philip and five other Christians filled with the Spirit. Then, they were presented to the apostles for their approval.

The apostles prayed, putting their hands on the seven deacons, and told them, "The work of the Lord is being carried out."

Thanks to that help, all the widows and orphans received the necessary food. The apostles had time to study the Word of God, preach, teach and pray. And more and more people heard the good news about Jesus and became Christians.

The church grew even more, because everyone worked together to fulfill God's work.

ACTIVITIES

Whose job is that?

Hand out the student worksheets for this lesson. Instruct the children to draw a line from each figure (the one of the apostles and the one of the seven deacons) with the things they did.

Ask them to circle the three jobs they consider most important.

When they are finished, explain that everything that is done in the church is valuable, however small it may seem. Remind them that this is the teaching of today's story: any work that is done for the Lord is important.

I can do it!

Ask them to go to the next page, and tell them: *There are many tasks that children can do to help in the work of the church. Can you give me some examples?* (Allow them to respond, some suggestions: help keep the church clean, invite our friends, participate in services and classes, sing for a special occasion in a choir, pray, help those in need.)

Ask them to look at the illustrations on the second page. Then, color the ones that show jobs they can do in the church. Then, ask them to make a drawing in the blank space about how they can use their talents and abilities to help in the church.

As they work, ask: *What do you think would happen if everyone in the church worked together to solve problems and help others?* Let them respond, and read Acts 6:7 as a conclusion.

Special guests

In advance, invite one or two church members who are actively serving in a ministry. Ask them to tell your students about the work they do in the church, and why their work is important. Remind them to keep it brief since the students' attention is short.

Memorization

Write the memory verse on the board and read it once with your students. Then, delete the first and last words, and ask for a volunteer to say it. Go on erasing words until the board is blank and your students say the text by heart.

To end

Form a circle to pray, thanking God for the people who work in the church. Ask each student to pray for a church leader during this week. If possible, give them a piece of paper with the name of the person they will pray for.

Sing a praise song before saying goodbye, and do not forget to invite them to the next class.

Lesson 21
The Church is persecuted

Biblical References: Acts 6:8—8:3.

Lesson Objective: That the students learn to trust in God when they have to suffer for defending their faith.

Memory Verse: *Go into all the world and preach the gospel to all creation* (Mark 16:15).

PREPARE YOURSELF TO TEACH!

As elementary students develop more friendships at school and in their neighborhoods, they become more sensitive to what others think of them. This makes them more susceptible to the influence of their peers, so they easily feel hurt when they reject or treat them badly.

In particular, they find it difficult to tolerate ridicule and rejection for doing the right thing. If they are not advised appropriately, they may stray from what they have been taught and adopt the behavior of others, with the sole reason of being accepted. This story will encourage them to know that they are not alone when they suffer for loving and serving God. Assure them that God is always with them and understands them when they face persecution. Christians around the world are facing increasing hostility, so this may be one of the most important lessons you teach. Encourage your students to be faithful witnesses of Christ wherever they are.

BIBLICAL COMMENTARY

Acts 6:8-8:3. The church in Jerusalem grew rapidly. There were men there filled with the grace and power of God, and one of them was Stephen. He was one of the leaders of the first Christians who, according to verse 8, "did great wonders and signs among the people."

Unfortunately, some people opposed his ministry, and continually argued against him. We know that it was the Holy Spirit who gave Stephen the wisdom to speak with authority, to the point that his opponents could not find an answer to his arguments.

Then some of them bribed certain people to raise false testimony against Stephen, falsely accusing him.

As the situation worsened, they brought him before the council. When the high priest questioned him, Stephen reminded them of what God had done in the past.

Starting from Abraham, he preached the greatness of God and His revelation of love through His Son Jesus, whom they had crucified, saying that he was now seated at the right hand of God. Stephen, full of the Holy Spirit, preached to them with power and confronted them with reality. They had rejected and crucified the Savior of the world, the one true Messiah, just as their ancestors had persecuted and killed the prophets that God had sent them.

This outraged his opponents so much that they gnashed their teeth against him. They then condemned him unjustly and stoned him. That trial, according to Jewish law, was illegal because the Sanhedrin had no right to sentence someone to death. It was the uncontrollable anger they felt that led them to lash out against Stephen and kill him.

Even with his last breath of life, Stephen prayed to Jesus and said, "Lord, do not take this sin into account." We see that Stephen followed Jesus' example, who also begged the Father to forgive his executors.

This lesson teaches us that those who follow Christ with true commitment will encounter difficulties along the way, but the Holy Spirit will equip and sustain them to face difficulties. The Lord needs fully committed servants of the Holy Spirit to serve in his church.

DEVELOPMENT OF THE LESSON

Choose some of the following activities to enrich the group work and encourage the participation of your students.

Who do we trust?

Ask the children to sit in a circle. Talk about people they can trust. Ask the students to name people in the community who help people (firemen, teachers, police, doctors, some neighbors, etc.). Talk about situations in which these people help (when a fire occurs, when we are lost, sick, etc.).

Tell them: *There is someone we can trust because He is always with us. Who?* (God). *Even when we have problems, God is with us. If someone at school bothers you or makes fun of you for doing the right thing, remember that you are not alone, God is with you.*

What is persecution?

On the blackboard or on a card, write the word PERSECUTION in large letters.

Ask the children: *Have you ever heard the word "persecution"? What do you think it means?* Allow them to respond. Then, supplement their answers by explaining that: *Persecution means bothering someone or making them suffer as much as possible. Some people are cruel to others for what they believe or what they are.*

Has someone ever mistreated you for what you believe or for being different from others?

Based on their answers, tell them: *Today's story is about a man who obeyed the great commission and spoke to the people who lived in Jerusalem about Jesus, although this cost him his life.*

BIBLE STORY

Stephen trusts in God

One day Stephen was preaching to many people. Suddenly, he heard angry voices approaching.

"Stop talking like that! You are speaking against God!" a man shouted.

"It is not right to speak badly about the temple," said another. "The temple is a sacred place."

"You are inciting people to disobey our religious law," others said. "Why don't you shut up!"

Stephen saw that everyone was very angry. But why did those people hate him so much? He hadn't done anything he was accused of. They were all lying. The only thing Stephen had done was to teach people about Jesus.

But that didn't matter to the people around him. They didn't want to love Jesus. They just wanted to get rid of Stephen.

That day, they attacked him and took him to the Sanhedrin, which was a group of religious leaders of the Jews. There these men told more lies about Stephen.

"The only thing he does is to speak badly about the temple and the law. We heard him say that Jesus of Nazareth will destroy this place and change the customs that Moses taught us."

The leaders of the Sanhedrin listened to all the lies the outraged men said. Afterwards, they looked at Stephen. He did not look angry. On the contrary, his face showed love, like the face of an angel.

Then the high priest asked him, "Is everything they say against you true?"

Instead of responding yes or no, Stephen began to remind them of all that God had done out of love for his people.

"God called Abraham to a new land and gave him a big family," said Stephen. "Later, God rescued his people from the bondage of Egypt. He gave them good laws to help them live well, and he sent prophets to teach them the way of God. Finally, he sent his Son Jesus to be our Savior. But you killed him, just as you killed the prophets. God has shown you His love again and again, but you do not want to hear it or obey it."

When the religious leaders heard that, they became enraged against Stephen.

"Blasphemer," they responded indignantly.

"Look," he said, looking at the sky, "I see the heavens open and I see Jesus at the right hand of God."

"Enough!" the leaders shouted, covering their ears and shouting loudly.

Then they took Stephen and dragged him out of the city. They threw him on the ground and started throwing big stones at him.

The pointy stones hit Stephen on the head, arms, legs and all of his body. Soon, blood began to flow down his face and his body.

Stephen looked at the men who were stoning him, and prayed, "Lord Jesus, receive my spirit, and do not take this sin into account." After that, he died.

Stephen's death did not cause these men to repent for what they had done. On the contrary, they wanted to destroy all Christians, so they started to persecute them and lock them in prisons.

To escape the persecution, many Christians fled from Jerusalem to other cities and countries. They had to leave their homes, their jobs and many of their possessions, but they did not give up their faith in Jesus.

Everywhere they went they talked about the good news of Jesus. Upon hearing the message, the people of those places also believed in Jesus. Enraged men could persecute Christians, and even kill them, but they could not stop the church from growing.

ACTIVITIES

The persecution of Stephen

Distribute the student worksheets and the strip of drawings for lesson 21 from the Cut-Out Section (p. 139).

Together read the Bible verse that is at the bottom. Then, help them cut the two openings marked on the figure of the Bible, and show them how to insert the strip of drawings. Ask some volunteers to use their finished work to relate what they learned in the biblical story.

Triumph over the persecution

Hand out the stars and squares with numbers from the Cut-out Section (p. 139).

Then ask them to choose a partner to play this game. Each person must place a star with his name in the start box. Then, put all the numbers in a bag. Then, each player must draw a number without seeing, and advance the spaces indicated by that number. If a player reaches a box where there is an order, he should read it out loud and do what is indicated there.

This game will help them identify occasions when they may be mistreated for doing the right thing, or persecuted for loving and serving God. Assure them that they can trust in God, because he will be with them in difficult times and give them the courage they need to defend their faith in Christ.

The persecuted church

Get a world map and mark with a visible color the following countries: China, Vietnam, Egypt, Iran, Pakistan, Afghanistan, Libya, Nigeria, Sudan, Somalia and Malaysia.

Explain to your students that in many of these countries, Christians are persecuted, and many die because of their faith. In some of these places, it is forbidden to meet together to worship God and, if they do, the authorities destroy their churches.

Pray for Christians who suffer persecution around the world. Encourage your class to intercede every day for the persecuted church.

If you wish, prepare cards with the name of each country for the children to take home as "prayer reminders."

Memorization

Write the words of Mark 16:15 on a poster board. Then, divide the class into four groups and the verse into four sentences: (1) Go into all the world (2) and preach the gospel (3) to all creation (4) Mark 16:15.

Assign a phrase to each group to say when it is their turn. Then, rotate the phrases among the groups so that everyone learns the full text.

To end

Encourage your students to trust in God in difficult times. Pray for each other.

Lesson 22

The Church show God's love

Biblical References: Acts 9:36-42

Lesson Objective: That the students know that the church grows when believers show God's love to others.

Memory Verse: *Go into all the world and preach the gospel to all creation* (Mark 16:15).

PREPARE YOURSELF TO TEACH!

Children are self-centered by nature. But, with the proper guidance and instruction, they will learn to consider the needs and feelings of others. With this lesson, your class will realize that it is important to help others. By helping others in the name of Christ, we not only solve their immediate problems, but we also communicate to them God's message of love and salvation.

Your class will understand that they can show God's love by considering the needs of others. Cultivate in your students the desire to help. Soon they will realize that, even though they are small, they can use their talents and abilities in the name of the Lord.

BIBLICAL COMMENTARY

Acts 9:36-42. The early church continued to develop thanks to the power of the Holy Spirit. No one just sat around in this new community of believers. Common and simple people preached with authority the Word of God to the religious and authorities.

In addition, they developed a compassionate ministry that impacted Jerusalem and the cities around it. The first Christians showed the love of God in practical ways. The presence of the Holy Spirit in their lives gave them power to treat their neighbor with love and generosity. By the grace of God, they established a fellowship in which everyone cared for others with compassion.

That's what Tabitha did. She showed God's love by supplying the needs of the poor and homeless. God did not overlook what she was doing. Because of her faithfulness and commitment, He performed a miracle by restoring her life, which is why many people in Joppa believed in the gospel.

DEVELOPMENT OF THE LESSON

Use some of the following activities to enrich the development of the lesson.

How I can help?

Provide white paper and colored pencils. Ask your students to draw pictures of different ways they can show God's love by helping others.

Then, paste the drawings on a poster board to make a mural. Allow time for your students to decorate it and stick it on the wall.

Talk about the importance of being imitators of Christ by helping others.

BIBLE STORY

The church shows the love of God

"I just finished this dress for you," said Tabitha. "I hope you like it."

"Oh, Tabitha! Its beautiful. Thank you very much," said a young mother.

Almost all the people of Joppa knew Tabitha, especially the poor. She cared very much for the needy, and she showed them by making beautiful dresses for them. She knew how to sew very well, so she used her talent to help people.

"I did this for you," said Tabitha as she handed a beautiful dress to an old woman.

"Thank you very much, Tabitha!"

One day she became seriously ill, and soon after, she died. Her friends put her in a room.

"Why did such a good person have to die? We will miss her so much, we love her so much!" her friends said sadly.

"She did so many good things for us. What will we do without her?" they were asking each other.

"Peter is in Lydda," said one of Tabitha's friends. "Maybe he knows what to do."

"You two, go get him!"

Two men went from Joppa to Lydda. When Peter was told what had happened, he went immediately to Joppa.

Upon arriving at the house, he was surprised. There were many people crying!

"Peter! We are so glad you came. Poor Tabitha. She was so good to us. Look at the beautiful clothes she made us. We will miss her very much."

"Leave me alone," Peter told them. "Please, wait outside."

People went quietly into the other room. Then Peter knelt down and prayed. Then, he looked at the face of the dead woman and said, "Tabitha, get up!"

By the power of God, Tabitha opened her eyes. When she saw Peter, she sat up on the bed.

"You can go in now," Peter told her friends.

"Look everyone! Tabitha is alive! The power of God restored her life," Peter explained to the people.

The people were very happy. They praised and thanked God. And when the other people of Joppa heard about God's wonderful miracle, many believed in the Lord Jesus Christ.

ACTIVITIES

Project of love

Organize with your class a community support project, or compassionate ministry, to put into practice what they learned today. We suggest you collect food to donate to a family in need.

Or, if you know of some place where some tragedy has occurred, they could collect an offering and send it to the missionary or to the pastor who works there.

Let's show the love of God

Ask for some volunteers to help you distribute the student worksheets.

Allow time for the students to cut out the boxes at the bottom of the page and paste them in the blanks, according to the order of the Bible story.

While doing this activity, briefly review what they learned in this lesson.

I can also show the love of God

Encourage the children to put into practice the biblical principles they studied. Using their worksheet, ask them to write or draw each day how they demonstrated God's love to others.

Remind them that some ways to show God's love are: helping the elderly, sharing food with those who don't have, helping their parents, etc.

Tell them that next week they should bring the completed worksheet to class to report to the rest of the group what they did to show God's love to others during the week.

Memorization

Ask that some volunteers come forward and recall the memory verse of this unit. Prepare small prizes to recognize the effort of your students.

If you wish, invite the parents of the children, and prepare a demonstration of what they learned in these four lessons.

To end

Briefly review the stories they studied during the unit.

Then, form a circle and pray for the Lord to help you all love your fellow human beings.

Make sure everyone takes home the crafts they did.

Year 2 Introduction – Unit VI

THE GREAT COMMISSION

Biblical References: Acts 1:1-14; 10; 3:1-12; Philippians 2:25-30; 4:14-20.

Unit Memory Verse: *Therefore go and make disciples of all nations, baptizing them in the name of the Father and of the Son and of the Holy Spirit* (Matthew 28:19).

UNIT OBJECTIVES

This unit will help the students to:

- Recognize the importance of being witnesses of Christ.
- Learn that by supporting missionaries and serving Jesus, they respond to the call of the Great Commission.
- Support missionaries with their prayers and offerings.

LESSON UNIT A

Lesson 23: The Great Commission
Lesson 24: Peter talks about Jesus to Cornelius
Lesson 25: The Church sends Paul and Barnabas
Lesson 26: Offerings for the mission

WHY ELEMENTARY STUDENTS NEED THE TEACHING OF THIS UNIT:

Children of this age are beginning to show a marked interest in exploring the world. They are curious and want to know more every day.

This unit will help them know that God not only wants them to be saved, but also that they care about people all over the world. God desires that his Word be known even in the most remote and inhospitable regions.

Help them understand that each Christian is a "witness," and therefore has the responsibility to tell others the Good News of God's love. This is what we call "the great commission."

Taking advantage of the ingenuity and energy of your students, look for ways to transmit the Word of God in your community.

In these lessons they will also learn about the apostles. They will study the work they did to achieve the growth of the early church and spread the message of salvation through Jesus.

Use this lesson as an opportunity to involve them in missionary work, and teach them to pray for those who work preaching the gospel around the world.

Lesson 23
The Great Commission

Biblical References: Acts 1:1-14

Lesson Objective: That the students learn that the Holy Spirit helps us talk to others about God's love.

Memory Verse: *Therefore go and make disciples of all nations, baptizing them in the name of the Father and of the Son and of the Holy Spirit (Matthew 28:19).*

PREPARE YOURSELF TO TEACH!

It is likely that your students have friends or have met people who profess other religions or beliefs. They may have noticed that they go to other churches or that their holidays are different from the ones that Christians celebrate.

Through this lesson they will understand that it is necessary for them to speak to others about Christ's love. Help them develop ideas for inviting their friends to the Sunday School class. It is important that they know that God wants to use them to guide others to him.

BIBLICAL COMMENTARY

Acts 1:1-11. 43 days passed between the crucifixion of Christ and his ascension. During that time, the disciples were expectant and had many doubts in their hearts. The Gospels relate that in the days following the resurrection, Jesus appeared to his disciples at least 11 times.

In the book of Acts we read about God's plans for the apostles: to take the gospel to Jerusalem, Judea, Samaria and "to the ends of the earth" (1:8). Surely, it seemed an impossible task to perform. And, although it was, they could do it through the promise of the Holy Spirit. Jesus promised that the Holy Spirit would empower all believers to tell the gospel to all the people of the world, regardless of their race.

It is evident that God's plan is to reach all nations with the message of his love. The apostle Peter tells us in his second letter: "The Lord does not delay his promise, as some count slowness, but he is patient with us, not willing that any should perish, but that all should come to repentance" (3:9).

Just as the disciples were given the power to witness, we can also ask the Holy Spirit to fill us with his presence to speak to others about the great love of Christ.

DEVELOPMENT OF THE LESSON

Choose some of the following activities to make your class more enjoyable.

Introduction

The four lessons of this unit are aimed at teaching your students about missions and its importance. Therefore, prepare in advance some resources that make learning more meaningful. For example, contact a missionary to visit your class and talk to them about their work, or prepare a project for a missionary.

Worldwide

For this activity you will need a large black and white world map and colored pencils.

Stick the map on the wall and ask your students to identify some countries. Each one will choose a country to color. Then, talk to them about the need to take the gospel to other regions of the world.

Ask them: *What can we do to help people in these countries to know Christ?* Listen to their answers and use them as an introduction for the next activity.

Missionaries

Ask the students if they know what it means to be a missionary. Tell them that a missionary is a person who dedicates his/her life to preaching the Word of God in faraway places. Talk about missionaries who work away from their extended families, and in many cases, in countries where the people speak a different language. Sometimes they find it difficult to buy food and get other things they had in their home country.

If possible, show a photo of a missionary family, and point to the map where they live and minister.

BIBLE STORY

The Great Commission

"He lives, He lives!" the disciples repeated, giving the good news. It was incredible. Some still doubted that it was true, but Jesus was patient. He showed them the marks on his hands where the nails had pierced, and also the wound in his side. After he spoke to them, he ate and walked with them. And he said to them, "Do not leave Jerusalem; wait for the promise of the Father."

"A promise? What promise?" asked the disciples. They did not understand what Jesus was saying.

They thought that he was going to have a kingdom here on earth, like the other kings. In addition, they wanted to be an important part of that kingdom.

Jesus tried to explain to them one more time: "You do not know the day or the hour in which it will happen, but you will receive power when the Holy Spirit comes upon you and you will be my witnesses in Jerusalem, in Judea, in Samaria and to the ends of the earth."

Later, Jesus was taken to heaven, and the astonished disciples watched him ascend, until a cloud hid him.

They stayed there, looking towards the sky. They could not believe what their eyes had seen! "What does this mean? Where did he go? How can we be his witnesses?" they asked each other.

While they were still looking toward the sky, two men appeared in white robes standing next to them, asked them, "Galileans, why are you looking at the sky? This same Jesus, whom they have seen ascend to heaven, will come again in the same way."

Then the disciples returned to Jerusalem. After a long day on the journey, they arrived at a room on the second floor of a house and stayed there.

Then they prayed, asking God to help them understand the meaning of what Jesus had told them before he had left.

ACTIVITIES

Adopt a missionary!

Get in touch with a missionary who works in your area to invite them to your class. If he or she cannot come, ask them to provide you with information about their job and family, including photographs, birthday dates, and their mailing or e-mail address.

Make the presentation of the missionary to your students, and explain what their work consists of and what their main needs are. During this unit, gather a special offering, and make drawings or write letters to send to the missionary.

Acts 1:8

Distribute the student worksheets and the figure of Jesus that corresponds to lesson 23 in the Cut-out Section (p, 133). Then on the worksheet, have them make a cut in the black line in the center to form an opening, and insert the figure of Jesus. Show them how to fold the page on the dotted line, and review the bible story.

Turn the page over, and ask: *Do you know anyone who needs to hear the message of Jesus?*

Use the illustrations on the worksheet to help them think of people they could talk to about Christ. Allow time for the children to write those names on the lines.

Memory verse

We suggest that you write the text on colored cards, putting some words on each card. Explain that the passage they will learn is known as the "great commission," and that it was the special work Jesus gave his disciples before going to heaven. Have your students repeat the text several times. Then, give a card to each child, and ask them to line them up so that the verse can be read.

To end

Thank them for having attended, and remind them that in the next class they will continue talking about the "great commission".

Help them pick up the materials they used, and end up singing a song.

Lesson 24
Peter talks about Jesus to Cornelius

Biblical References: Acts 10

Lesson Objective: That the students understand that God's love, shown through Jesus Christ, is for everyone.

Memory Verse: *Therefore go and make disciples of all nations, baptizing them in the name of the Father and of the Son and of the Holy Spirit* (Matthew 28:19).

PREPARE YOURSELF TO TEACH!

Elementary-aged children are beginning to discover that the world is bigger than their homes and their community. They still have difficulty understanding the concepts of time and space. They are learning that some places in the world are far away, and that not all people speak, act or look the same way.

Your students should understand that Jesus died for all the people of the world, and that the mission of the church is to tell everyone about the love of Jesus.

Emphasize the teaching of Acts 10:34: "God does not show favoritism." When your students understand that God loves all people wherever they are, it will be easier for them to reach others for Christ, and tell them about his love.

BIBLICAL COMMENTARY

Acts 10. Christianity spread very rapidly, and the time had come when the gospel of Christ would cross the barrier that separated Jews from Gentiles.

In this story there are four important aspects that we must highlight:
1. The first Jewish Christians were reluctant to take the gospel to the Gentiles.
2. God himself incorporated the Gentiles into the church of Christ, and in doing so showed his approval.
3. God did not use Paul, but Peter, to open the door of the kingdom of God to the Gentiles.
4. The acceptance of the Gentiles into the church in Jerusalem, even though they had no connection with Judaism, was a sign that God himself had adopted them as part of his family.

In this passage we find two different visions: that of Cornelius in Caesarea and that of Peter in Joppa. In both cases, God worked separately with each of them for the meeting they had.

Cornelius lived in Caesarea, the main port of Palestine. Being a centurion of the Roman army, he had under his command 100 soldiers. He was gentle; He did not belong to the Christian church or the synagogue of the Jews. However, he was faithful in his worship of God. Cornelius received his vision at 3:00 in the afternoon when an angel of the Lord approached him while praying.

The next day, Peter had a vision that questioned his belief in strict Jewish laws regarding pure and unclean foods. While meditating on the meaning of the vision, the messenger of Cornelius arrived, coming from Caesarea. No one could have imagined that Peter would receive Gentiles as guests. The fact that he received them indicates that the vision produced a significant change in his life.

Another evidence of the change was that he entered the house of Cornelius when he arrived in Caesarea. And his reaction when Cornelius prostrated himself before him showed that he did not consider himself superior to him because he was a Jew and they were Gentiles.

Cornelius invited his family and friends to listen to Peter's important message, and received him with joy in their hearts. The outpouring of the Holy Spirit upon the Gentiles stunned the Jews who were present. Peter understood that God accepted Gentiles, as well as the Jews, in his kingdom, and baptized them in the name of the Lord Jesus.

DEVELOPMENT OF THE LESSON

Use some of the following activities to focus the attention of the class on the topic of study.

Our friends

Tell your students: *Everyone here are friends. I would like some of you to tell me how you met your best friend.*

Give opportunity for the children to participate. Then, ask them: *How do you choose your friends?* (Help them understand that friends often have similar interests. (sports, games, etc.))

Emphasize that although friends usually like to do the same activities together, we can also be friends with people who are different or do not have our same interests.

Ask them: *What do you think friends can have in common, even if they like different things?* (Something we have in common is that God loves us all equally, and sent his Son Jesus to die on the cross for all the people of the world.)

Make a poster with the memory verse, and ask your students to decorate it. Then, stick it on the wall and repeat the verse together a couple of times. Ask that some children read it aloud and then say it by heart.

Mysterious characters

Write on a card the names PETER and CORNELIUS, and cut out each letter. Keep them in a bag, and ask your students to draw out the letters and try to put together the names of the two characters. If you wish, make two sets of letters; Divide your class into two groups and tell them that the group that forms the names in the shortest time will be the winner.

BIBLE STORY

Peter talks about Jesus to Cornelius

One day Cornelius was in his house. Suddenly, he saw an angel of God enter where he was and said, "Cornelius!"

Cornelius was amazed, and looking at the angel, asked him, "What do you want, Lord?"

The angel replied, "God has heard your prayers and knows everything you have done to help those in need. Send some men to Joppa to bring Peter. You will find him in a house near the sea."

Cornelius was a centurion, that is, a Roman soldier who was in charge of many men. So he called two of his servants and a soldier and communicated the angel's message to them. They knew that Cornelius was a good man, so they immediately obeyed and left for Joppa to look for Peter.

The next day in Joppa, Peter went to the roof of his house to pray. While there he had a vision. He saw a large cloth that descended from the sky, hanging from the four corners. In it were all kinds of animals, including reptiles and birds.

Then, a voice said to him, "Get up, Peter, kill and eat."

When Peter looked at what was in the cloth, he saw that all the animals it contained were those that the Jews did not eat.

"No, sir, by no means! I have never eaten anything impure or prohibited," Peter answered firmly.

"Do not call impure what God has cleansed," the voice answered.

This happened three times. Then, the cloth rose again to heaven.

Peter was still on the roof when the men sent by Cornelius arrived at his house.

"Does a man named Peter live here?" they asked.

While Peter was still thinking about the vision, the Spirit said to him, "Peter, three men are looking for you. Get up and do not be afraid to go with them because I have sent them."

Peter obeyed and came down from the roof. The men who waited for him were Gentiles. The Jews thought that Gentiles were impure people and did not want to be with them. They were never invited to their homes, but Peter remembered the words of the vision: "Do not call impure what God has cleansed."

Then Peter invited them to rest at his house that night. The next day he chose some friends to accompany him, and they left for Cornelius' house in the city of Caesarea.

When they arrived the next day, Cornelius was waiting for them with a group of relatives and friends he had invited.

Peter told them, "You know that according to our law, we Jews must not visit Gentiles, but God has shown me that I should not call anyone impure. That's why I came when you called for me. Could you tell me why they came for me?"

Cornelius replied, "Four days ago I was praying at my house, about 3:00 in the afternoon. Suddenly, I saw before me a man in shining clothes who said to me, 'Cornelius, God has heard your prayers and has seen your alms for the poor. Send men to Joppa to bring Peter. He is in a house near the sea.' So I sent for you, and you have done well to come.

Now we are here in the presence of God to hear all that God has commanded you."

Then Peter began to say to them, "Now I understand that in truth God does not favor certain people, but accepts people of all nations who fear him and do what is right." Then, he spoke to them about Jesus and his love for all people.

Cornelius and his friends began to praise God. While they were doing that, the Holy Spirit descended on all those who had heard the message.

The Jews who had gone with Peter were surprised to see that the Gentiles were also receiving the gift of the Holy Spirit.

Then, Peter said to them, "They have received the Holy Spirit just as we received it." Then he told them to be baptized in the name of Jesus Christ.

Cornelius was happy to know about Jesus, so he invited Peter to stay at his house for a few more days.

ACTIVITIES

God loves Peter and Cornelius

Pass out the student worksheets for Lesson 24. Discuss the differences and similarities between Peter and Cornelius. Ask the children to draw a line by joining the point of each sentence with the character it describes. Some phrases refer to Cornelius, some to Peter, and others to both.

God loves all people

Turn to the page of the student worksheets, and explain to your students that in the first frame each one must draw himself; in the second, someone they love; and in the last one, a person whom they don't know very well.

A second option is that in the first frame glue a piece of aluminum foil to simulate a mirror; in the second they can draw their family; and in the third one, they can paste clippings from magazines that show other people. As they work, talk about God's great love for humanity and the responsibility we have to tell others the message of salvation, just as Peter did in Cornelius' house.

We are all the same

Prepare a poster with photographs or drawings of people of different races, and allow your students to look at them.

Tell them: *In today's story, we learned that God has no favorites. He loves us all equally and wants everyone to know and trust in Jesus.*

Encourage them to talk about Christ to all people, regardless of who they are.

Memorization

Place the cards you made for the previous class on the table. After repeating the verse a couple of times as a group, ask a volunteer to order the words in 10 seconds. Then call another, and so on until everyone participates.

To end

Praise God and give thanks for loving all of us equally. Exhort your class to be witnesses of Christ wherever they are, and to invite their friends and family to Sunday School.

Lesson 25

The Church sends Paul and Barnabas

Biblical References: Acts 13:1-12

Lesson Objective: That the students know that God calls some people to be missionaries.

Memory Verse: *Therefore go and make disciples of all nations, baptizing them in the name of the Father and of the Son and of the Holy Spirit* (Matthew 28:19).

PREPARE YOURSELF TO TEACH!

The world of elementary children is expanding beyond their home through school, their friends, sports, etc. As they discover the needs of others, they will learn to respond to those needs according to the will of God.

This lesson will help them understand that all Christians have the mission to communicate the love of Christ to our neighbors, but also that God calls some people for a specific task. We know these Christians as missionaries. He calls them through the Holy Spirit to take the gospel to other countries and cultures. Although we must all communicate the love of God, the call of missionaries implies leaving their homes and taking the good news of salvation to other cultures and places of the world.

BIBLICAL COMMENTARY

Acts 13:1-12. The Holy Spirit called Paul and Barnabas for a special mission, a new stage in evangelism. And the church confirmed the call through fasting, prayer and the laying on of hands. The Holy Spirit and the church worked together to set them apart as leaders of the church.

God made the call, but he wanted the church to support and send them. Therefore, the church sent Paul and Barnabas to fulfill the mission entrusted by the Holy Spirit.

When Paul and Barnabas crossed the sea to the island of Paphos, they faced the first opposition to the gospel of Christ. Verses 6-12 tell us that the proconsul invited Paul and Barnabas to hear Jesus' message first-hand.

But Barjesus, who was a magician and false prophet, wanted to keep the proconsul from the faith. Paul, filled with the Holy Spirit, fixed his eyes on him and said, "You are a child of the devil and an enemy of everything that is right! You are full of all kinds of deceit and trickery. Will you never stop perverting the right ways of the Lord? Now the hand of the Lord is against you. You are going to be blind for a time, not even able to see the light of the sun." He was instantly blind and needed someone to guide him.

The Bible tells us that when the proconsul saw what had happened, he believed, marveling at the gospel of Jesus. The power of the Holy Spirit was manifested to witness about Jesus Christ and his love.

This was the first of many of Paul's missionary journeys. The key to his ministry with Barnabas was the guidance of the Holy Spirit. In addition, they were faithful and obedient to the holy calling of God.

DEVELOPMENT OF THE LESSON

Choose some of the following activities to complement the development of today's class.

Adopt a missionary!

Collect an offering that will be sent to a missionary, and ask one of the children to pray, giving thanks to God for the opportunity to participate in missionary work.

Prepare some cards (follow the recipe suggested at the beginning of the book), or hand out white paper for your students to make cards and write a message to send along with what has been collected.

Missionary trips

Look in magazines for some travel illustrations (for example: suitcases, boats, airplanes, cars, etc.).

Place the clippings on a table, along with a poster board and glue. Allow time for your students to make a poster related to travel. Talk to them as they work, and ask them how people prepare for a trip. Explain that in today's story they will talk about a mission trip.

BIBLE STORY

The church sends Paul and Barnabas

The leaders of the Antioch church were praying and fasting. Suddenly, the Holy Spirit told them, "Separate Paul and Barnabas to do the work to which I have called them."

For many years Paul and Barnabas had been witnesses of Jesus, speaking to many people about him. But now they would be missionaries. Missionaries are witnesses of Christ who go to other cultures or countries to preach the good news of God's love.

The leaders of the Antioch church prayed and sent them to fulfill the mission that God had assigned them.

The Holy Spirit led Paul and Barnabas to Seleucia, and from there they went by ship to Cyprus.

Upon arriving in Salamis, the new missionaries preached in the Jewish synagogues. Then they crossed the whole island, preaching in each city. After a while they came to Paphos, on the other side of the island, where the governor of Cyprus lived.

"Bring Paul and Barnabas to me," the governor ordered. "I want to hear the Word of God."

When the missionaries arrived to meet the governor, there was Elymas, a wicked magician who did not want the governor to believe in the teachings of God.

When Paul saw what the evil man was doing, he said, "You are a child of the devil and an enemy of everything that is right! You are full of all kinds of deceit and trickery. Will you never stop perverting the right ways of the Lord? Now the hand of the Lord is against you. You are going to be blind for a time, not even able to see the light of the sun."

At that moment Elymas shouted, "I cannot see!" and staggered away, looking for someone to guide him.

The governor was amazed at what God had done and by Paul's teachings. So he believed in Jesus and became a Christian.

ACTIVITIES

The call of God

Pass out the student worksheets, and ask the children to cut out the strip with illustrations on the right side of the page. Give them time to cut out the figures and paste them into the scenes, according to the order of the biblical story.

Then, have them go to the next page and complete the crossword puzzle using the words listed beside the puzzle. Help them if they have difficulty filling in the blanks.

Biblical review

Organize a competition to review the following questions:
- What were the leaders of the Antioch church doing when the Holy Spirit spoke to them? (They were fasting and praying.)
- What did the Holy Spirit tell them? (God wanted Paul and Barnabas to do a special job.)
- What do we call the people that God calls to preach and teach people from other cultures and countries? (Missionaries)
- Name some missionaries you know.
- What island did Paul and Barnabas go to preach? (To Cyprus)
- Who did the missionaries meet in Pafos? (The governor and the magician Elymas)
- What did Elymas do when Paul and Barnabas arrived to meet the governor? (He tried to prevent the governor from believing in Jesus.)
- Who gave Paul the power to announce to the evil magician that he would be blind? (The Holy Spirit)
- What did the governor do when he saw what God had done and had listened to Paul's teaching? (He believed in Jesus.)
- What do we call people who communicate the love of God in their own land? (Witnesses)

Memorization

Hand out the cards with the memory verse. After repeating the words several times, say the first sentence and ask those who have those words to come forward. Continue to the end, and repeat the biblical text together.

To end

Have your students sit in a circle and tell them: *Today we learned that God calls some people to be missionaries. Although not all of us will be missionaries, we can help the growth of the kingdom of God. We fulfill the great commission when we obey God and tell others about the love of Jesus.*

Say goodbye with a prayer and intercede for the missionaries around the world.

Lesson 26

Offerings for the mission

Biblical References: Philippians 2:25-30; 4:14-20

Lesson Objective: To encourage the students to want to help missionaries accomplish the work that God has entrusted to them.

Memory Verse: *Therefore go and make disciples of all nations, baptizing them in the name of the Father and of the Son and of the Holy Spirit* (Matthew 28:19).

PREPARE YOURSELF TO TEACH!

It is likely that your students are not familiar with missionary work. Some may think that the "great commission" is something that the apostles did in the past and that the missionaries do today. Others may have never heard that term. With certainty, your students have not prepared their backpacks to go to talk about Christ to the most remote places in the world. However, this lesson will teach them that the task of the great commission is for every Christian, not only for missionaries or evangelists. Your students can learn to participate in the mission of the church "now." They do not have to wait until they're adults! God can use them even at an early age.

BIBLICAL COMMENTARY

Philippians 2:25-30; 4:14-20. Paul wrote this letter to the Philippians while he was in prison. The church of Philippi was the one that had responded to God's message by sending help to the apostle Paul.

The Philippians chose Epaphroditus to take gifts to Paul and accompany him for a time. Epaphroditus knew that when making that trip, his life could be in danger, and so it was. When he was with the apostle, he became seriously ill and was about to die. When the Philippian church heard about it, the congregation became very concerned. For that reason, Paul decided that Epaphroditus would return to Philippi. With him he sent a letter, asking the church to welcome him with joy because he had fulfilled his task with excellence and deserved a great welcome.

In his letter, Paul thanked the brothers and sisters of Philippi for the offering they had sent him, explaining clearly that he did not express gratitude so that they would continue sending offerings, but to teach them that it is more blessed to give than to receive.

The most important thing for Paul was that the members of Philippi, knowing his need, made it theirs and responded immediately and with love. Their disposition was such that they accepted Paul's affliction as their own and decided to act. Their spiritual growth was the fruit that Paul wanted to see; for this he did an arduous job. The offerings of the Philippians pleased God because they were born of obedient hearts and attentive to need.

God continues to work in the same way today. The offerings and prayers that Christians send are a blessing and help for missionaries around the world.

DEVELOPMENT OF THE LESSON

Choose some of the following activities to enrich the group work during this lesson.

Offerings

Prepare a poster that illustrates various ways in which missionaries invest the offerings they receive: food, shelter, and clothing, for people who don't have sufficient resources: materials to evangelize; teaching; preaching; medicines, etc.

Show it to your students, and talk about the importance of supporting missionary work through offerings and gifts.

A special offering

For this activity you will need small boxes, colored paper and glue.

Give a box to each student, and ask them to decorate them with colored paper. When they are finished, let the glue dry. Tell them to take their boxes home and put their offerings they will send to the missionaries in their boxes. That little box will be a reminder that they should give an offering for missionary work.

BIBLE STORY

To tell this story we suggest that you write it on paper and keep it in an envelope, as if it were a letter. Open the letter in front of the children and tell them that you are going to read them the message that Paul sent to the church in a place called Philippi.

The Christians of that church were very worried. Some time ago, upon learning that Paul was in prison, they had sent a man named Epaphroditus with some gifts for Paul.

"Epaphroditus, please take these gifts to Paul and stay with him to help him in whatever he needs," the members of the church had told him.

He gladly carried out what was asked of him. But after a while, they received bad news: "Epaphroditus is very sick, about to die!"

Paul knew that the members of the Philippian church were worried about their friend. So, when Epaphroditus had the strength to travel, Paul told him, "I think you should go back to Philippi. Our friends want to see you and know that you're better."

Epaphroditus agreed, but before traveling, Paul wrote a letter for his friend to take to the believers of the Philippian church.

Dear brothers and sisters of Philippi:

I think it's time for my friend Epaphroditus to come back to be with you. He is like a brother to me.

You sent him to be with me when I needed him the most. You sent him as a messenger to take care of me; now he is eager to return. He does not want you to worry about his health.

He was very sick, but God had mercy on him and me. I want you to see him so you know he's okay. Receive him in the Lord with much joy. He almost died for the work of Christ, risking his life to do what you could not do for me.

Thank you for participating in my sufferings. You were the only ones who sent me help. Thanks for everything you did for me. I no longer expect to receive more gifts. I am happy because you learned to give and help others with joy. I received everything you sent me and I have an abundance. Your offerings please the Lord.

My God, then, will supply everything you lack according to his riches in glory in Christ Jesus. To God and our Father be glory for ever and ever. Amen.

A servant of Christ,
Paul

ACTIVITIES

Epaphroditus and Paul

Hand out the student worksheets. Have the children number the pictures according to the Bible story. As they work, talk with them about the importance of helping in the missionary work by giving our offerings.

Obedient hearts

Hand out the 5 hearts for lesson 26 from the Cut-Out Section (pg. 133) and paste them in the appropriate spaces. Next, ask several volunteers to read the entire sentence. Tell them to bring the worksheet home to tell their family members what they learned in the lesson.

Adopt a missionary!

Together with your students, develop a plan to help a missionary from your area or from another part of the world. Establish the monthly or annual amount that they will send as an offering. Write on a calendar the dates of their birthdays or wedding anniversary to send them a greeting card. Explain to the students that by adopting a missionary, they are committing to praying and supporting their ministry constantly.

Memorization

Close the unit by making a collective review of the biblical text. Give opportunity for those who have learned it by heart to come forward and say it out loud. If possible, reward them with a treat, a pencil or a bookmark for their Bible.

To end

Briefly review the unit lessons, and stress the importance of fulfilling the Great Commission that Jesus left us. Form a circle and pray for missionaries from around the world.

Give them the work they did during the unit, and encourage them to attend the next class to start a new unit, which is titled: "Great stories of God's power."

Year 2　　　　　　　　　　　　　　　　　　　　　　　Introduction – Unit VII

GREAT STORIES OF GOD'S POWER

Biblical References: Genesis 11:1-9; Exodus 13:17—15:2; 2 Kings 5:1-15; 6:8-23; Jonah; Daniel 3:1-30.

Unit Memory Verse: *Great is our Lord and mighty in power; his understanding has no limit.* (Psalm 147:5).

UNIT OBJECTIVES
This unit will help the students:

- ❖ Know that God has control of the world, even though situations are difficult.
- ❖ Feel thankful for God's wisdom, love, patience, and forgiveness.
- ❖ Trust in God in whatever situation they find themselves.
- ❖ Know that God guides and sustains us.

LESSON UNIT A
Lesson 27: God is in control
Lesson 28: God rescues His people
Lesson 29: God honors Naaman's obedience
Lesson 30: God's invisible army
Lesson 31: God is patient and forgiving
Lesson 32: God is more powerful than the fiery furnace

WHY ELEMENTARY STUDENTS NEED THE TEACHING OF THIS UNIT:

Elementary-aged children learn about God through the Bible stories and the testimony of the believers around them. Children have learned to consider God as Father, friend or pastor, taking into account His loving qualities. However, it is important to balance that perception with emphasizing His great power and majesty. This unit will deal with the power of God.

Your students need to feel safe, so they seek refuge with their parents, friends and teachers.

With these lessons, you can teach them that God is sovereign and controls all situations in the world. Even when situations seem complicated, God shows his fidelity to those who love him.

Lesson 27
God is in control

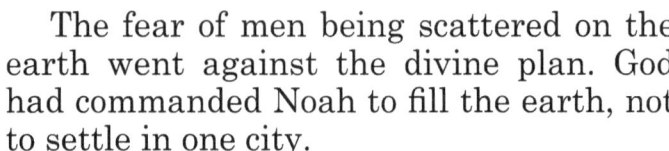

Biblical References: Genesis 11:1-9

Lesson Objective: That the students learn that God is in control of every situation.

Memory Verse: *Great is our Lord and mighty in power; his understanding has no limit* (Psalm 147:5).

PREPARE YOURSELF TO TEACH!

Elementary-age children are aware of the evil that exists in the world. In many occasions, evil seems to dominate; furthermore, it would seem that often people who reject God prosper, while those who believe in Him suffer.

It is important that your students know that no matter how big evil may seem, God is sovereign. He gave us the freedom to choose between good and evil, but sometimes God intervenes and says, "Enough!" Knowing that God has control over everything that exists will help your students trust him. God has been working with humanity since its creation; we can see it through all of history. Help them understand that God is greater than evil, and that he has absolute control over everything.

BIBLICAL COMMENTARY

Genesis 11:1-9. After the flood, God blessed Noah and his children, telling them to multiply and fill the earth. It is incredible that, having seen the power and sovereignty of God in the flood, the descendants of Noah thought that they could live without him and decided to disobey him.

However, after settling on a plain, they decided to build a city and a tower for all to know. Thus, if they were scattered on the earth, people would know where they came from.

This story reflects a clear image of humanity in rebellion against God. They sought exaltation through their ingenuity, skills and cunning. They were not interested in God's command to multiply and fill the earth. They wanted to create a powerful nation that would reign on earth.

The fear of men being scattered on the earth went against the divine plan. God had commanded Noah to fill the earth, not to settle in one city.

God does not oppose unity when it is based on fidelity to him. In this case, the descendants of Noah suffered the consequences for disobeying the divine mandate. Because of their pride and false security based on their self-sufficiency, they received the judgment of God.

Seeing what people wanted to do, God confused their languages so they could not communicate to continue their plans.

We can say that the tower remained as a monument to the impotence of the creature before its Creator. The different languages remind us of the retribution to human pride. Help your students understand that, even if all of humanity were united against God, he would always have absolute control over everything.

DEVELOPMENT OF THE LESSON

Choose some of the following activities to focus your students' attention on today's study topic.

Do you understand me?

As your students enter the room, welcome them by saying "good morning" in different languages. Use these examples: bonjour (French); good morning (English); buona mattina (Italian); bom dia (Portuguese); guten morgen (German).

Tell them: *It is difficult to communicate when other people speak a language that we don't understand. Did any of you understand what I said?* Listen to their answers and explain that in today's Bible story, they will study about some people who could not understand each other.

Let's work together

Ask your students to work together without communicating through speech. Divide the class into groups of two or three. Whisper to one of the members a simple task to do with everyone in their group (for example: move a table, arrange the chairs, make a tower with blocks, etc.).

Give them time to try to complete the task. After a few minutes, ask them to stop and ask them why they did not complete the activity. Based on the answers, tell them that the same thing happened to a group of Old Testament people when they tried to do a project.

BIBLE STORY

Tower of Babel

When Noah and his three sons left the ark, the world was clean. It was a whole new world, ready to be inhabited.

Noah and his children built new houses. Then, Noah's children and their wives had children. And these in turn had children.

Later, some families went to live in another region, where they found a great and beautiful place to live.

There those people decided that they wanted to be together forever. They did not like the idea of going to different places. God had commanded them to settle the earth, but they did not want to obey.

Some said, "Let's build our own city, with a big tower that reaches the sky. That way we will be famous and we will all be together, and not be scattered all over the world."

Some started making bricks; others prepared the mixture to join them; others brought the bricks and the mixture to the builders.

Seeing what the people were doing, God became sad. They were not obeying what he had commanded. Instead of filling the land, they were building a big city and a tower to be all together.

God had promised them that he would not destroy the earth again with a flood. The rainbow was a reminder of that promise he had made to Noah. But despite that, God was in control of the situation.

At that time, everyone spoke a single language and used the same words. But since the people decided to disobey God, he made them speak different languages. Those who were making bricks suddenly did not understand each other anymore. Nor did they understand those who loaded the mortar. And those who loaded the mortar did not understand those who carried the bricks. Also those who were building spoke different languages.

Soon people had to abandon their plans. They stopped building the city with the big tower, and they moved to other places and filled the land, just as God had told Noah.

ACTIVITIES

Confusion!

Distribute the student worksheets for this lesson. Allow time for your students to cut out the figure following the outline. Then, ask them to bend it along the dotted lines and glue the small tabs on the large tabs.

Encourage them to use their finished work to tell their families the story of the Tower of Babel.

Memorization

On a poster, draw the figure of a tower and write the memory verse inside. Allow time for your students to color the figure and decorate the edges of the card. Hang up the finished poster in the classroom, and repeat the verse a couple of times. Cut out the Verse of the Month club cards corresponding to this unit, and ask the students to take them home to review the verse of this unit.

To end

Tell your students that this lesson taught us that God controls all situations, even when people are disobedient. Encourage the children to observe signs that God controls the world around them.

Then, pray giving thanks to God because he has control over everything. Invite them to the next class, and encourage them to invite a friend or friend.

Lesson 28
God rescues His people

Biblical References: Exodus 13:17—15:2

Lesson Objective: That the students know that God uses His power to take care of his kids.

Memory Verse: *Great is our Lord and mighty in power; his understanding has no limit* (Psalm 147:5).

PREPARE YOURSELF TO TEACH!

It is not unusual for the children of our church to spend hours in front of the television, watching cartoons of superheroes with fantastic powers. Sometimes it is difficult to distinguish where fantasy ends and reality begins. Therefore, they must understand that God is the only one who has the power to perform supernatural events, because He is the Creator and sustainer of all that exists.

They must be sure that God's power is real and that he is willing to help His children, even in the most difficult trials. The history of the liberation of the chosen people of God will increase their confidence in the care and protection of God.

BIBLICAL COMMENTARY

Exodus 13:17-15:2. The story of the Exodus allows us to see God's great power. First, he saved little Moses from dying in the Nile River; years later he called Moses in a supernatural way, speaking to him from a burning bush in order to give him specific instructions for saving His people. God had a plan to free his people and for everyone to know that He is the only almighty God.

The Hebrews also needed to be convinced that they could be free. They did not want to leave the benefits they enjoyed in Egypt, even though they were slaves, since they did not know another way of life. Therefore, Moses had to earn their trust as a leader.

God showed himself to Moses by turning his rod into a serpent; and, when the sorcerers of Egypt tried to copy that miracle, the Lord sent plagues that attacked the power of the Egyptian gods.

The plague of the water turned into blood was a direct attack on the god Hapi, god of the Nile. The plague of the frogs was a mockery against the god Hept, an Egyptian frog-like god, symbolizing fertility and birth. The plague of darkness showed the falsity of Ra, god of the sun. To show that Hat-Hot (god in the form of a cow) and Apis (in the form of a bull) were false idols, God sent the plague of cattle death. The military symbol of the Egyptian people was a hornet, and God demonstrated his power over these gods by sending them the plagues of lice and flies. With each plague, the true God demonstrated his great power over the false Egyptian idols.

God showed his power by freeing his people from the most powerful empire of that time. When the Egyptians changed their minds and pursued the people of Israel, God showed himself during the night as a pillar of fire, and during the day as a cloud, reminding them of his presence every day.

What God did when opening the Red Sea was one of the most impressive events in the history of the Jews. Often, the prophets and apostles reminded the people of this fact as a sign of God's faithfulness.

Help the children understand that God is bigger than any problem or difficulty we face on our way.

DEVELOPMENT OF THE LESSON

Use some of the following activities to enrich the development of the lesson and facilitate the learning of your students.

What is the sea like?

Show your class pictures or illustrations of the sea, and ask if anyone has ever visited it. Allow some children to relate their experiences. Complement their information by talking about marine animals and plants. Emphasize that only God has the power to control the sea, as they will learn in today's story.

Superpowers

Talk with the children about television characters who demonstrate superpowers or perform extraordinary activities. Allow everyone to participate, and if possible, allow time for them to give a brief description of the character they most admire.

We suggest that you bring cut-outs from magazines or drawings of characters that the children consider "fantastic" to class. Show them, and ask them to say which is real and which is fiction.

If you notice that some are confused, explain that most of these characters are the product of someone's imagination and that they do not exist in reality. The only one who can do supernatural things is God.

Treat this topic tactfully, helping them to understand that it is important to trust only in the miracles that God can perform.

Then tell them: *Today we will talk about a very special topic. We will study one of the miracles that God did to free his people from slavery.*

Follow the path

Using cardboard or poster board, make 16 footprints. In each one write one of the words of Exodus 15:2. Then, stick them on the floor to form a path around the room. Tell your students that this verse is part of today's story, and encourage them to repeat it while following the path, trying not to step on the tracks.

BIBLE STORY

God rescues his people

"No, you will not leave here! I will not let my slaves leave Egypt!" cried Pharaoh.

Then, he ordered his officers, "Increase their workload."

Moses and his brother Aaron went before Pharaoh many times to ask for the freedom of God's people, but he refused to let them go. Time after time, God showed him His power. He caused the waters of the Nile River to turn to blood, and covered the earth with frogs. But the sorcerers of Pharaoh copied those miracles with their magic tricks.

Later, God sent a terrible plague of lice. This time the Egyptian magicians could not imitate what God had done. However, the king's heart was still hardened.

Then God sent a plague of flies.

Next, the Egyptians and their cattle were filled with sores that produced intense pain.

God sent other plagues to punish the Egyptians for their stubbornness: hail, locusts and darkness on the earth.

Finally, God sent the angel of death to strike the firstborn of all the families and cattle of the Egyptians.

Then Pharaoh called Moses and said, "Tell the Hebrews that I will set you free. Get out of my country!"

The people were happy with the news. They all quickly followed Moses, because God had promised to take them to a beautiful land. The people praised God because at last they would be free from Egyptian slavery.

God made a special plan to guide the Hebrews to the land of Canaan. To help them know that he was with them, a pillar of cloud guided them during the day, and at night a pillar of fire lit them as they walked.

When they reached the shores of the Red Sea, the village decided to camp, and that's where the problems began.

"The Egyptians are coming!" someone shouted. "Look at the dust their carriages are raising! They are getting closer!"

"We should have stayed in Egypt!" others shouted. "Why did you bring us to die in the desert?" they asked Moses.

God had told Moses that the Egyptians would go after them, but Moses knew that the power of God was greater.

"Do not be afraid! You will see that the power of God will free us from danger!" Moses proclaimed to the people.

The noise of horses and chariots was heard closer and closer.

When it began to get dark, God moved the pillar of cloud and placed it between the Hebrews and the Egyptians. The people of God would have clarity to continue traveling, while the Egyptians would remain in darkness.

"Lift up your rod over the sea," God commanded Moses.

Moses obeyed God, and the wind blew so hard that it split open the sea in two, forming a dry road for the Israelites to cross upon.

Very early in the morning, the whole group began to cross over in the middle of the sea. When they looked back, they saw that the Egyptians were following them the same way.

However, God caused the wheels of the Egyptian chariots to break, and everyone shouted, "We must get away from the Hebrews! Their God is fighting against us!"

When all the Hebrew people had safely crossed to the other side, God told Moses to raise his staff again. Then, the waters of the sea returned to their place, covering the Egyptian soldiers, their horses and their chariots. God saved his people with his great power.

Moses and all the people praised God, singing the words that we find in Exodus 15:2: "The Lord is my strength and my defense; he has become my salvation. He is my God, and I will praise him, my father's God, and I will exalt him."

ACTIVITIES

The crossing of the Red Sea

Pass out the worksheets for Lesson 28, and have your students cut out the action figures of the soldiers and Hebrews at the edges of the page. Then, cut out the figure of the Red Sea and shorelines along the solid lines, and fold it along the dotted lines. This will create a stage for the biblical story.

Tell them to take it home, and encourage them to tell their family members what they learned in class using the action figures and stage.

True or false

Put a strip of tape on the floor, or use a rope to divide the room into two sections. Tell them which side will represent the word "true" and which word will be "false."

When you read one of the following phrases, they should be go to the side of the room that represents the correct answer. Those who choose wrongly twice will be eliminated and must sit down.

- Pharaoh was happy because God's people left Egypt.
- God sent a plague to punish the Egyptians.
- Moses was a disobedient man.
- God chose Moses to free his people from slavery.
- God sent a plague of lice to Egypt.
- The Hebrew people liked being slaves.
- Moses and the people camped on the shores of the Red Sea.
- The Egyptians decided to remain calm when the Israelites left.
- God protected his people with a pillar of fire during the night, and a cloud during the day.
- The Hebrews crossed the Red Sea by swimming.

Memorization

Form a circle, and place yourself in the center with a sponge ball and throw it to one of your students. The child who receives it should say: "I can trust that God will help me because 'Great is our Lord and mighty in power; his understanding has no limit.'" (Psalm 147:5). Continue with other kids.

To end

Ask your students what they liked most about the story. Remind them that we also belong to the people of God, and in the same way that He helped the Hebrews, he cares for us and keeps us from danger. Explain that our God can do supernatural things because his power is immense.

Pray, giving thanks to God for who He is and for what everyone learned today. Conclude by singing praises about God's great power.

Lesson 29
God honors Naaman's obedience

Biblical References: 2 Kings 5:1-15

Lesson Objective: That the students learn to trust in God's great power.

Memory Verse: *Great is our Lord and mighty in power; his understanding has no limit* (Psalm 147:5).

PREPARE YOURSELF TO TEACH!

Through this lesson your students will learn that they can trust in our great and powerful God.

At this stage of physical and emotional changes, it will give them stability to know that they are children of a God who does not change and who is willing to help them.

Emphasize that Naaman was a real person, not the product of someone's imagination like the characters they see on television. Naaman learned to trust in God when he faced a difficult illness and, as a reward for his obedience, God restored his health.

Help them understand that although Naaman was a very important official in the Syrian army, he submitted to the power of the one true God.

BIBLICAL COMMENTARY

2 Kings 5:1-15. Naaman was an important man in the Syrian army, a man whom everyone honored and respected. However, he suffered from leprosy, a disease that threatened his life.

Bible scholars believe that the type of leprosy that Naaman had was not the one we know today, but a more aggressive one that completely disfigured the person.

In this story, God showed his great power through people and common objects.

First, through the young Hebrew girl who served Naaman's wife. Despite being a slave, she had the courage to talk about her faith in God because she knew that He was with his people Israel and that Elisha was a prophet.

Second, through the messenger. He brought specific instructions to Naaman from Elisha, who did not speak directly with the Syrian general.

Third, through the Jordan River. This river had an important meaning for the Hebrew people, but for Naaman it was only a muddy and ordinary river.

Fourth, through the prophet Elisha. Having been a disciple of the prophet Elijah, now God was using him to guide His people.

History tells us that after Naaman appeared before the king of Israel, he went to the prophet's house. Elisha was not impressed by the Syrian captain's elegant caravan, nor all his titles or recommendations. He simply sent his servant with simple instructions so that Naaman would obey them and be healed. Maybe Naaman had his own idea about how the miracle would occur (verse 11), but God showed him that He controlled the situation and that He had the power to heal him, as long as he obeyed.

Naaman went away from Elisha's house enraged, refusing the prophet's instructions. Finally, after his servants convinced him, he finally obeyed and was healed.

Something that we must emphasize is that the absence of the prophet in this miracle gives all the credit to God. Naaman recognized Jehovah as the only living God.

God honored his obedience, and not only restored his skin but also his heart.

It is important that your students know that God has control over everything that exists and honors His children when they obey Him.

DEVELOPMENT OF THE LESSON

Choose some of the following activities to make the development of the lesson more and fun.

Sick!

Look in magazines or newspapers for illustrations of medicines, hospitals, doctors, sick people, etc.

Show them to your students and talk about the various diseases that affect children. Give opportunity for two volunteers to share a brief experience of being sick. Tell them that today's lesson will be about a person suffering from a serious illness.

Trust walk

For this activity you will need pieces of cloth to blindfold the eyes of your students.

Ask the children to line up and blindfold their eyes. Tell them they should walk around the room, trusting you to guide them so they do not get hurt. Remove objects that may cause accidents. If the weather permits, do this activity in a place with grass.

Guide them on a walk through the room.

Then, get together to talk about the experience. Ask them: *How did you feel about having to depend on someone to guide you?* *"How did it feel to trust the leader, even without knowing where I was leading you?*

God wants us to trust him, even though we often do not understand what is happening around us. He wants us to trust that he will take care of us and guide us on the right path.

Today's Bible story tells us about a person who trusted God.

BIBLE STORY

Naaman's trust

Naaman was a general in the army of the king of Syria. The king valued him very much because he was a good man and a brave soldier. But unfortunately, Naaman had leprosy and nobody knew how to cure that disease.

In the house of Naaman a girl worked. She had been taken captive from the land of Israel. One day, she told Naaman's wife, "If my lord Naaman asked the prophet who lives in Samaria for help, he would heal him of his leprosy."

Naaman's wife told him what the girl had told him: "My servant says there is a prophet in Israel who can heal you."

Naaman immediately went to see the king of Syria, and said, "Your Majesty, my wife's servant says that in Israel there is a prophet who can cure me of leprosy."

"Then, go," said the king. "I will send a letter to recommend you to the king of Israel."

In this way, Naaman was ready to go on his journey, carrying much gold, silver and clothing as gifts. The letter that he brought to the king of Israel said: "I am sending you this letter through my servant Naaman so that you may heal him of his leprosy."

When the king of Israel read the letter, he became very worried and said, "I cannot cure leprosy. Why does the king of Syria want to fight with us?"

When the prophet Elisha heard what had happened in the palace, he sent a messenger to the king of Israel: "Tell Naaman to come to my house and he will know that there is a prophet in Israel."

Naaman got into his carriage and went to Elisha's house, but there he got a big surprise. Although Naaman was a very important man in his country, Elisha did not go out to meet him. Rather, he sent a messenger to instruct him.

"Go and wash yourself seven times in the Jordan River. Then your flesh will be restored and you will be clean, and completely healthy from that disease."

When Naaman heard the message, he left angry and told his servants, "I thought the prophet would come out and talk to me. I thought that he would pray to God and touch my wounds, and that would cure me of leprosy. Also, he wants me to wash in the

Jordan River when there are many better rivers in my country. Can't I wash in one of them to be healthy?"

When preparing to return to Syria, one of his servants said to him, "Lord, if the prophet ordered you to do something difficult, wouldn't you do it? However, he has asked you to do something very simple. Why don't you try it?"

So Naaman went down to the Jordan River and submerged himself seven times, just as the prophet had commanded. After the seventh time, Naaman saw that his body was completely healthy.

"I'm healed!" shouted Naaman with joy.

So he returned with his servants to Elisha's house and said, "Now I know that in the whole world there is no God but in Israel. From now on, I will not worship another God, but only the God of Israel who has healed me."

ACTIVITIES

The story of Naaman

Distribute the student worksheets and scissors. Ask the children to cut out the pieces of the puzzle and arrange them according to the order of the Bible story. Then tape them together with clear tape. When the puzzle is finished, a "T" will be formed.

Turn the puzzle over and they will find a special message.

Another option is to distribute a bag or envelope to each student so that they take the pieces of the puzzle to their house, and they put it together with their friends and family.

The king says ...

Gather your students in front of you and tell them: *Let's play 'The King says.' If I say, "The king says touch your nose," you must touch it. But if I just say, "Touch your nose," without saying "The king says," and you do, you must sit down.*

Repeat the game several times (jump, run, sing, etc.) until most children lose and sit down.

Explain that when they follow the rules of the game, they are being obedient. In the same way, God wants us to always obey His Word and His commands, just as Naaman did.

Memorization

Write the words of the memory verse text on different cards and hide them in the room. Tell the children they should look for them. As they find them, they are to assemble the verse and repeat it aloud together. Reward them by giving them time to play their favorite game.

To end

Gather your students and tell them: "This month we have heard Bible stories about the power and majesty of God. He is so powerful that He can do anything. He created the world, confused the languages of the people who built the tower of Babel, and healed Naaman from leprosy. God also wants to show His power in your life and wants you to trust Him with all your heart."

Lead them in a prayer, and intercede for those with special needs. Encourage them to attend the next class, where they will study about an invisible army.

Lesson 30
God's invisible army

Biblical References: 2 Kings 6:8-23

Lesson Objective: That the students know that God is always with them.

Memory Verse: *Great is our Lord and mighty in power; his understanding has no limit* (Psalm 147:5).

PREPARE YOURSELF TO TEACH!

Elementary students are aware that there are people in the world who do not treat others well. They know that injustices are committed, and they are disturbed by situations that are beyond their control. Through this lesson they will have the assurance that God controls everything that exists, although sometimes there is pain and injustice. Help them understand that God cares for those who trust him. When the Christian trusts God, he can feel His care and protection, even when others do not care about him. This does not mean that the believer never experiences discouragement, but faith will help him in those difficult times. Although it is sometimes difficult to perceive the presence of God, it comforts us to know that he is always with us.

BIBLICAL COMMENTARY

The Israelites and the Syrians often waged battles on their borders. The Syrians attacked the Israelites with lightning offensives and fled. However, the Israelites did not remain passive. Through the prophet Elisha, God helped his people by informing him of what the enemy army planned to do. The king of Syria came to suspect that there was a spy in his army who carried information to the king of Israel, but one of his servants said to him, "The prophet Elisha is in Israel, and he tells the king of Israel the words that you speak in your most secret chamber" (v. 12).

The king of Syria, full of anger, sent troops to capture the prophet who was in Dothan. Seeing that the Syrian army had surrounded them, Elisha was not disturbed, demonstrating his confidence in God's power. His servant, on the other hand, was worried and fearful, as is the case when we trust in man and not in God.

In the biblical passage we see that Elisha did not pray for God to rescue them. He knew that he did not need to ask because God was in control of the situation. Rather, he prayed that God would open his servant's eyes so he could see that there were more on their side than those who were against them. The miracle happened immediately, and when his spiritual eyes opened, he noticed that the mountain was full of people on horseback and chariots of fire around them.

While looking with fear and distrust, he seemed to see no hope. But when he saw everything with the eyes of faith, victory was assured. Nowadays, the world affirms that it is necessary to "see to believe", but in everything related to God, we must first "believe to see."

DEVELOPMENT OF THE LESSON

Use some of the following activities to encourage the participation of your students and focus their attention on biblical learning.

Invisible message

Before class, prepare the following message for each of your students. On white paper write with a white crayon (wax pencil): I love you and I am always with you! God.

Give your students the notes with the invisible message and a marker.

Tell them: *Sometimes we feel alone and think that our enemies are stronger than us. But not everything is always as it seems. Use the markers to color the note and you will find a secret message.*

Allow your students to do the activity and read the message they discovered.

We can trust in God even when situations are very difficult. In today's Bible story, you will learn about someone who trusted God in the midst of terrible danger.

BIBLE STORY

The invisible army of God

The king of Syria was at war against the king of Israel. Together with their officers, they organized secret plans for the battle. "We will hide in this place, and when the Israelites come, we will attack them," said the king.

Although the plans were secret, God knew them and warned the prophet Elisha. Then Elisha warned the king of Israel: "Be careful because the Syrians have planned a trap against you!"

The prophet told the king the exact place where the Syrians planned to attack. He was right!

Time after time, Elisha warned the king, and thus the Hebrew army was prepared and successful. One day the king of Syria shouted angrily, "Why does the king of Israel always know where we are going to attack? Surely there is a spy among us!"

Then he gathered all his officers and asked them, "Which one of you is on the side of the king of Israel? Who is the spy?"

"None of us is a spy," said one of his officers. The prophet Elisha is the one who tells the king of Israel everything you say in secret.

"Go and find out where that man is!" the king ordered. "I will send men to capture him."

After a while they told the king that Elisha lived in Dothan, so he sent chariots, horses and a large army. It was still night when they arrived at that place.

The next morning, Elisha's servant got up early and saw that the enemy army was surrounding the city.

"What will we do now?" he asked Elisha.

"Do not be afraid," the prophet answered. "There are more who are with us than those who are with them."

Elisha's servant did not understand what his master was telling him. All he saw was the Syrian army surrounding the city and ready to attack them.

Elisha prayed, saying, "God, I beg you to open his eyes so that he sees." Then God opened the eyes of the servant, who saw that in the hills between the Syrians and Dothan, there was a multitude of soldiers mounted on horses and chariots of fire.

When the enemies advanced towards Elisha, he prayed to the Lord saying, "I pray you will strike them with blindness."

Instantly God made all the Syrian soldiers go blind, as Elisha had requested. Then the prophet came to them and said, "This is not the way or the city that you seek. Follow me and I will take you to the man you are looking for."

The soldiers were blind and confused, so they followed Elisha to Samaria, the capital of the kingdom of Israel. After they entered the city, Elisha prayed again and said, "Lord, open their eyes so that they may see."

When God opened their eyes, they realized that they were in the city of Samaria. They were prisoners of the Israelites because Elisha had captured them!

"Elisha, should I kill them?" asked the king of Israel.

"No, do not kill them!" replied the prophet. "Would you kill a prisoner of war? Give them food and water. In this way they will recover their strength and will be able to return to where their king is."

The king of Israel prepared a great banquet for the Syrians, and when they had finished eating and drinking, sent them back to their country. After that day, the armies of Syria did not attack the territory of Israel again.

ACTIVITIES

An invisible army

Hand out the student worksheets. Ask the children to cut out the figure, following the solid line, to detach the figure of Elisha and his servant. Then, fold this figure along the dotted line and glue the base so that it remains standing.

Allow time for your students to cut the stage following the perpendicular line. Then, bend one of the triangles backwards and another forward, so that the part of the army remains standing.

Encourage them to use their finished work to tell the Bible story they learned today.

God takes care of us through ...

Make a list with your students of ways God cares for us. Write them on the board or on a poster board (for example: God cares for us through our parents, teachers, doctors and hospitals, the members of the church, the laws of the country, the traffic laws, providing food and clothing, through of the prayers of other Christians, etc.).

Memorization

Ask the students to open their Bibles to Psalm 147:5. Give the opportunity for girls to read it first, then the guys, then those who have black shoes, and so on, naming different groups. Look for other fun ways to do the reading that will help them review the memory verse.

To end

Sing praises to God in gratitude for His constant love and protection.

Let the class express their prayer requests, and intercede for each other.

Then, distribute the craft that they made.

Do not forget to visit or call those who did not attend the class or are sick.

Lesson 31
God is patient and forgiving

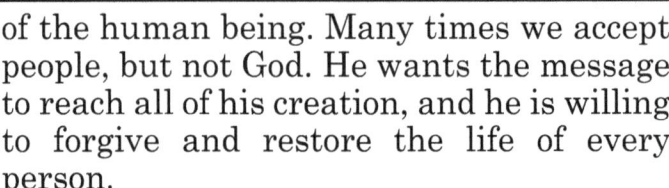

Biblical References: Book of Jonah
Lesson Objective: That the students know that God is patient and forgives us.
Memory Verse: *Great is our Lord and mighty in power; his understanding has no limit* (Psalm 147:5).

PREPARE YOURSELF TO TEACH!

Many people have the wrong idea about God. They believe that he is a rigid and severe being who is eager to punish the disobedient. However, seeing the story of Jonah, we learn that it is the opposite. The nature and love of God are unique. He is patient, understanding and forgiving, and is willing to lift and restore those who have fallen.

Elementary students are learning to recognize their mistakes and repent for their wrongdoing. Emphasize Jonah's disobedience, its consequences and God's reaction to it. Through this story, help them understand that if they are wrong, God is willing to forgive them and give them a new opportunity.

BIBLICAL COMMENTARY

Jonah. To describe the book of Jonah, we could use Psalm 103:8, which says: "The Lord is compassionate and gracious, slow to anger, abounding in love."

To understand this story, we need to see it from God's perspective. This story emphasizes the character of God, and his desire for all to repent and change their way of life. It also shows that the servants of God can not simply disobey an order from the Lord without receiving a wake-up call.

On the other hand, it reminds us that God is faithful, patient, merciful and forgiving. Despite Jonah's rebellion and disobedience, God stayed with him, and he finally repented and took the Lord's message to Nineveh.

We also see that Jonah received God's forgiveness with pleasure and relief, but he did not want the people of Nineveh to receive him. This shows us the character of the human being. Many times we accept people, but not God. He wants the message to reach all of his creation, and he is willing to forgive and restore the life of every person.

The people and king of Nineveh believed in God, and proclaimed a general fast. From people to animals, everyone was to cry out to the just and forgiving God. God heard their plea and forgave them.

God is faithful and merciful, and does not reject the contrite and humble heart.

DEVELOPMENT OF THE LESSON

Use some of the following activities to enrich the study of today's lesson.

Introduction

It is likely that most of your students already know the story of Jonah. Therefore, in this lesson, focus your attention on God's forgiveness and patience instead of focusing on the big fish.

Emphasize in particular that the big fish was a resource that God used to keep Jonah from drowning, but what really matters is that God was patient and forgave Jonah for his disobedience, giving him a second chance.

Patience

This activity will help you test the patience of your students by trying to write a sentence without making a single mistake.

Hand out pens and paper. Ask them to write a complete sentence without making any mistakes. If they make a mistake, they must start the sentence again from the beginning. Encourage them to work with patience and care so they can write the sentence without making a mistake.

Elementary students often use the eraser in their homework. At this stage they are developing and perfecting their writing skills, so most of them want to do it without mistakes. This exercise will help them test their level of patience and tolerance for frustration.

The phrase they should write is: God is patient and forgiving.

Give them five minutes to complete the activity. Then ask them: *What does it mean to be patient?* Listen to their answers and supplement the information. *It is often difficult for us to be patient, but God is always patient and willing to forgive us when we are wrong.*

Jonah in the sea

For this activity, distribute play-doh. Ask your students to make a figure of Jonah and another of a big fish. While doing that, ask them to tell you everything they know about the Bible story. Based on that information, narrate today's story with an emphasis on God's forgiveness and patience.

BIBLE STORY

God forgives

One day God told Jonah, "Go to the great city of Nineveh. I have seen that the people there only do bad stuff and I am tired of their behavior. You must go and tell them to repent of their sins."

But Jonah did not want to obey God. So he escaped to hide in the city of Tarshish, which was the opposite direction of Nineveh. Jonah went to the port of Joppa, where he found a ship bound for Tarshish. After paying for his ticket, he went aboard and was prepared to flee as far as possible from the Lord.

While Jonah was traveling, God sent a strong wind and a terrible storm. The wind was so strong that it looked like the ship was going to be split in half. All the sailors and passengers were very worried, and each one cried out to their gods to protect them.

To lighten the weight of the ship, they threw part of the luggage into the sea.

And where was Jonah while all this was happening? Sleeping!

Finally, the ship's captain found Jonah and asked, "How can you sleep? Get up and pray to your God! Maybe he will see what is happening and protect us so we don't die."

The sailors said, "Let's see if we can find the reason for this terrible storm."

When they learned that Jonah was the reason for the storm, they said to him, "Tell us, who is responsible for this happening to us? Who you are? What do you do? Where do you come from? From which country do you come from?"

"I am a Hebrew and I fear Jehovah, God of heaven, who made the sea and the land," answered Jonah.

When they heard this, they were afraid and asked, "What have you done to make this terrible storm try to finish us? What should we do to calm the sea?"

"Take me and throw me into the sea," said Jonah. "Only then will it calm down. I know that this terrible evil has come upon you because of me."

The sailors did not want to throw Jonah into the sea, but the situation was getting worse. In the end, they threw Jonah overboard and the sea calmed down. When the sailors and passengers saw that the storm had ceased, they realized the great power of God and praised Him.

Meanwhile, God had prepared a big fish to swallow Jonah.

Jonah spent three days and three nights inside the animal. There he prayed to God, and promised that he would not disobey him again. In addition, he apologized for running away and promised to do God's will, going to Nineveh as he had been ordered.

God heard Jonah's prayer and forgave him for his disobedience. Then he ordered the fish to throw Jonah up on dry land. Jonah was very happy to have another opportunity to obey God.

Then God spoke to Jonah a second time and said, "Go to the great city of Nineveh and proclaim the message I have given you."

This time Jonah obeyed! He went to Nineveh and told the people that God was going to destroy the city in 40 days. Upon hearing that message, the inhabitants of Nineveh believed in God, and the king sent this message to all his subjects: "Cry all to God. Stop doing bad and violent things. Maybe God will decide not to destroy us. Maybe he will feel sorry for us and we will not die."

When God saw that the inhabitants of Nineveh were repentant, He had compassion on them and did not destroy them.

When Jonah realized that God had forgiven the people instead of destroying them, he became very angry. "God, I knew that this would happen! That's why I ran away. I knew you were compassionate, patient and forgiving, and that you would not destroy our worst enemies. Now it would be better if you killed me!"

Then God answered him, "Do you have the right to be so angry? You are only thinking of yourself, but in Nineveh there are more than 120 thousand people. Don't you think I should worry about such a big city?"

God wanted Jonah to learn an important lesson. God is patient, forgiving and merciful. He loves all people, no matter who they are or what they have done. When someone repents and leaves sin, God gladly forgives them. How wonderful our God is!

ACTIVITIES

Jonah learns a lesson

Distribute the worksheets so that your students can make the booklet suggested in this activity. Help them follow the instructions to complete the project.

When they have finished, choose several children to come forward and, using their little books, relate what they learned in the Bible story.

Memorization

Prepare in advance the figure of a large fish and write the memory verse on it in large letters. Ask the children to sit in a circle and read the verse several times. Then, hand the fish to one of them and tell them to pass it to the person on their right, who passes it to the person on their right, and so forth. When you say "STOP", the one with the fish must say the verse. Continue the game until everyone has participated.

To end

If the Holy Spirit leads you to do so, give your students the opportunity to confess their sins and ask God for forgiveness. If possible, ask each one if God has already forgiven him for the bad actions he has done. Explain that this is a personal decision, and present them with the message of God's forgiveness.

Pray with those who decide to ask for forgiveness, and also intercede for others.

Remember that it is important to keep track of new students, so try to keep in touch with them during the week.

notes

Lesson 32

God is more powerful than the fiery furnace

Biblical References: Daniel 3:1-30
Lesson Objective: That the students learn to do the correct thing and trust in God.
Memory Verse: *Great is our Lord and mighty in power; his understanding has no limit* (Psalm 147:5).

PREPARE YOURSELF TO TEACH!

According to Sinclair Ferguson, "having faith means trusting in God and in his Word. Faith does not mean that we know or understand God's specific purpose for our life. It means that we are willing to follow him whatever it is. "

Trust is an essential Christian principle. We must trust in God when we decide to follow him and serve him. Often, we talk with elementary students about trust. However, the lessons of this unit focus on exercising their trust in God. Recognizing the power of God will inspire confidence in your students, and help them understand that they are not alone in difficult times.

However, it is important that they learn to always trust God, not only when he uses his power to protect them. Genuine confidence continues even "inside the fiery furnace."

BIBLICAL COMMENTARY

Daniel 3:1-30. The main theme of the book of Daniel is God's authority over earthly kingdoms. The young Hebrews knew that God was in control and that only he could save them.

In the outcome of this story, the king confessed his faith in the only living God who was powerful to save his servants from the terrible furnace of fire.

This story reveals the conflict in the royal court between the king and the three young Jews. As we all know, Nebuchadnezzar had built a golden statue for all the people to worship. He thought he was the most powerful and majestic king in the world, and whoever did not worship the statue when the music played would be executed in a furnace of fire.

Some Chaldeans took the opportunity to accuse the Jews of bad intentions, and filed a complaint with the king. Upon hearing it, the king was offended, and immediately sent for Ananias, Mishael and Azariah.

They presented themselves before the king, bearing witness to their trust in the one true God. Nebuchadnezzar wanted to give them the opportunity to reconsider, but they told him it was not necessary. Their decision was made, and even if God did not save them from death, nothing would change their minds.

King Nebuchadnezzar became so angry that he ordered the furnace to be heated seven times hotter than normal. The heat was so hot that the men who threw the Hebrews into the furnace were burned to death.

The king was shocked when he saw the young Hebrews walking around inside the furnace, and greater was his amazement to notice that there weren't only three but four walking around inside. God honored the faithfulness of his servants and delivered them with a mighty hand. The passage mentions that "not even the hair of their heads had burned; their clothes were intact, and they did not even smell of fire" (v. 27).

Nebuchadnezzar then blessed the God of the Hebrew youth, and issued a decree: that any people, nation or language that blasphemed against the God of the Hebrews would be dismembered.

Just as God saved his servants who trusted him, he can also save us from adversity and danger if we are faithful and obedient.

DEVELOPMENT OF THE LESSON

Babylonian maps

For this activity you will need: a container to mix the ingredients, a spoon, a dropper, 2 tablespoons of salt, a tablespoon of flour, ¾ cup of water, 3 drops of oil, a small shallow mold and a pencil.

Tell your students: *The story we will tell today happened many years ago in Babylon. Today we will learn to make maps like those used in that city in ancient times.*

Read the instructions out loud for your students to follow. If your class is very large, divide it into groups of three or four children to facilitate cooperative work.

Instructions: First, mix the salt and the flour. Then, add the water little by little while mixing with a spoon. Add the oil with the dropper, mix it and pour the dough into the mold. Press the mixture until it is well flattened. Now using a pencil, draw mountains, rivers, the city of Babylon, the palace of the king, etc.

Fire Fire!

Do this activity with great caution to avoid accidents. Light a candle and put the edge of a piece of paper over the flame so that it starts to burn.

When the paper is burning, extinguish the candle. Talk with your students about the characteristics of fire and what it can do to things.

Tell them: *Fire is very dangerous. Just as it burned the paper, it can burn everything in its path: trees, buildings, people, etc. However, there is someone more powerful than fire. Do you know who that is? Exactly! God! And in today's story, we will learn how he cared for his servants in a blazing furnace.*

BIBLE STORY

Freed from the fiery furnace

The king of Babylon was an arrogant man. His name was Nebuchadnezzar. He was very proud of all the great endeavors he had made, and he liked that other people thought he was great.

One day, King Nebuchadnezzar had a new idea. He ordered his servants to make a giant statue, all covered with gold.

Then he put it in a place where everyone could see it, and sent a messenger throughout the kingdom to announce: "Come to the dedication of the beautiful golden statue."

During the dedication, the king's messenger said loudly, "When you hear to the music, everyone should bow down and worship the golden image that King Nebuchadnezzar has made. Whoever does not kneel and worship it will be immediately thrown into a blazing furnace."

In those times it was very dangerous to disobey an order from the king, so when the music began, everyone prostrated themselves on the ground and worshiped the golden statue.

All did, except three Jewish men named Ananias, Mishael and Azariah, who worshiped the only true God.

Then, some servants of the king saw the three Jews who had remained standing, while all the others were kneeling, so they went to tell the king.

"King, live forever," the servants said. "We know that you have made a law that requires that when hearing the sound of the musical instruments, everyone must go and worship your golden statue. And you warned that those who disobey would be thrown into the fiery furnace. However, some Jews didn't pay attention to your orders. They have important positions in your kingdom, but they don't worship your gods and they don't bow before your golden statue."

King Nebuchadnezzar was furious, and ordered that Ananias, Mishael, and Azariah be brought before him.

"Young Hebrews, is it true that you do not serve my gods or worship the golden statue that I have built?" asked the enraged king. "Now when you hear the sound of musical instruments, you must bow and worship my statue. If you refuse, you will be thrown into a blazing furnace."

"King Nebuchadnezzar, if you throw us into the furnace of fire, the God we serve has the power to save us, and he will rescue us from your hands. And even if he doesn't, we want you to know, O king, that we will not serve your gods or worship the golden image you have made," the three young men replied.

King Nebuchadnezzar became even more angry and shouted at his servants, "Heat the oven seven times hotter than usual! Then tie Ananias, Mishael and Azariah and throw them in." The oven was so hot that the flames killed the soldiers who threw the three friends into the oven.

King Nebuchadnezzar and his servants watched closely at what was happening. Suddenly, the king got up surprised and asked, "Were there not three men tied and thrown into the fire?"

"Yes, that's the way it was," the servants replied.

"Look!" said the king with amazement. "I see four men walking in the middle of the fire. They aren't tied up and seem to be well, and the fourth man looks like a child of the gods."

Nebuchadnezzar approached the furnace and shouted, "Shadrach, Meshach, Abednego (the Babylonian names of the young Hebrews), servants of the Most High God, come out of there!"

Everyone looked at them in amazement. The three young men were unharmed from the furnace. The fire hadn't burned a single hair. They didn't even smell of smoke!

Nebuchadnezzar recognized that the God of Shadrach, Meshach, and Abednego was more powerful than the gods he worshiped, so he made a new proclamation.

"Praise be to the God of Shadrach, Meshach and Abednego, who sent his angel and rescued his servants! They trusted him and disobeyed the king's order, being willing to die rather than worship another god. Therefore, I order that if a person of any nation speaks against the God of these men, their heads will be cut off, and their house will be destroyed, because no other God can save in this way."

Nebuchadnezzar did something more. He gave the Hebrew youth new jobs, more important than the previous ones. He knew he could trust these brave men because they served an almighty God.

ACTIVITIES

Trust and obey

Distribute the student worksheets. Ask the students to cut along the solid line to detach the strip with the instructions. Trim around the edges so you have a square within a square. Then, fold the 4 triangles up along the dotted line to cover the figure. Ask that some volunteers read aloud the words of the triangles. Open them and review the biblical story using the illustrations.

Then, take time to cut out the figure of the angel on the back of the instruction strip and stick it inside the fiery furnace, next to the young Hebrews.

Encourage them to use their finished work to tell their family members what they learned in class.

Memorization

Use the sheet from the student worksheets to review the biblical text of this unit. If time permits, invite parents to listen to their children say the text by heart. This encourages the children to continue participating and learning in the class.

To end

Since this is the last class of the unit, briefly review the previous lessons. Emphasize the importance of knowing that our God is almighty and willing to help his children.

Encourage your students to tell their friends this great truth and to invite them to participate in Sunday School.

Conclude by praying for one another.

JESUS TEACHES US TO PRAY

Biblical References: Luke 6:12-16; 11:1-4; John 17:6-26; Matthew 26:36-46.

Unit Memory Verse: *I call on you, my God, for you will answer me; turn your ear to me and hear my prayer* (Psalm 17:6).

UNIT OBJECTIVES

This unit will help the students:

- ❖ Recognize that Jesus teaches us to pray, giving us an example and specific instructions.
- ❖ Pray for themselves and other people.
- ❖ Develop the habit of prayer.
- ❖ Believe that prayer is the way that God provided for us to communicate with Him.
- ❖ Know that God responds to the prayers of his children.

LESSON UNIT A

Lesson 33: Jesus prays before deciding
Lesson 34: Jesus teaches his disciples to pray
Lesson 35: Jesus prays for others.
Lesson 36: Jesus prays when he is sad.

WHY ELEMENTARY STUDENTS NEED THE TEACHING OF THIS UNIT:

It is necessary for elementary-age children to learn to pray. They should know that they can ask for God's help when they make decisions or when they have to choose between the good and the bad.

Your students need to be heard, either by their friends, their parents or other family members. It is important for them to know that God is willing to listen to them when they pray. No matter the place or circumstances, God is never too busy to help them.

During this unit you will learn some important aspects of prayer and the basic teachings we see in the Lord's Prayer.

At this age, caring about others is important. So elementary students will know that they can express their love and concern by interceding for other people.

These lessons will teach them to face their fears and concerns with the help of prayer, and to express gratitude and love to the Lord when they talk to him.

Lesson 33
Jesus prays before deciding

Biblical References: Luke 6:12-16
Lesson Objective: That the students learn to pray before making decisions.
Memory Verse: *I call on you, my God, for you will answer me; turn your ear to me and hear my prayer* (Psalm 17:6).

PREPARE YOURSELF TO TEACH!

Prayer is the cornerstone of the lives of Christians. Through it, our communication and relationship with God is nurtured and strengthened. Children should exercise the habit of prayer from an early age. It is sad to see that many people consider prayer synonymous with boredom, or that they simply do not know what to say to God.

Use these lessons to teach your class how important it is to talk to the Lord, following Jesus' example, approaching the Father with reverence, and finding in Him the answers for all our needs.

It is difficult for some children to think about the needs of others. Suggest that they pray asking God to help them remember to share, instead of being selfish; that it is important to be friendly instead of discourteous; and that being kind will help them have more friends.

Elementary-aged children will have to make more and more decisions. Therefore, encourage them to pray and ask for God's direction to know how to act.

BIBLICAL COMMENTARY

Luke 6:12-16. This passage reminds us that Jesus' ministry revolved around prayer. The evangelist Luke was careful to include this important aspect in his record of the Master's life. Jesus was baptized after a time of prayer (3:21); when he was surrounded by crowds, after ministering he retired to pray (5:16); before choosing his twelve disciples he spent time in prayer (6:12); when he climbed the mountain of transfiguration he went to pray (9:28).

Jesus spent time in communion with God before choosing his disciples. He knew that the decision was of the utmost importance, because they would be the basis of the church. They would be responsible for bringing the message of salvation to the whole world. Jesus knew that spending time alone with his Father, far from the distractions of the world, was the best thing before making such a decision.

The passage does not say that Jesus went before the Father and prayed hastily to ask for his direction. It also does not say that Jesus tried to pray all night and could not do it. Rather we are told that Jesus went away to that hill to spend the whole night talking with his Father. It was a time of communion with God, when his thoughts became like those of the Father, and he received the help he needed to make the right decision.

Jesus taught us not to make decisions before consulting with our heavenly Father. However small the decision we have ahead, it is always better to ask for God's guidance and wisdom to make the right decision.

DEVELOPMENT OF THE LESSON

My prayer book

Give each child cardboard or poster board and four white pieces of paper. Ask them to fold the card in half and write on the front: "My prayer book." Fold the paper in half, and put them inside the cardboard. Fasten or stick the sheets along the fold to make a notebook. Allow time for your students to write their name there and decorate the outside of their prayer books. Keep them in the room to use during this unit.

When can we pray?

Ask the children when they or their parents pray. They may say that they pray when they are in church, before eating or before going to sleep. Tell them it is important to pray on those occasions, but emphasize that God always listens to us, and we can pray at all times and in all places.

Decisions

For this activity you will need a bag of sweets or candies of two different colors.

Show the sweets to your students and ask them to choose one of the color they prefer to take home with them at the end of the class. Allow everyone to come forward and take the candy of their choice.

Ask them to save it, and ask if it was difficult to choose the correct color. Tell them that many times the decisions we make are simple and we do not need to think too much. However, there are other decisions that are much more important. Through this biblical story, God wants to teach us to ask for his advice before deciding.

BIBLE STORY

Jesus prays before making a big decision

"I need help," thought Jesus. "Many people want to know God, and I have to train some men to help me do that job. Who do I choose?"

Crowds of people followed Jesus everywhere. They wanted to hear his teachings and know how to live to please God. Later, some of these people could be leaders who would teach others.

"This decision is important and there is only one way I can make it," thought Jesus. "I will ask my Father to help me decide."

The decision was so important that Jesus went alone to a mountain to pray. Do you know how much time he spent praying?

All night! While the people were sleeping, he prayed. Perhaps he began to pray about nine o'clock at night, and when midnight came, he continued to pray. At two o'clock in the morning Jesus was still praying, and this continued until four in the morning. "Father, whom should I choose?" he asked in prayer.

Then, Jesus knew who he should choose and prayed for each one.

He prayed for Simon Peter. Peter would be strong as a rock and would preach to many people about the kingdom of God.

Then he prayed for Andrew, Peter's brother. Andrew was the one who brought Peter to know Jesus. Surely he was going to guide many other people to know Jesus.

When he prayed for James and John, he prayed for Peter again. Peter, James and John were going to be Jesus' best friends. Then he prayed for Philip, Bartolomew, Matthew and Thomas.

Among the twelve apostles there was another Jacob and another Simon, so Jesus prayed for them too.

Also, he prayed for two men called Judas. One would be a faithful follower, but the other would one day betray Jesus and deliver him to his enemies.

When it was already morning, perhaps like seven or eight, Jesus came down from the mountain to look for the men that God had chosen for this special work.

ACTIVITIES

Pray before deciding

For this activity you will need paper fasteners with two legs and scissors.

Hand out the worksheets for Lesson 33, and have the children cut out the three circles following the contours.

Read the instructions together, and explain in detail each of the steps to do the activity. After trimming the circles, they should place the circle of the title on the top, the circle of words in the middle and the circle of figures below, and join them in the center with the paper fastener. Make sure everyone follows the instructions so the circles spin easily.

As they work, tell them: *Jesus prayed before making important decisions. God wants us to pray and ask for wisdom before deciding.*

It is important to pray

Hand out the prayer books that your students made at the beginning of the class. Ask them to write down the title of the lesson and then draw or write an important decision for which they should pray. Then, talk with them about the importance of making wise decisions in light of God's Word.

Tell them they will use the prayer books during class and they can take them home when they finish the unit.

Encourage them to pray during the week when they have to make decisions.

Memorization

Write the memory verse on a piece of poster board, and show it to your students. Teach them the following gestures to accompany each phrase of the verse, as they review it: I call on you (place your hands around your mouth as if calling someone), my God (point above); for you will answer me (point to yourself), turn your ear to me (put a hand behind your ear), and hear my prayer (point to your mouth) (Psalm 17:6).

Guide your students to make these gestures each time they repeat the memory verse.

To end

Lead the class to sing a song about prayer. Then, have some volunteers offer short prayers to conclude.

Lesson 34

Jesus teaches His disciples to pray

Biblical References: Luke 11:1-4

Lesson Objective: That the students know that Jesus was an example for his followers about how to pray.

Memory Verse: *I call on you, my God, for you will answer me; turn your ear to me and hear my prayer* (Psalm 17:6).

PREPARE YOURSELF TO TEACH!

Many students of this age are experiencing growth in their relationship with God. Through this lesson they will learn how to talk to God in prayer.

Children appreciate the people who listen to them. So understanding and experiencing prayer in their daily life will strengthen their relationship with the Lord. Above all, it will encourage them to know that God is always willing to listen to them when they talk with Him.

For children of this age, it is easy to memorize, and maybe some already know the Lord's Prayer. Although the memorization of the Lord's Prayer is not one of the objectives of this unit, those who are interested can do so. The emphasis of this lesson is to help children follow the pattern of the Lord's Prayer.

BIBLICAL COMMENTARY

Luke 11:1-4. The disciples had the opportunity to observe Jesus many times while praying, so they approached him to ask him to teach them how to pray. To answer this request, Jesus taught them a model prayer, known as the Lord's Prayer.

It was not unusual for the rabbis to teach their disciples to pray. In fact, John the Baptist taught his followers to pray.

This passage considers prayer as something that can be learned. Jesus taught his disciples that when speaking with God, they should address him as their Father, using simple and sincere words. If we could divide the Lord's Prayer into sections, we could say that in the first, the purpose of prayer is to give honor and glory to God. Next comes the request for daily needs, leaving each day in the hands of God.

Forgiveness is a fundamental part of prayer. We must seek forgiveness from God and we also forgive those who have offended us. Forgiveness is based on the grace of God, and as we have been forgiven, we can also forgive.

In the last part of the model prayer we ask God to protect us from the temptations and trials that come into our lives. The Lord has promised that He will not let us be tempted beyond what we can resist with His power. The apostle Paul reminds us of this in his letter to the Corinthians when he tells the Christians that there is no temptation that has overtaken man that is not common to man, but that God is faithful, because in the face of temptation He will provide the way out.

DEVELOPMENT OF THE LESSON

My prayer book

Ask a volunteer to distribute the prayer books. Help them write on the second page some model prayers to give thanks for the food. Allow them to include some drawings.

Tell them that at the end of the month they will have a collection of model prayers. This book will serve as a guide for when they need to talk to God.

Decisions that Jesus took

This game will help your class review the names of the disciples that Jesus chose after praying all night. In the last lesson the names of the disciples were mentioned. Children like this type of information, and they will surely enjoy this activity.

Write the names of the 12 apostles on the board. Then, write each name on a piece of paper and place them in a bag. Explain that each child should draw a name, but should not show it to anyone (if you have more than 12 students, ask for volunteers to take a name, if you have less than 12 students, some should get two pieces of paper).

Ask a child to come forward and pretend that he/she is the disciple mentioned on their paper. The others should guess their name by asking questions such as: How many letters does your name have? With what letter does your name begin? Etc.

God's phone

For this activity you will need several phones. Ask your students: *Have you ever talked on the phone with a friend?* Allow them to respond, and then tell them: *When you talk to a friend, you don't need to use special or difficult words, but you speak naturally and can say whatever you want. God wants to be your best friend. You can talk to him confidently, using simple words. God knows everything about you and wants you to talk to him, just as you do with your friends.*

Allow them to take turns saying a small prayer on the phone. Remind them that God hears their prayers and is never busy. He always has time to listen to his children.

BIBLE STORY

Write the Lord's Prayer on the board or on a card to use as you tell the Bible story.

Jesus' prayer

When Jesus prayed, his disciples listened to him and watched him closely. One day when he had finished praying, one of his disciples said to him, "Lord, teach us to pray. John the Baptist taught his disciples to pray. Please, teach us to pray as you do."

Jesus told them, "This, then, is how you should pray: 'Our Father in heaven, hallowed be your name, your kingdom come, your will be done, on earth as it is in heaven. Give us today our daily bread. And forgive us our debts, as we also have forgiven our debtors. And lead us not into temptation, but deliver us from the evil one, for yours is the kingdom, and the power, and the glory forever. Amen (Matthew 6:9-13).'"

When Jesus taught this prayer to his disciples, he did not mean that we should always use the same words when praying. It was an example for us to know how to talk to God. In many places, this prayer is known as the "Lord's Prayer," or the "Our Father" prayer.

We can say the Lord's Prayer as part of our prayers, but it is also necessary that we use our own words to speak with God.

ACTIVITIES

My prayer box

Distribute the student worksheets and the prayer hands for lesson 34 that are in the Cutout Section (p. 135) and write their name on the line.

Then have them cut along the solid lines of the figure of Lesson 34. Show them how to fold the sheet along the dotted lines to assemble the prayer box. Help them to glue their prayer hands in the marked spaces. Then glue the sections that make up the box.

Explain that this box will help them keep their prayer requests. In addition, they can invite their family and friends to add other requests to intercede for them.

Our Father

Elementary children are becoming familiar with this prayer, and it is important that they begin to memorize it. Therefore, devote a special time to explain its meaning and make sure they understand it well.

Talk to them about the meaning of each phrase. Allow them to express their ideas and add information when necessary.

Our Father: When we address God in this way, we express that he represents a loving and wise father. It shows us that we are part of the family of God.

Hallowed be your name: Show respect and honor to God. It means that the name of God is holy.

Your kingdom come: Recognize that the ways of God are the best option.

These first phrases express honor and worship to God. There are also other ways to refer to God and to worship him, such as: God is wonderful, powerful, loving, Most High, etc.

Give us today our daily bread: By setting these words as an example, Jesus wanted us to know that God is the one who provides everything we need to live each day. If we go through times of need, we can ask for God's help. He promised that he would provide for our needs.

The next part of the sentence is very important:

Forgive us our debts, as we also have forgiven our debtors: When we do something that does not please God, we should ask for forgiveness. It's the only way we can come back to him. God always forgives us when we ask him with sincerity. In the same way, we must forgive those who do us wrong.

Memorization

Review the memory verse using the gestures learned in the previous lesson. Ask that some volunteers come forward and lead the group while repeating the verse a couple of times.

Hand out the Verse of the Month Club cards so that the class takes them home and reviews the text during the week.

To end

Give your students all the work they did, and form a circle to pray. Write the petitions on a card, and intercede for them.

Say goodbye by singing a song about prayer, and encourage them to attend the next class.

Lesson 35
Jesus prays for others

Biblical References: John 17:6-26

Lesson Objective: That the students follow Jesus' example and pray for others.

Memory Verse: *I call on you, my God, for you will answer me; turn your ear to me and hear my prayer* (Psalm 17:6).

PREPARE YOURSELF TO TEACH!

Elementary-aged children are increasingly interested in the people around them. It is the ideal time for them to learn to think about the needs of others and to pray for them.

Children have a lot of memory, as they demonstrated in learning the memory verses. This will help them remember that they should pray for others. Teach them to use their memory to develop an effective prayer ministry.

Your example regarding prayer is important for children. Include prayer for others as part of your class. Also, let your students know that you pray for them during the week, and encourage them to pray for each other.

BIBLICAL COMMENTARY

John 17:6-26. This passage is known as "Jesus' prayer for his church." It is the most extensive prayer of Jesus that appears in the Bible. He begins praying for himself, then he prays for his disciples, and in the end, for those who would believe in him through the message of his disciples. This includes us, so we can say that Jesus prayed for us.

This prayer shows the close relationship that existed between Jesus and his Father, and is a preamble to the final stage of Jesus' earthly ministry. Although he was aware that the cross awaited him, in his prayer he expressed hope and joy, instead of despair. Jesus had his eyes fixed on the future, and he knew that his disciples would carry the message of salvation with boldness, surrendering their own lives out of love for him.

He also knew that many would believe because of the testimony of the apostles; that is why he prayed that they be protected in this world.

In that prayer he included three specific requests: protection for believers, unity among them and their sanctification.

Jesus also prayed for his twelve disciples, whom he had chosen to represent him on earth. These men, after having left everything to follow Jesus, were willing to give their lives for him. And knowing that they would face opposition and danger in carrying the message of salvation, Jesus asked the Father to protect them from the evil one.

He also prayed for the unity of his followers. He knew that they would face divisions and that the enemy would try to destroy them, but he trusted that God could free them from all evil.

DEVELOPMENT OF THE LESSON

Choose some of the following activities to teach your students the Bible story.

Prayer hands

Give each child a piece of paper, and show them how to fold it in half to make a card. On the front of the card, have them draw an outline of one of their hands with their fingers together, as if they were in an attitude of prayer. Then, they can color it and decorate it.

On the inside, they are to write a letter to a person they know who needs prayer.

Let them write their own notes or give them a small sentence. Tell them to take their card after class, and not to forget to give it to the person they chose.

Prayer partners

In advance, make figures of different shapes on poster board. You will need two of each figure, and enough figures for all your students. Cut out the figures, and place them in a basket. Ask each child to take one. Then tell them that they should look for the person who has the matching figure of the one they picked.

When everyone has found their partner, ask them to stay together, because they will be prayer partners in the next activity. Each child should write their prayer request on the figure, and then give it to their partner to take home and pray for that request during the week.

My prayer book

Hand out prayer books, and give time for your students to make a list of the people they should pray for. Do not forget to include the pastor of the church and the missionaries.

Ask them to write as a title: "I must pray for ...", and decorate the page to their liking.

BIBLE STORY

Read the following passages from John 17, and explain to the class that they are part of the prayer that Jesus prayed to God shortly before he died. If you wish, ask them to open their Bibles and follow the reading with their eyes, or if you have good readers in your class, assign them a part to read out loud.

Jesus prays for others

"I have revealed you to those whom you gave me out of the world. They were yours; you gave them to me and they have obeyed your word. ... they believed that you sent me.

I pray for them ... Holy Father, protect them by the power of your name, the name you gave me, so that they may be one as we are one. While I was with them, I protected them and kept them safe by that name you gave me....

My prayer is not that you take them out of the world but that you protect them from the evil one. They are not of the world, even as I am not of it. Sanctify them by the truth; your word is truth. As you sent me into the world, I have sent them into the world ...

My prayer is not for them alone. I pray also for those who will believe in me through their message, that all of them may be one, Father, just as you are in me and I am in you ...

Righteous Father, though the world does not know you, I know you, and they know that you have sent me. I have made you known to them, and will continue to make you known in order that the love you have for me may be in them and that I myself may be in them."

ACTIVITIES

Remember Jesus' prayer

Ask two children to represent Thomas and Matthew. They will read the following dialogue that illustrates the content of today's lesson. Or if you want you can use puppets for this activity.

Thomas: Jesus told us many things we should think about now.

Matthew: I learned a lot from Jesus. I really want to tell others everything he taught me.

Thomas: Me too. But I'm afraid because I don't know how to do it or what to say.

Matthew: Don't you remember the prayer he prayed for us after the Passover dinner? He prayed for us! He asked God for each one of his followers. He was happy because we believed he was the Son of God! Isn't that amazing?

Thomas: That's right, but when he finished praying, he told us he would have to leave, although we didn't know where he would go. I always felt safe when he was close. He always took care of us and protected us.

Matthew: None of us knew what would happen next, and maybe it was better that way. We never would have believed that they were going to crucify him. But good thing he asked the Father to protect us! When we travel, teach or preach we know that we are not alone because God is with us.

Thomas: Yes, I often think of that prayer. I'm so glad that Jesus prayed for us before he left.

Matthew: Even though we all went to different places, the Master prayed that we would be united in our faith in him.

Thomas: We have a great job to do.

Matthew: That's right.

Thomas: I'm glad Jesus prayed for us and for all those who would believe in him when we preached to them.

Matthew: I know. Jesus prayed for all believers, even for those who never saw him in person.

Thomas: Jesus loved us very much and prayed that the Father would take care of us. That's why I want to tell everyone about that love he gave us.

Matthew: Thomas, you're already doing it because you live as Jesus taught us and you want to teach others about the kingdom of God.

Thomas: Thank you, Matthew.

Why did Jesus pray?

Hand out the strip with the Prayer Hands from the Cutout Section (p. 135) and then look at their worksheet for this lesson.

Give them time to write their names in the blank circle, and tell them: *A moment ago we read in John 17 the prayer Jesus prayed for others. According to what you learned, stick a prayer hands in each circle that represents the people Jesus prayed for.*

Instruct them to complete the sentence, "Jesus prayed for ..." Then, explain that Jesus prayed first for himself; later, for his disciples; and he concluded by praying for people all over the world who would become Christians.

Then tell them: *John 17:20 says, 'But I do not pray only for these, but also for those who will believe in me through their word.'*

Who do you think is included in this sentence? Allow them to respond, and let them know that Jesus prayed for all who believed, and would believe, in him as their Savior and Lord.

I will pray for my neighbor

Have the students find the worksheet entitled "I will pray for my neighbors." Encourage them to use this sheet to pray for each other during the week. Remind them that Jesus prayed for his disciples and for all believers. Show them how to use this prayer sheet. Ask them to write the names of the people they will pray for. If they have difficulty choosing these people, suggest that they may be relatives, friends, the pastoral family, leaders, missionaries, etc.

Encourage them to pray each day for the people on their list, and draw a star in the box that corresponds to the date they prayed.

Memorization

Use a puppet to review the memory verse. Have the puppet talk with the children so that they have to say the verse to correct the puppet's mistakes. For example, the puppet could say: "I do not remember the verse, can you help me?"

Another option is that the puppet says the verse incorrectly and then the class must correct its mistakes. When the puppet finally says the verse without errors, invite your students to repeat it with him.

To end

Ask if it is better to pray long or short prayers: *In our lesson today we learned that Jesus prayed a long prayer, but sometimes he prayed short prayers. Do you think Jesus listens to us better when we pray long prayers?* Explain that the length of our prayer does not matter. God always listens to us and understands our needs.

Ask for two volunteers to lead the class in prayer before saying goodbye.

Lesson 36
Jesus prays when he is sad

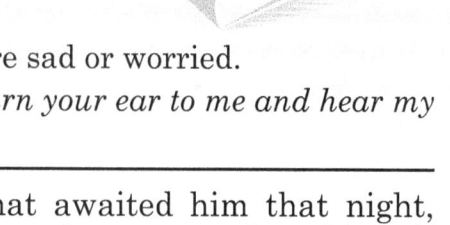

Biblical References: Matthew 26:36-46
Lesson Objective: That the students learn to pray when they are sad or worried.
Memory Verse: *I call on you, my God, for you will answer me; turn your ear to me and hear my prayer* (Psalm 17:6).

PREPARE YOURSELF TO TEACH!

Since children often think that Jesus never had problems, this lesson may surprise them. Knowing that Jesus also sometimes felt distressed by circumstances will comfort them to know that he understands how we feel when things are not going well for us. After all, he experienced the same feelings as us: sadness, anxiety and anguish.

Elementary students face more and more fears. They have passed the stage where their home was their little world and their parents were the main people. Even the smallest children go through situations that are out of their control and frighten them.

Elementary-aged children are afraid to face new situations, to be rejected, to get lost, to be alone, to change their routine or to fail. Therefore as a teacher, you have many opportunities to show them that they must surrender their fears to God, just as Jesus did.

By teaching them about God's love and care, it will give them the security they need to confront complex situations.

With this lesson your students will also understand that sometimes God does not free us from difficulties, but gives us the strength to face them. By learning to submit to the will of God, they will understand that God wants the best for them.

BIBLICAL COMMENTARY

This lesson on Jesus' prayer in the Garden of Gethsemane shows us both his humanity and his divinity. The road that leads to death is one that we all must travel. Jesus was on that path and, in Gethsemane, he realized how close he was to the end of his earthly life. The Son of God was not a mysterious ghost who was not affected by circumstances. On the contrary, he was God incarnate, the one who experienced the greatest human suffering and pain.

Knowing what awaited him that night, Jesus felt the need to strengthen himself through prayer. Therefore, leaving eight of his disciples outside of the garden, he entered with Peter, James and John.

The impact of the cross began to weigh on Jesus. Mark describes it very clearly: "My soul is overwhelmed with sorrow to the point of death," he said to them. "Stay here and keep watch" (Mark 14:34). Jesus' prayer shows his fear as a human being, as well as his love for God and submission to the divine will. As a man, he wanted to escape the cross and the separation from the Father that this would cause; but as the Son of God, he knew that he must fulfill the plan of salvation for humanity.

How often do we look for ways to avoid God's will to follow our own desires! This lesson reminds us that God calls us to strengthen ourselves in prayer and to fulfill his will, which is holy and perfect.

DEVELOPMENT OF THE LESSON

Introduction

Be creative in telling this story, emphasizing the pain and difficult situation that Jesus faced. Ask them what they do when they are sad. Then explain that they can go to God in prayer, just as Jesus did.

Emphasize that Jesus was honest with God and did not hide what he felt, so when we pray, we must trust that God not only hears us but also understands us.

My prayer book

Distribute the prayer books to your students. Ask them to write the words from Psalm 120:1 and draw a picture to illustrate it.

Tell them that prayer is how we talk with God about our sadness and troubles. Review the prayers they wrote during the unit, and give them time to finish the drawings or fill in the missing information. They should take the books home after class today.

Sad or worried?

Ask the children to briefly tell about an experience in which they felt sad or worried. Listen carefully, and ask them: *Do you think Jesus was ever sad or worried?*

Based on their answers, tell them: *Although Jesus was the Son of God, he felt the same as us: fear, pain, worry, etc.*

In today's story we will hear what he did one day when he was very sad.

BIBLE STORY

Jesus took his disciples to a very special and peaceful place called the Garden of Gethsemane. When they arrived, he said, "Sit here. I will go to pray. Peter, James and John, please come with me."

As they walked, Jesus began to grieve and worry. Then he told his best friends, "My heart is so sad that I feel like I'm going to die. Stay here and pray with me." Then, he walked on a little more to pray.

Some people frown when they are sad; others cry, and some do not want to talk to anyone. When Jesus was sad, do you know what he did? He knelt on the ground and prayed, "My Father, if it's possible, I don't want to suffer. But, if it's not possible, let your will be done."

Jesus knew that soon he would suffer a lot. He did not want to, but he knew it was the only way to save people from their sins. So he prayed, "Father, your will be done. Do what is best for everyone."

When he finished praying, he returned to where his three friends were. And what do you think they were doing? Were they waiting and praying as Jesus had told them? No, they were asleep.

"Couldn't you stay awake for an hour?" asked Jesus. "Pray that you can resist the temptation."

Jesus again left his disciples and went away to pray. After kneeling, he said, "My Father, if it is not possible to remove this suffering from me, may your will be done."

When Jesus returned to where his disciples were, he found them sleeping again. Although they tried to stay awake, sleep had overcome them. Jesus let them sleep and went to pray to the Father, just as he had done before.

When he returned and found his disciples still asleep, he told them, "Sleep now and rest. Soon the suffering will begin."

Finally he said, "Get up, come on. The man who will deliver me to my enemies is coming."

ACTIVITIES

Thy will be done!

After distributing the activity sheets for this lesson, ask the children to fold the page along the dotted line to remember what Jesus did when he was sad.

Then, have them go to the next page and fill in the blanks to review the memory verse.

Let's teach children to pray

What is prayer?
- Prayer is one of the ways God chooses to communicate with us.
- To pray means to talk to God with freedom, from the depths of our hearts.
- To pray is to express our fears and concerns to God.
- To pray is to talk with him about our problems, needs and questions, and also about our dreams and joys.

Essential concepts about prayer that children should learn:
- I can pray at any time, day or night.
- I can pray anywhere.
- God always listens to our prayers.
- God knows our weaknesses and strengths. He knows what makes us happy and what makes us sad.
- God knows about our lives and those of all the people around the world.
- God has a purpose for answering our prayers according to his will.

Memorization

Prepare a contest in which your students show their ability to memorize and say the full verse. Have simple prizes to stimulate them to continue learning the Word of God.

Option: Ask the pastor to allow your class to participate in the worship service to recite the memory verse they learned.

To end

Pray for each one, interceding for their family, studies, health, and above all, for their spiritual growth. Pray also for the sick and those who did not attend the class.

Distribute all the work they did during the unit, and remind them that in the next class they will begin to study the unit on the Bible.

Year 2　　　　　　　　　　　　　　　　　　　　　　　　　　Introduction - Unit IX

THE BIBLE

Biblical References: Jeremiah 36; Luke 4:16-44; 2 Chronicles 34; Acts 16:1-5; 2 Timothy 1:1-7; 2:1-6, 16-18; 3:10-17; 4:13-22.

Unit Memory Verse: *Your word is a lamp for my feet, a light on my path* (Psalm 119:105).

UNIT OBJECTIVES

This unit will help the students:

- ❖ Love and respect the Bible as being the Word of God.
- ❖ Discover the origin of the Bible and its passage through time.
- ❖ Develop the skill to locate the Old and New Testaments, the Gospels, the Psalms, Genesis and Revelations.
- ❖ Realize that God changes our lives when we study His Word.

LESSON UNIT A

Lesson 37:　The Bible is God's special book
Lesson 38:　The Bible tells us about Jesus
Lesson 39:　The Bible helps us to do the right thing
Lesson 40:　The Bible teaches us every day

WHY ELEMENTARY STUDENTS NEED THE TEACHING OF THIS UNIT:

It is likely that many of your students have prior knowledge of the Bible; maybe they even know some memory verses. However, this lesson gives them the opportunity to go deeper into the study of this precious book. They will learn to locate the Old and New Testaments, as well as some other books of the Bible.

Through these lessons they will follow the journey of the Bible through time to the present day. They will also understand that through his Word, God reveals his love to us and teaches us how to live correctly.

The first lesson, based on the story of how God revealed his Word to Jeremiah, teaches them that the Bible is "inspired by God."

In the second lesson, they will learn that the Bible reveals God's love for people; and in the last two they will study that God wants to change lives through his Word.

Help your students discover the spiritual truths we find in the Bible. While listening to the Bible stories, elementary students will learn more about God.

Lesson 37
The Bible is God's special book

Biblical References: Jeremiah 36
Lesson Objective: That the students know that the Bible is special because it contains God's message for us.
Memory Verse: *Your word is a lamp for my feet, a light on my path* (Psalm 119:105).

PREPARE YOURSELF TO TEACH!

This stage of your students' development is ideal for them to become familiar with the stories of the Bible and the message of God they contain.

Most elementary students know how to read, so you can encourage them to enrich their minds with the Word of God.

Through today's lesson, your students will learn that God inspired the Bible so we can know His will. It is important that they understand that God speaks to us through biblical stories and gives us guidelines for living correctly.

BIBLICAL COMMENTARY

Jeremiah 36. When Jeremiah was very young, God called him to be his prophet. He loved God, listened to him and obeyed with all his heart for more than 40 years. He told the people what God wanted them to do, and also what the consequences (good and bad) of their actions would be, even at the cost of his own life.

One day, the Lord asked Jeremiah to write down all the messages he had given to His people during the time of his ministry. Soon God's prophecy for the people of Israel, in which He said they would be taken captive, would be fulfilled; and even at that moment God wanted them to repent. He hoped that by listening to His Word, people would stop their bad behavior and ask for forgiveness.

By making known the message of the Lord, Jeremiah suffered abuse and persecution. Many times he had to hide to protect himself from attacks. The people did not want to leave their sin, and ignored the Lord's calls for attention. However, this lesson reminds us that the Word of God can not be silenced; it will always be truthful and effective. As a teacher, you have a very important ministry: to convey to your students the message of love and hope that God has for humanity.

DEVELOPMENT OF THE LESSON

Choose some of the following activities to help your students have more meaningful learning.

The Bible

Put your Bible in a visible place, and say: *The Bible is the Word of God, but that does not mean He physically wrote it. What He did was inspire many faithful people to write what He wanted His people to know. In the Bible we find laws that guide our lives, stories of miracles and healing, lots of faithful and courageous characters, and God's plan of salvation for us.*

Ask them how many of them read their Bible during the week, and what passages they know. Listen to their answers, and explain that in this unit, they will learn more about the Word of God.

Scrolls

Explain to your students that scrolls were used in ancient times to write on. Many times they were made of animal skins, and that made them resistant and durable.

During the week, prepare some blank pages as follows: sprinkle some with water with lemon, dry them in the sun to make them wrinkle and give the appearance of being old. Then lightly pass a lit match along the edges to turn them brown.

Bring those sheets to the class, and give one to each member of your group. Ask them to write the biblical text on them and decorate them. Tell them that today's story tells us about a prophet who used scrolls to write very special messages.

Attendance sheet

Record the attendance of your students during this unit using the attendance sheet found after Lesson 36 of the student worksheets. Tell them that the Bible is divided into the Old Testament and the New Testament. In this unit they will study stories from both sections.

Hand out the figure corresponding to this lesson (world) (Cut-Out section pg. 129) and paste it in the place marked on the sheet. Encourage them to attend regularly to complete their project.

BIBLE STORY

God gives a message to Jeremiah

"Leave us alone!" shouted the enraged Hebrews at the prophet Jeremiah. "We'll do what seems best to us. We don't need your advice."

Jeremiah was a prophet of God. This meant that he was someone to whom God gave messages to be communicated to people.

The Hebrew people did not want to hear the message that God wanted to give them through the prophet. However, Jeremiah knew that he must obey God and continue proclaiming His messages.

"Why do you worship these idols?" Jeremiah asked. "If you continue to disobey God, the enemy army will come to fight against you and take you to a distant place where you will be enslaved. Leave your bad behavior and ask God for forgiveness!"

However, the people and King Jehoiakim refused to listen to the prophet's warnings, and continued to disobey God.

After the fourth year of Jehoiakim as king of Judah, God told Jeremiah, "I want you to write down all the messages I have given you. Maybe when they hear the punishments that I plan to send upon them, they will stop disobeying me. If they do, I will forgive all their sins."

God did not want to punish his people. He loved them and wanted them to listen to his warnings and obey him.

Writing all the messages was going to be an arduous job, so the prophet asked his friend Baruch to help him. Baruch got animal skins, because in biblical times, skins were used to write on instead of sheets of paper.

"Baruch, please come here," Jeremiah called him, "and write down all the messages I'm going to dictate to you." For more than a year, Jeremiah dictated God's messages to Baruch to write on parchments.

Do you know what a parchment is? It's a roll of animal skin that people used to write on, just like we use paper now. Jeremiah and Baruch finally finished their work.

"You know I am forbidden to enter the temple," Jeremiah told Baruch, "so you will have to do it. Go to the house of God and read to the people everything I have dictated to you. "

Baruch obeyed, and went to the temple to read the contents of the scroll.

Micah, one of the king's officers, heard what Baruch was reading and went to tell the other officers.

"I just heard the message that God gave to the prophet Jeremiah," Micah said. "God says we will be punished if we keep disobeying his commandments."

When they heard that, they sent to tell Baruch to bring the parchment and read it.

Then Baruch read to them. When he finished reading, the officers looked at each other, and with great fear said, "The king must hear this. But you and Jeremiah must hide or the king will kill you."

So the officers went before the king to tell him what had happened. One of the officers, named Jehudi, read the scroll to the king and to all the leaders who were with him.

Since it was winter and very cold, the king was sitting near the fire to warm up. When Jehudi read three or four sections of the parchment, the king cut them with a knife and threw them into the fire. He continued doing that until he had burned up the whole roll. Some officers begged him not to burn it, but the king paid no attention.

Then he ordered Baruch and Jeremiah to be arrested, but the officers who went to look for them could not find them because God had hidden them and kept them safe.

God spoke again to Jeremiah and said, "Find another parchment and rewrite everything that I dictated to you before.

Also, add these new messages for King Jehoiakim and for the people. Tell them I will take their land because they did not listen to my words. Also, no member of King Jehoiakim's family will reign in Israel."

Jeremiah and Baruch obeyed God and wrote all the messages again. We can read them in our Bible. These messages remind us that God loves us and wants us to be obedient to His Word.

ACTIVITIES

Phylacteries

For this activity you will need scissors, glue, pencils and a piece of yarn or wool for each child.

Distribute the student worksheets and guide them to make their phylacteries by following the instructions.

Explain the meaning of the phylacteries by saying: *The phylactery is a small box containing biblical verses. The Hebrews put them on their foreheads or on their arms as a permanent reminder of the commandments and the promises of the Word of God.*

Unit Project

One of the purposes of this unit is for your students to become familiar with the books of the Bible and to know some of their divisions. Therefore, we suggest you use this activity to achieve that goal.

You will need: ten cardboard boxes of the same size (for example, shoe boxes), 66 cards (10 x 4 cms.), 99 plastic forks, earth or sand, colored paper and pencils.

Before the class, cover each box with a different color. Write on each the name of a division of the Bible (Pentateuch, History, Poetry, Major Prophets, Minor Prophets, Gospels, History, Paul's Epistles, General Epistles, Prophecy). Then, fill each box half way full with dirt or sand. Write the name of a book of the Bible on each card.

Put the cards with the names of the Old Testament books on the tines of the forks. Ask your students to arrange them in the boxes in the correct order, with the handles of the forks in the dirt.

In this first class, guide them in placing the cards in the correct box. As they advance in the development of the unit, they should do it without help. Next week, the New Testament books will be added to the game.

Memorization

Hand out the Verse of the Month Club card corresponding to this unit, and read the biblical text together. Then, ask the all girls to read the verse, then all the guys, then by those who are 8 years old, etc. Remind them that the card will help them review the verse of the unit during the week.

To end

Give thanks to God in prayer for having given us His Word to learn more about Him. Sing songs about the Bible, and invite the children to the next class. Do not forget to tell them that it is very important that they bring their Bibles.

Lesson 38
The Bible tells us about Jesus

Biblical References: Luke 4:16-44
Lesson Objective: That the students know that the Bible teaches them about Jesus, the Son of God.
Memory Verse: *Your word is a lamp for my feet, a light on my path* (Psalm 119:105).

PREPARE YOURSELF TO TEACH!

Many elementary students think that the Bible is a collection of stories; others know that the Word of God contains rules and commandments; and some have heard that the Bible speaks of God and Jesus.

This information is valuable to them, but the most important thing is that they begin to recognize that the Bible is a unique book, unlike all other history books or manuals with rules. This book talks about God's love and gives the right answers to many of our questions. The message of the Bible is unique and available to everyone.

This lesson will help them understand that Jesus is more than a great teacher who lived a long time ago. He is the Son of God and, through many biblical stories, they can learn about the great miracles he performed.

Guide your students as they learn not only to read and memorize passages of the Bible, but to love, respect and above all, obey it.

BIBLICAL COMMENTARY

Luke 4:16-44. One year after his baptism, Jesus returned to Nazareth, the town where he had grown up, and went to the synagogue, as was customary on the Sabbath. In biblical times, going to the synagogue was very important for Jewish families. The services in the synagogue were divided into three parts: prayer, reading of the Law and the Prophets, and the explanation of the Scripture.

This would be a special service. It was the ideal time and place for Jesus to begin his ministry. In the synagogues there were always preachers, and it was customary to ask a visiting teacher to read the Scripture and explain it. After the explanation of Scripture, there was a time of questions and debate.

Jesus' sermon in the synagogue of Nazareth was one of the many episodes in which Jesus showed clearly that he was the fulfillment of the Old Testament prophecies. He read Isaiah 61:1-2 and surprised everyone present when he said, "Today this Scripture has been fulfilled before you" (Luke 4:21).

The passage of Scripture was clear. Jesus was the Messiah that the Hebrew people had been waiting for for hundreds of years. However, people rejected that message.

The Bible repeatedly declares to us that Jesus is the Son of God and that he has a special plan of salvation for all mankind. However, as happened in Nazareth, each person has the option of rejecting or accepting him.

DEVELOPMENT OF THE LESSON

Bring your Bible

Thank the students who brought their Bibles to class this week, and ask them to open it to the first page. Explain that the Bible is divided into two major parts: the Old Testament and the New Testament.

Ask them to locate where one Testament ends and where the other begins. Repeat this several times until the children locate the divisions with ease. Ask them what is the first book of the Old Testament and which is the last. Help them become familiar with the divisions and books of the Bible as they study these lessons.

Attendance sheet

Hand out the figure from the Cut-Out section that corresponds to this lesson (books - pg. 129). Have them put the figure in the correct space on the attendance sheet. Encourage them to not miss any classes in order to complete their attendance sheet.

Ten things that I know about Jesus

For this activity you will need a plastic ball.

Ask the children to sit in a circle, and tell them: *Today's Bible story tells us about Jesus. Let's see how quickly we can say ten important things we know about Jesus.*

Begin the game by saying: *I know that Jesus loves us all.* Then, hand the ball to one of your students to say something different, and then they pass the ball to another person, etc. Continue the game until 10 children or more have participated.

BIBLE STORY

Jesus in the synagogue

"Look who came back to the city!" people said. Jesus had come to Nazareth to visit the place where he had grown up.

Jesus went to the synagogue and looked for a place to sit.

"Isn't that Jesus, the son of Joseph, the carpenter?" some asked.

"Yes, it's him," someone answered. "His mother will be happy to see him. I would like to hear him read the Scriptures. They told me that he taught in some Galilean synagogues and that he is a great teacher."

So they invited Jesus to come forward to read the Scriptures. The people who were there wanted to hear him, and they were attentive while Jesus opened the scroll and began to read.

"The Spirit of the Lord is on me, because he has anointed me to proclaim good news to the poor. He has sent me to proclaim freedom for the prisoners and recovery of sight for the blind, to set the oppressed free, to proclaim the year of the Lord's favor."

The people recognized the portion of the Scripture that Jesus was reading. Many years ago, the prophet Isaiah had written those words, announcing the fulfillment of a promise. That passage referred to the Savior of the world, whom God had promised to send.

Jesus closed the scroll and said, "Today the Scripture that you have just heard has been fulfilled."

"What?" said the people. "Is it true what he is telling us?"

"Isn't he Joseph's son?" they asked each other.

Jesus tried to explain more about the Word of God and what it said about the Savior, but they didn't want to hear it.

Rather, all who were in the synagogue became angry with Jesus. So they took him out of there to the top of a hill to throw him off. However, Jesus passed through them and went to Capernaum. There he performed many miracles, healed the sick and taught many about the love of God. Jesus showed the people that he really was the promised Messiah.

"Do not leave us!" the inhabitants of Capernaum asked him.

But Jesus answered, "I have to go. It is necessary that I go and tell others the good news of the kingdom of God. For that I have been sent."

So Jesus went to many others, healed the sick and taught in other synagogues the message of God's love.

Although it was very sad for Jesus to have been rejected by his own people, in other places many believed in his Word.

The Bible tells us about Jesus

Ask a volunteer to help you distribute the student worksheets. Instruct the class to look at the pictures and number them according to the order of the biblical story. As they work, tell them that the story they learned is in the Gospel of Luke.

Next, ask them: *Is Luke in the Old or New Testament?* Listen to their answers. If you see that many are still confused, ask them to open their Bible and locate the Gospel of Luke.

Let's play!

On the next page, read the instructions for this game together. Have them find a partner to play the game with. To each pair give a set of x's and o's and questions for the game from the Cut-Out section (pg. 129) and let them start playing. Observe them while doing the activity, and help those who have difficulty answering the Bible questions.

Unit Project

Allow time for your students to arrange the Old Testament cards in the corresponding boxes. Then, distribute the New Testament cards and forks and guide them to arrange them in the correct order. Make sure all your students participate in this activity to learn the divisions of the Bible.

When finished, keep the cards and sand boxes for use in the next class.

Memorization

Write the words of Philippians 4:19 on different cards. Tape them on a wall or blackboard, so that you can peel them off and put them back on. Read the text several times, and ask your students to repeat it. Change the cards for your students to reorder them. Repeat this activity several times and say the text each time the cards are ordered.

To end

Pray for your students, and give thanks to God for allowing us to know Jesus more through his Word. Remind them to pray during the week and bring their Bibles to the next class.

Lesson 39
The Bible helps us do the right thing

Biblical References: 2 Chronicles 34

Lesson Objective: That the students know that God uses his Word to teach His children to do the right thing.

Memory Verse: *Your word is a lamp for my feet, a light on my path* (Psalm 119:105).

PREPARE YOURSELF TO TEACH!

Your students are beginning to understand that the Bible is a special book because it is the Word of God. They understand more of the Bible than we suppose. They do not question its teachings, nor compare them with ideologies or philosophies as many adults do. The time you spend ministering to them and telling them Bible stories will be of great value for their spiritual formation. Remember that not only will you impart knowledge, but you will develop in them the spiritual sensitivity and desire to learn more about the kingdom of God.

This unit focuses on the response of people when they hear the message of the Word of God. Take advantage of this lesson to teach your class that the Bible is not just a book to read; we must believe it and put it into practice.

BIBLICAL COMMENTARY

King Josiah was cleaning up the nation, removing all the pagan idol altars. In addition, he began preparations to restore the temple of God. During the reconstruction work, the priest Hilkiah found the book of the law, where they could read about the covenant that God had made with his people. This book perhaps contained the Pentateuch or just the book of Deuteronomy.

When Shaphan the scribe read the book to the king, the king was troubled to hear the law of God. Realizing the difficulty and captivity that would come upon them because of their sins, Josiah asked the spiritual leaders of the people to consult God about the message of the book. God, pleased to see the king's concern for the sins of his people, promised not to punish the people as long as Josiah reigned.

Instead of re-hiding the covenant book, Josiah called all the people to a meeting in the temple in Jerusalem to read the Word of God publicly. The king wanted his people to live according to the divine commandments. Upon hearing the words of the book, the Israelites renewed their commitment to fidelity to God.

In gratitude to God, King Josiah increased his efforts to cleanse the country of every idol. In addition, he consecrated the people, the leaders and their government to God. While he lived, this king led all the people to obey the Lord.

DEVELOPMENT OF THE LESSON

Where is the Bible?

Before your students arrive in the classroom, hide your Bible in a place where it is not easy to find it. After welcoming the children, tell them you need to find your Bible, and ask them to help you find it. When they locate it, ask them how they felt while they were looking for it. Tell them that today's story is about a king who found the Word of God and how that changed the course of his life and the country he ruled.

Attendance sheet

Hand out the attendance figure for this lesson (David playing harp - pg. 129) and have the children paste it in the correct space. Use the attendance sheet to review what they learned in the previous lessons.

My Bible

Review the divisions of the Bible with the children. Ask them to locate the Old and New Testaments in their Bibles. Then, ask them to locate some books (for example: Genesis, Matthew, Revelation and Psalms). Then, tell them to look for 2 Chronicles, because that is the location of today's story.

BIBLE STORY

Josiah finds the Word of God

Josiah began to reign in Israel when he was only 8 years old. His father and his grandfather had been evil kings who built idols of wood and other materials, and put them in the temple of God.

Josiah's grandfather killed some of his children, offering them as sacrifices to the idols he worshiped.

When Josiah turned 16, he decided to follow and obey God. He did not want to do evil like his ancestors, but to follow the one true God.

Four years later, he removed the altars where false idols were worshiped and destroyed all the images.

In addition, he asked his messengers throughout the kingdom to give the following announcement: "From now on, no one in this kingdom will worship idols. We will only obey the living God, the only God of Israel."

But Josiah's work was not over. He knew that the temple of God was in ruins, so he ordered a man named Shaphan to repair it. He asked him to look for the best builders and carpenters to restore the temple so it would look as beautiful as before. A large number of people worked hard in the repair and decoration of the house of God.

Suddenly, the priest Hilkiah saw something in the rubble. "What is this?" he asked as he lifted a large scroll and shook off the dust.

Hilkiah could not believe what he had in his hands. It was the book of the Law of God! On that scroll were written the laws that God had given Moses long ago. These laws taught the people how God wanted them to live before him.

"Look what I found," Hilkiah told Shaphan, showing him the parchment. When he recognized the book of the Law of God, Shaphan said, "We must show it to King Josiah at once!"

Upon receiving the news, the king was very moved and asked Shaphan to read it to him. That scroll said that God wanted his people to love him, obey him and serve faithfully.

Upon hearing these words, Josiah became very sad, knowing that everyone in Israel had disobeyed God.

The king tore his clothes in sadness and said to Shaphan, "God is angry with us because we have not listened to his Word or obeyed his commandments."

Then he told Hilkiah and others to pray and ask what would happen to the kingdom.

Hilkiah and his companions went to speak with the prophetess Hulda, a woman who loved and obeyed God. The Lord showed her what she should say to the messengers of King Josiah: "God does not like it when people do not listen to him or obey his words. Therefore, he had decided to send a great punishment upon the people of Israel. But now he has seen the heart of Josiah and knows that this king wants to obey him and love him. God wants all people to listen to him, obey him and love him."

Then King Josiah called all the people together to read them the Word of God.

Then he promised: "I will do everything God wants me to do."

And the people also promised: "We will obey and love God."

The people of Israel followed God and obeyed him during all the time that Josiah reigned.

The Bible helps us know the right thing

Hand out the student worksheet for Lesson 39. Ask the children to cut out the shape following the outline, and fold it along the dotted lines. Then they should cut out the small lines in sections 1 and 5.

Explain how to assemble the figure by inserting section 1 into section 5. Review the biblical story, discussing how the study of the Bible helps us to be different.

Unit Project

Allow time for your students to review the divisions of the Bible books using the cards and boxes of sand. Divide them into groups of two or three to use the materials, while the others conclude their work on the student worksheets or sing a song.

Memorization

Ask the children to sit in a circle. Give a Bible to one of them, who must pass it to the next, and so on. When you say STOP, whoever has the Bible should say the verse. Let the group help the child who has difficulty memorizing it.

Lesson 40
The Bible teaches us every day

Biblical References: Acts 16:1-5; 2 Timothy 1:1-7; 2:1-6; 16-18; 3:10-17; 4:13-22
Lesson Objective: That the students know that the Bible teaches them to live correctly.
Memory Verse: *Your word is a lamp for my feet, a light on my path* (Psalm 119:105).

PREPARE YOURSELF TO TEACH!

The Bible is a practical book that guides us to live according to God's will. In this unit, your class will learn that the message of the Bible is for them, and that will help them differentiate good from bad.

In this unit, the children have learned basic biblical concepts which will help them understand that the Bible is a book in which they can find all the answers they need. They have also learned to easily locate the books that compose it. Take advantage of this last class to reinforce the importance of reading, studying and loving the Word of God.

BIBLICAL COMMENTARY

Acts 16:1-5; 2 Timothy 1:1-7; 2:1-6, 16-18; 3:10-17; 4:13-22. Timothy was a young man who lived in Lystra with a Jewish mother and a Greek father. His mother Eunice and his grandmother Lois were converted to Christianity during Paul's ministry. Timothy accompanied Paul on many of his missionary trips. He went with him when he traveled to Jerusalem and also accompanied him to Rome.

The two letters to Timothy are known as "pastoral epistles." Although they were personal letters written by Paul, they demonstrate deep love and pastoral care.

Paul was imprisoned in Rome when he wrote the second letter to his friend and collaborator, who was in Ephesus. They became very good friends, and after Paul died, Timothy was in charge of the church in Ephesus.

In his second letter, Paul asked Timothy to be faithful to his call and thanked him for his prayers. He told him that his faith assured him the way to reach Christ. In addition, he encouraged him to work in the ministry. Paul confirmed that God inspired the Scriptures and that they would help Timothy in his daily life.

Through these epistles, Paul reminds us that the source of all wisdom and understanding is the Word of God.

DEVELOPMENT OF THE LESSON

Use some of the following activities as support material to teach the Bible story to your students.

Registration of attendance

Pass out the last figure for this unit attendance sheet (cloud - page 129). Looking at the figures, review what they learned in the biblical stories, and if possible, reward those who had perfect attendance throughout the unit.

Reminder

During the week, draw figures of open Bibles on a piece of poster board and cut them out. Make enough for all your students. Make sure that the size is large enough for the children to write the memory verse in it. Provide pencils or colored markers to decorate them and have them take them home as a reminder of the unit theme.

BIBLE STORY

Photocopy the Bible story and keep it in an envelope, as if it were a letter. Open it in front of your students and tell them that they are going to read a very important letter that the apostle Paul wrote to his friend Timothy.

The letter to Timothy

Paul was in prison while awaiting his trial in Rome. His "crime" had been to tell others about Jesus. To make matters worse, many of his friends had left him alone and winter was coming. But Paul, without being discouraged himself, wrote a letter to his friend Timothy.

Dear Timothy,

I feel very grateful for your friendship and I pray for you every day. You are like my son and I am glad to know that you are a good Christian, just like your mother and your grandmother.

Be strong always and follow God's direction. I know that hard times will come, but remember that athletes run the entire race, regardless of the difficulties.

Many bad things happened to me while I was preaching, but God rescued me from all of them. Those who serve God and obey Him will face problems. They are likely to be persecuted, just as I am in prison! However, it is worth serving Jesus.

Be careful, because many people will preach false teachings and deceive many, but don't be confused. Continue to believe in what you know is right. Remember that you can trust the Scriptures because God inspired and guided the people who wrote them.

Don't forget that the Scriptures teach us to do the right thing, exhort us when we are wrong and show us what God's will is for us. Studying the scriptures will help you prepare for God's work for you.

I am waiting with great excitement for your visit. When you come, please bring me the coat that I left at Carpus' house. Also bring my books, especially the scrolls.

I'm still waiting for the day of my trial. In my first defense before the authorities, nobody helped me. They all left me alone. I ask God not to punish them for that. But the Lord Jesus was by my side, giving me strength and peace. I know that the Lord will deliver me from all evil and will protect me until I am brought to his heavenly kingdom.

Say hello to all my friends. Do everything possible to come before the winter begins. All the brothers here send you greetings.

God bless you!

Sincerely,

Paul

The Bible helps us know what we should do

Distribute the student worksheets and read the instructions out loud for the class to do the activity. Encourage them to reflect and make wise decisions in light of the Word of God.

Turn to the next page and cut out the figures on the drawing strip; Then fill in the blanks in the biblical text.

Unit Project

Do a little competition to reinforce the learning of the divisions of the books of the Bible. Form teams and give everyone the opportunity to use the cards and sandboxes. The winning team will be the one that puts all the books, from Genesis to Revelation, in order in the shortest time.

Memorization

Since this is the unit's last lesson, prepare some prizes for those who have learned the memory verse. Hand out Bible-shaped cards or bookmarks with the memory verse. Give the opportunity for those who wish to do so to say the verse by heart.

To end

Do a brief review with the class of the lessons they learned in this unit. Ask which of the stories they liked best. Emphasize how important the Bible is to all Christians. Invite them to read it and study it, but, above all, to obey it and love it. If possible, invite the parents of your students to see the work their children did. Encourage them to foster love and respect for the Word of God in their children.

Pray before saying goodbye, and give thanks to the Lord for the blessing of having the Bible as a guide for our lives.

Year 2 — Introduction – Unit X

THE POWER OF JESUS

Biblical References: Matthew 20:29-34; Mark 10:46-52; Luke 5:17-26; Matthew 4:1-11; Luke 19:1-10.

Unit Memory Verse: *Therefore, if anyone is in Christ, the new creation has come: The old has gone, the new is here!* (2 Corinthians 5:17)

UNIT OBJECTIVES

This unit will help the students:

- Understand that Jesus, the Son of God, can change the lives of those who approach him and get to know him.
- Know that Jesus' presence makes a big difference in people's lives.
- Learn to resist temptation.
- Trust in Jesus' power and help.

LESSON UNIT A

Lesson 41: Jesus heals the two blind men
Lesson 42:   Jesus shows that he is the Son of God
Lesson 43:   Jesus defeats temptation
Lesson 44:   Jesus visits Zacchaeus

WHY ELEMENTARY STUDENTS NEED THE TEACHING OF THIS UNIT:

By studying this series of lessons, your students will learn that Jesus transformed the lives of many people during his ministry on earth. They will also know that he can do many wonders because he is the Son of God, and there is no one who can match his power.

Jesus has the power to heal a sick body, forgive sins and transform a sad soul into one with hope and joy.

This stage of the development of your students is crucial for their spiritual formation. During this stage, they adopt role models and tend to imitate people they consider "special." Therefore, take every opportunity to teach them that Jesus is the primary model they should follow. Guide them to understand that they need to have a personal encounter with Christ and walk always hand in hand with the Lord.

Lesson 41
Jesus heals the two blind men

Biblical References: Matthew 20:29-34; Mark 10:46-52

Lesson Objective: That the students develop compassionate feelings, following Jesus' example.

Memory Verse: *Therefore, if anyone is in Christ, the new creation has come: The old has gone, the new is here!* (2 Corinthians 5:17)

PREPARE YOURSELF TO TEACH!

Your students are growing up in a world where compassion is often secondary. Help is conditional: they help only if they receive something in return. Thus it is important that they learn that Jesus was compassionate and helped others in a selfless way.

If we teach them to respond to the needs of others with compassion, they will grow up with a healthy perspective of the Christian life and love of neighbor.

BIBLICAL COMMENTARY

Matthew 20:29-34; Mark 10:46-52. When Jesus left Jericho, he went to Jerusalem to fulfill the purpose for which he came to earth: to give his life to save people from eternal damnation.

On the way, he was surrounded by a large crowd following him. Suddenly, he heard desperate screams that clamored for help.

Two blind men tried to approach the crowd to reach the Master. Mark's book focuses on one of them, Bartimaeus.

When Bartimaeus heard Jesus approaching, he began to shout, "Jesus, Son of David, have mercy on me!"

It was the first time that Jesus was publicly called "Son of David." This humble sick man proclaimed before the crowd who Jesus really was: a descendant of the royal house. In addition, he gave the key to the triumphal entry. The Jews considered David to be chosen of God, and they knew that one of his descendants would be the Messiah.

Then Jesus asked the people to take him to Bartimaeus. The Lord told this man to take a step of faith and trust in his power. Instantly, Jesus performed the miracle, and Bartimaeus regained his sight.

Jesus had walked a lot and he knew the suffering that awaited him, but he did not hesitate to show compassion towards the needy. Therefore, with love he healed the two blind men. Jesus is the greatest example that compassion is not an option, but a way of life.

DEVELOPMENT OF THE LESSON

A dark room

If there are windows in your class room, before class cover them with newspapers or cloth so that the light does not come in. Arrange all the chairs along the wall, and in each place a card with the name of each student. Remove all objects that may hurt children, and greet them at the door. Tell them that for the activity they will do, it is necessary that the lights are off, so you will need their cooperation and understanding.

Instruct them to enter the room and remain standing. Then, lead them in a time of praise. Then ask them to look for the chair with their name and sit down.

When they are in place, turn on the lights and ask them how they felt in the dark. After listening to their answers, tell them that in today's class they will talk about some men who could not see because they were blind.

Identify the objects

Have several objects (balls, dolls, a book, a brush, etc.) in a bag for your students to identify through touch. Ask several volunteers to come forward, put their hands in the bag and try to say what object they are touching.

Explain that blind people depend on their sense of touch to identify many of the objects that surround them. In today's story we will learn what some men did to recover their sight.

BIBLE STORY

Jesus and his disciples traveled many kilometers to teach and heal people. How do you imagine they traveled from one city to another? By car? By bus? On a train? By plane? At that time there weren't all those means of transport that we have now, so people walked great distances to go from one place to another. Only those who had money could travel on a cart or on horseback. In today's story we will learn what Jesus did while walking to Jerusalem.

Jesus heals two blind men

One day Jesus and his disciples left Jericho and headed to Jerusalem, and a large crowd followed them on the road. Everyone wanted to hear the teachings of Jesus.

"I'd like to hear what Jesus says," one man said.

"It's wonderful to see people's happiness when Jesus heals them," said another one.

"Did you hear that?" the blind man Bartimaeus asked his friend.

"Hear what?" answered the friend.

"What people are saying. I heard someone say that Jesus is coming along the way. Listen! Here he comes. Jesus is coming here!" Bartimaeus continued talking excitedly. "I heard that Jesus does miracles. Maybe he can heal our eyes so we can see!"

As the crowd approached, the two blind men stood up and began to shout as loud as they could, "Jesus, Son of David, have mercy on us!"

"Shut up!" someone shouted at them. "You're making a lot of noise."

"Keep silent! Show a little respect," others demanded.

But the two blind men did not shut up. On the contrary, their voices were heard louder and louder. "Jesus, Son of David, have mercy on us!"

Then Jesus stopped and called the two blind men.

"Have confidence, Jesus is calling you," a man told them.

The two men left their cloaks and walked towards Jesus as fast as their legs allowed.

"What do you want me to do for you?" Jesus asked.

The blind men felt their heart beat faster and faster. They were so excited! What they had wanted so much was about to become reality.

"Sir, we want to see!" the blind men pleaded.

Jesus realized that these two men believed in his power, and he had compassion on them. So, he extended his hand and touched their eyes. At that moment, the two men could see Jesus. They could see everything! The trees, the blue sky. What a wonderful day!

The two men, jumping with joy, praised Jesus and followed him along the way.

ACTIVITIES

Where is Matthew?

Tell the children to look for the book of Matthew in their Bibles and mark the place with bookmarks. Ask them to identify which book is before Matthew and which is after. Explain that this Gospel is the first book of the New Testament and contains wonderful teachings about the life and ministry of Jesus. In fact, today's story is found in this book.

Compassion mural

For this activity you will need white paper, colored pencils, glue, and a large piece of cardboard or paper.

Write the word "COMPASSION" as the title on the card. Ask the children to draw pictures of how they can show compassion to others (visiting the sick, helping the needy, sharing food, etc.). When they are finished, have them stick their drawings on the poster board. Place the mural on the classroom door so parents can see the work they did.

Jesus shows compassion

Hand out the student worksheets and ask the class to trace the written words. Then, fold the page along the dotted line to see what happened when the two blind men approached Jesus.

Turn to the next page and explain that next to "What the blind man said" they should copy the letters in the red boxes in order; and next to "What Jesus did" they must copy the letters of the yellow boxes.

When the activity is over, read the answers together, and talk about how Jesus showed compassion in today's Bible story.

Memorization

Divide the children into three groups and assign them a part of the memory verse. Follow this example: (Group 1) Therefore, if anyone is in Christ, (Group 2) the new creation has come: the old has gone; (Group 3) the new is here (2 Corinthians 5:17).

Each group must say its part in the correct order to complete the text. Repeat the exercise a couple of times, have groups trade parts, repeat, and then encourage them to say it together.

To end

Form a circle with your students and allow each one to say a short prayer of thanksgiving if they want to. Conclude, praising God for the miracles of healing he does in the midst of his people, and asking that he help all of you to be compassionate and loving to one another. Sing a song before saying goodbye, and invite the children to the next class.

Lesson 42
Jesus shows that He is the Son of God

Biblical References: Luke 5:17-26

Lesson Objective: That the students understand that Jesus has the power to do amazing things because he is the Son of God.

Memory Verse: *Therefore, if anyone is in Christ, the new creation has come: The old has gone, the new is here!* (2 Corinthians 5:17)

PREPARE YOURSELF TO TEACH!

Today, as happened in biblical times, many people believe that Jesus was only a teacher and prophet. However, he is the Son of God; His presence and love made a great difference in the ancient world and in today's world. His birth divided history into two periods and transformed the lives of countless people. He alone has the power to forgive sins and restore the relationship between people and God. He was the only one who performed amazing miracles, such as giving sight to the blind and healing the paralyzed.

Jesus made a difference because his life represented the beginning of the redemption of mankind and the destruction of sin.

At this stage, elementary students are easily impressed, and tend to imitate behaviors and fashions. Sometimes the models they follow are not the most appropriate. However, you have the opportunity to teach them that Jesus is the perfect model. In these lessons, by emphasizing the qualities of Jesus' character, encourage children to be imitators of Christ in their daily lives.

BIBLICAL COMMENTARY

Luke 5:17-26. This well-known passage reminds us of the great love of some men who took their sick friend to Jesus. But above all, it tells us about the power and mercy of God through Jesus Christ.

Evading all obstacles, these four bold friends opened a hole in the roof of the place where Jesus was teaching. Thus they achieved what they wanted: a miracle of healing. But the most interesting thing is that Jesus declared his authority, not only to heal the body, but also to restore the soul through the forgiveness of sins.

Jesus knew that the time of his sacrificial death would soon come, and that the redemptive work would be consummated. Therefore, he took this opportunity to make it clear that he was not just a doctor, but that his mission on earth was to save humanity that was condemned by their sin.

Jesus healed the man, and he got up, took his bed, and left the house walking and praising God. This miracle not only shows us Jesus' compassion towards the paralytic, but it gives us a convincing proof that he is the Messiah.

DEVELOPMENT OF THE LESSON

Use some of the following activities to focus your students' attention on the topic of study.

Special capabilities

After telling the children to sit in a circle, talk about people who have special needs. It is likely that in your class or in the congregation there is someone with a certain disability. It is important that your students learn to respect and love all people equally, regardless of their condition.

Let them know that these people have a physical limitation due to different factors: illness, accidents or birth problems.

Tell them that today's story tells us about a person who had a physical disability. He was paralyzed, that is, he could not walk. However, God loved him and had a special plan for him.

Figures with stones

For this activity you will need small stones of different sizes and textures, cardboard or poster board, scissors, glue, colored markers and wool/yarn.

Place all the materials on a table and have the students sit in chairs around the table. Ask your students to observe the shapes, textures and sizes of the stones. Then ask them to draw a person or animal on the card. Then, they are to use the stones to make the eyes, nose, mouth, etc.

Tell them to complete the work with other materials, such as wool/yarn for hair, whiskers, etc. The important thing is that they do all the activity without getting up from their chairs even once. It does not matter if they drop the material or need something else; if they need help, they should raise their hands and you will help them.

When the jobs are finished, let them dry and ask them: *How did you feel when you could not get out of your chair?* Listen to their answers, and tell them that people who cannot walk often feel frustrated and helpless. However, God takes care of them because he loves them. In the Bible Story, we will learn more about this.

Note: You can substitute the activity of the stones for another craft that suits the needs of your group.

BIBLE STORY

Invite a young man from your congregation to represent one of the friends who brought the paralytic to Jesus. Provide him with a robe, and ask him to tell the story. Give the study materials in advance and allow him to interact with the children.

Jesus heals a paralytic

The people of Capernaum were happy because Jesus was with them. Many wanted to hear his teachings, so the house where he was had filled with people. Many had stayed outside, but they could look in through the door and the windows.

Four men passed near the house and saw the large crowd.

"What's happening here?" asked one of them.

"Jesus is in that house," someone answered.

Then, one of the four men said, "I know what we can do. Let's go bring our friend. I'm sure Jesus can heal him."

"You're right. Let's go get him!" called another.

Everyone agreed, so they went looking for their friend who could not walk.

"You must come with us to see Jesus," they said to him after they found him.

"But I can't go," said the paralytic. "I can't walk; how could I get there?"

"We'll take you. You must listen to the teachings of Jesus and see the miracles he does."

"Ok, let's go!" he said excitedly.

Each of the friends held tightly to one of the corners of the mat on which their friend was lying and set out on the road.

When they arrived near the house, one of them said, "There are too many people in front of the door and we'll never reach the place where Jesus is. What can we do?"

"Look! There is a stairway that leads to the roof," said another of the friends.

Everyone knew what they should do, so they very carefully held their friend and climbed the ladder to the roof. One by one they began to remove the tiles that covered the roof until they made a big hole. Then, they tied the mat with ropes and carefully lowered their friend, until they put him in the middle of everyone, right in front of Jesus.

Some people who were in the house began to say things about the paralytic.

"Poor man! Surely he did something very bad to deserve such punishment," thought someone.

Then Jesus approached the paralytic and said, "Friend, I forgive you of all your sins."

Upon hearing those words, many people became angry and began to speak badly of Jesus.

"Who do you think you are to forgive sins?" they said annoyed. "Only God can do that."

Jesus knew what they were thinking, so he spoke again to the man, saying, "Get up, take your mat and go home."

Then in front of the whole crowd, the man stood up, rolled up his mat and headed for the door. While walking, he shouted, "Glory to God! Look what Jesus did for me. He healed me!"

Everyone was amazed to see the man walking, and they began to praise God saying, "What wonders we have seen today!"

ACTIVITIES

A hole in the roof!

Hand out the worksheets for Lesson 42, and give each child a piece of wool/yarn. Explain that they must cut off the strip on the bottom of the paper and cut out the bed and the figure of the paralytic.

Then, tell them to fold the mat in half, following the dotted line (the colored part should face outwards), and place the figure of the paralytic inside.

Help them make the four holes marked on the bed of the paralytic, and one in the roof opening of the house. Pass the piece of yarn through the holes in the bed and roof opening, to simulate that the paralytic is descending.

On the next page, ask the children to draw a line that links the circle, the star, the square and the triangle to the people who can do what the phrases say. Talk about what only Jesus can do because He is the Son of God. Then, decipher the mysterious message.

True or false

Use this game to review with your students what they learned in the story. Form a row with the chairs, and ask them to sit down. Then, read the following statements. If the statement is true, they must stand up; if it is false they must remain seated. Those who lose must leave their chair and leave the game:

- Very few people went to see Jesus in Capernaum.
- The house was full of people.
- Three men had a friend who could not walk.
- Jesus went to Capernaum to visit relatives.
- When the friends saw that they could not enter through the door, they decided to enter through a window.
- Four men made a hole in the roof to lower their friend.
- Jesus can not forgive sins.
- Jesus healed the paralytic.
- The man was very worried because he had been forgiven of his sins and could walk.
- Jesus is the son of God.

Memorization

Pass out the Verse of the Month Club card for the unit (pg. 137). Then, tell them to divide into pairs to review the memory verse. Each person should say the text to his or her partner using different voice tones. Pay attention and choose the most creative to come to the front and tell others the text, modulating their voice in different ways.

To end

Lead the children in prayer, thanking God for having sent his Son Jesus to save us from our sins.

As your students prepare to go home, remind them to use their activity sheet to tell their family members the Bible story. Encourage them to study the biblical text during the week and not miss the next class.

Lesson 43
Jesus defeats temptation

Biblical References: Matthew 4:1-11

Lesson Objective: That the students learn what they must do when faced with temptation.

Memory Verse: *Therefore, if anyone is in Christ, the new creation has come: The old has gone, the new is here!* (2 Corinthians 5:17)

PREPARE YOURSELF TO TEACH!

As elementary-aged children learn to differentiate good from bad, they need to know how to deal with temptations that pull them toward evil. They must learn how to resist the impulses that guide them to sin.

Use this lesson to teach them how to resist temptation through Jesus' example. Help them understand that although Jesus was the Son of God, he was also human, and was subject to the same feelings and emotions that we have. Explain that, like them, Jesus felt hunger, cold, and fear. He had worries and faced temptations. However, he clung to God's promises and was able to resist temptation, even in the most difficult moments.

BIBLICAL COMMENTARY

Matthew 4:1-11. Those who witnessed Jesus' baptism were not the only ones who heard the voice from heaven that said, "This is my beloved Son, in whom I am well pleased" (Matthew 3:17). Apparently, Satan also heard that proclamation. Therefore, he believed that it was time to spoil the divine plan of redemption for the human race. For this, he would try to make Jesus give in to temptation and sin.

In the Scriptures we see Satan as an ambitious opponent of God and his purposes. He is the father of lies (John 8:44), and his job is to make those who believe in God stumble.

In this passage, we observe that Satan, knowing human weaknesses very well, tried to take advantage of them. However, Jesus showed that through the Word of God, we have the authority to resist the devil and make him flee from us.

The enemy knew that Jesus had just spent 40 days in the desert without eating food. That is why he did not hesitate to appeal to his human needs, tempting him to turn stones into bread.

When Satan did not get the answer he wanted, he asked Jesus to prove the authenticity of God's promises and throw himself from the pinnacle of the temple; for the angels would come to his aid. Again, Jesus quoted Scriptures to reject the attacks of the evil one.

Finally, Satan wanted to tempt Jesus with power, offering him all the kingdoms of the world. However, aware of his purpose on earth, Jesus clung to the promises of the Father to overcome temptations.

In this passage Jesus teaches us that through the Word of God, we can overcome Satan's deceptions and tricks.

DEVELOPMENT OF THE LESSON

Choose some of the suggested activities to reinforce biblical learning in your students.

What would happen if...?

Read this story to your students:

Mark found it difficult to study geography. Although he tried to learn what his teacher said, when the time came for the exam, he forgot everything he had learned. One afternoon, Mark and his mother spent hours memorizing the names of countries and capitals.

On the day of the exam, Mark remembered almost nothing of what he had studied. He tried to remember, but time was running out. Suddenly, he heard a voice inside his head saying, "Why don't you copy Steven's exam? He has all the right answers."

Ask your students to suggest the ending they would like for the story. Would it be correct for Mark to copy Steven's answers?

Tell them: *When Mark thought about copying Steven's exam, he was being tempted. In today's Bible story we will learn more about temptations and how to overcome them.*

The deception

For this activity you will need an empty jar or container with something wonderful on the outside wrapper, and a toy snake (plastic or a picture), which should be placed inside the jar.

Show the container to your students and ask them: *What do you think this container contains?* Allow them to respond. Then, ask a volunteer to uncover the jar.

Then tell them: *The package does not contain a delicious sweet, but a horrible snake. This serpent represents Satan, because he is hiding behind something that may seem good.*

Talk to the children about the sins that at first seem innocent, but make us fall into Satan's trap.

Tell them that in today's class, they will learn how to deal with temptations.

BIBLE STORY

The temptation of Jesus

Before starting to preach and teach people, Jesus went to see John the Baptist to be baptized in the Jordan River.

After his baptism, Jesus had to face a difficult test. The Holy Spirit took him to the desert, where he spent 40 days and 40 nights without food.

Of course, Jesus was very hungry and weak. Then Satan decided to tempt him. So he approached him and said, "If you are the Son of God, command these stones to become bread."

Jesus looked at the stones, and it is very possible that he thought about the hunger he felt, but he answered with courage, "It is written: Man shall not live by bread alone, but by every word that proceeds from the mouth of God."

Jesus refused to yield to temptation. However, Satan tried to tempt him in another way. This time he took him to the highest part of the temple in Jerusalem. There he said to him, "If you are the Son of God, throw yourself down. For it is written: 'He will command his angels concerning you, and they will lift you up in their hands, so that you will not strike your foot against a stone.'"

It would be a spectacular way to begin his ministry! The temple was full. Surely the religious leaders would recognize him as the Son of God if the angels came to rescue him. But knowing that this was not God's plan, Jesus said to him, "It is also written, 'You shall not tempt the Lord your God.'"

Thus, Jesus used another verse from the Old Testament to overcome temptation.

But Satan did not give up, and once again he tempted Jesus. He took him to a high mountain so that he could see all the kingdoms of the world and its riches, and said to him, "All this I will give you if you will bow down and worship me."

It seemed so simple! Jesus knew that his ministry on earth would not be easy. People expected the promised Messiah to be a great leader. They wanted a king, and Satan was promising that he would make him king. People would not listen to the carpenter's son of Nazareth, but if Jesus became king, they would all listen to him, and everything would be very easy.

Then Jesus said to him, "Go away, Satan, for it is written, 'You shall worship the Lord your God and serve him only.'"

The enemy had used his best temptations when Jesus was weakest. But for the third time, Jesus used a verse to destroy the devil. Satan knew that Jesus had defeated him, and seeing that he could not overcome him, Satan left.

Jesus stayed in the desert, alone, exhausted and hungry, but he had passed the test, resisting the temptations of the enemy. Suddenly, angels from heaven came to where he was to serve and help him.

ACTIVITIES

How do you recognize temptation?

Pass out the student worksheets for Lesson 43. Ask the children what image comes to mind when they think about the tempter.

Perhaps many of your students think that the enemy is a character dressed in red, with horns and a long tail. Explain that this is the way many cartoonists and caricaturists represent Satan. Many draw the devil as if he were a sympathetic being, while others draw him frightfully.

What really matters is that they know that Satan is an enemy of God; therefore, he is also our enemy. The only thing he wants is for people to disobey God and turn away from Jesus.

He tempts us in different ways to make us fall. Sometimes he does it through a friend who encourages us to do something bad; other time he temps us through the images we see on television.

Ask your class to circle all the temptations they find on the page, and talk about what they should do. Make sure your students understand that it is not bad to be tempted, even Jesus was tempted. Temptation becomes sin if we give in and do wrong.

Tools to overcome temptation

For the next activity, pass out the next student worksheet and the 8 rectangles or cards for this activity (pg 131 - the Bible, the running child, the balloons, etc.).

They must fold the worksheet along the dotted lines and glue both sides to form a bag or pocket. The children are to look at the cards and choose the ones that represent tools that help us overcome temptation.

Read the following situations, and ask your students to choose the tool they should use to defend themselves against that temptation.

- You really want to eat a candy, but you don't have money to buy it. Nobody is watching you and you are tempted to take it without paying. What should you do? (Example: Remember that the Bible says "Thou shalt not steal" [Exodus 20: 5], pray and ask for God's help.)
- You are very angry because a child hurt you and you are tempted to take revenge on him. What would you do?
- You did something wrong and you know that your mom will get mad. If you tell a little lie, she may not realize it was your fault. What should you do?
- A friend offers you a cigarette. You don't want him to think you're not brave, so you're tempted to accept it. What should you do?

Conclude this activity by reading together Hebrews 2:18.

Memorization

Draw a line on the floor, or place a string, which will be the "memory line." Make a circle with your students. Ask one of them to stand outside of the circle with his/her back to the others. Give him/her a tambourine or other musical instrument, and tell them to make it sound without looking at their classmates.

The others should start walking in a circle, going over the memory line. When the child with the tambourine stops playing, everyone should stop. The person who is on the line or just in front of it will have to say the memory verse. Continue the game until most students have said the biblical text.

To end

Get together to thank God for today's class. Pray also for your students, asking God to give them the strength and wisdom to resist temptations.

Encourage them to attend the next class, and call or visit the ones who were missing.

Lesson 44
Jesus visits Zacchaeus

Biblical References: Luke 19:1-10

Lesson Objective: That the students understand that people's hearts change when they decide to follow Jesus.

Memory Verse: *Therefore, if anyone is in Christ, the new creation has come: The old has gone, the new is here!* (2 Corinthians 5:17)

PREPARE YOURSELF TO TEACH!

The story of Zacchaeus illustrates very well the memory verse of this unit. It shows clearly that when Jesus comes into a person's life, he transforms it and makes it a new creation. Through this story, your students will learn that Jesus makes a difference in people's lives.

All children like to feel loved. In today's story, when Jesus stops to talk with Zacchaeus, we see the love of God in action. He seeks us, no matter what situation we find ourselves in. Through this story, your students will experience Jesus' love and acceptance. When they understand and accept Him, their attitudes and behavior will change, as happened with Zacchaeus, and begin to reflect the love of God in their lives.

BIBLICAL COMMENTARY

Luke 19:1-10. Zacchaeus was a Jew who lived in Jericho. That city was a large commercial center where tax collectors could prosper. These men earned their living by collecting taxes for the Roman Empire, to which they added their commissions because they were free to collect a certain percentage as payment for their work.

The amount of business that took place in that important city represented a source of temptation; That's why they charged large commissions and cheated people.

Zacchaeus had accumulated wealth by deceiving his clients. Apparently, this ambitious man heard something about Jesus that caused him to urgently want to meet him.

God's Holy Spirit was working in Zacchaeus' life, and although he was a rich citizen of Jericho, seeing Jesus was more important than keeping up appearances. This short man tried to make his way through the crowd, but since he could not, he decided to climb a tree to see Jesus when he passed by.

Knowing that Zacchaeus had a deep spiritual need, Jesus stopped under the sycamore tree and looked up. Then he called Zacchaeus and announced that he would go to his house.

Zacchaeus' encounter with the Master changed his life completely. He stopped being a swindler, and became a compassionate and giving person. The story of Zacchaeus helps us understand that Jesus makes a difference in people's lives because he not only forgives the past, but also changes the present, and blesses us with a future full of hope.

DEVELOPMENT OF THE LESSON

Choose some of the suggested activities to help your students better understand the biblical truth of this lesson.

Geometric figures

In advance, draw and cut out geometric shapes (diamonds, squares, circles, ovals, etc.) of different colors. Keep in mind that each student will need at least eight.

You will also need white paper or small pieces of construction paper, glue, scissors and colored pencils.

Give the materials to the children, and ask them to use the shapes to make a tree and a human figure. Allow them to identify the geometric shapes that would best serve to make the figures. Then, ask them to decorate the paper using the colored pencils.

Tell them that in today's story they will talk about a man who climbed a tree to see a very important person.

BIBLE STORY

We suggest that you invite a young man from your congregation to represent Zacchaeus. Ask him to read the parts that correspond to the character, while you tell the rest of the story.

Zacchaeus meets Jesus

"One, two, three ... how much money have I earned today!" Zacchaeus said. He was counting the tax money that the townspeople had paid him.

"I think I did a good job. I like to collect taxes because I can ask for the amount of money that I want. I give the Romans their part and the rest is for me. When people complain, I just tell them that taxes have gone up. I love this job!"

The people of the town knew that Zacchaeus deceived them, charging them more than they should. That's why nobody wanted him around.

While Zacchaeus kept his money in a safe place, he heard a great uproar in the streets of Jericho. "Almost certainly someone important is going through here," he thought as he tried to listen to what they were saying.

"Hurry up! Jesus is coming through the town. Let's see him!" someone said.

When Zacchaeus heard that news, he ran and joined the crowd that followed Jesus. He so wanted to meet him!

However, there were so many people that Zacchaeus could not get close, and since he was short, he couldn't see anything. He tried to jump to see better, but still he didn't succeed.

"I have to find a way to see Jesus," he thought. "I know! I will climb up that tree, and from there I will be able to observe everything."

Zacchaeus ran down the street to climb a large sycamore tree that was where Jesus was going to pass.

Although there were many people around him, Jesus knew that Zacchaeus was watching him from the tree. So, when he got to that place, he stopped.

"Why did Jesus stop?" the people asked each other.

"Zacchaeus, come down from there because I want to visit your house and your family," Jesus said.

Zacchaeus, happy that Jesus wanted to go to his house, came down from the tree as fast as he could.

"Isn't that man the cheater who charges taxes?" asked a man.

"Yes, it's Zacchaeus, the traitor who works for the Romans. Everyone here knows that he tricks us to get extra money for himself," they replied.

"So, why does Jesus want to go to his house?" they asked.

Jesus knew what Zacchaeus was like. He was aware that he cheated his neighbors to get money. However, Jesus loved him and wanted him to be different. He didn't accuse him or tell him he was a terrible person. Instead, he treated him with love and kindness.

For the first time in a long time, Zacchaeus was ashamed of what he had done. He was sorry for deceiving people and treating them badly.

He decided to follow Jesus and he wanted to do everything right. So he stood up and said, "Jesus, I want to follow you. I regret everything bad that I have done. I will give half of what I have to the poor, and those I cheated I will give them four times more than I stole from them."

Jesus was very happy and said, "Salvation has come to this house and your family. For that I came to the world, to seek and save what was lost."

ACTIVITIES

Zacchaeus meets Jesus

Distribute the student worksheets and the strips and the Zacchaeus figure from the Cut-out Section (pg. 129). Explain that they must join the two strips, gluing them on the spaces marked with the letters A and B. Then, glue the figure of Zacchaeus on the strip vertically, so that his belt covers the letters. Help them cut the openings in the black lines on the tree, and insert the two ends of the strip into them. Tell them to move the figure of Zacchaeus up and down to pretend to climb up and down the tree.

I can change!

Ask your students to look at the second page of Lesson 44 and look at the illustrations. Ask them: *What do you think Zacchaeus is doing?* (Returning the money to people). Explain that Zacchaeus tried to repair the damage he had done by deceiving the people.

Then, focus their attention on the second illustration. Ask them to say what they think is happening in that scene. (The child took something from the store and realized that he had acted badly, asked God for forgiveness and went to return it.)

Allow your students to color the figures and talk about what happens in people's lives when they meet Jesus.

Memorization

Prepare an exhibition with the work your students did during the week. Ask everyone to say the memory verse by heart as special participation. They can also sing a song or dramatize the story.

For parents it will be very interesting to see what their children do in class, and will motivate them to continue taking with them.

To end

Thank them for their attendance during these four weeks, and tell them that in the next class they will start studying a new unit about a very special family.

Year 2 Introduction – Unit XI

A FAMILY CHOSEN BY GOD

Biblical References: Genesis 12:1-7; 13; 15:1-5; 17:1-5, 15; 18:1-12; 21:1-7.

Unit Memory Verse: *And the people said to Joshua, "We will serve the Lord our God and obey him"* (Joshua 24:24).

UNIT OBJECTIVES
This unit will help the students:

- Learn that God's children must love and trust in Him.
- Be considerate of others.
- Always trust in God.
- Know that God helps us make decisions.
- Value and respect the members of their families.

LESSON UNIT A
Lesson 45: God calls Abraham
Lesson 46: Abraham lets Lot choose first
Lesson 47: Abraham believes in God
Lesson 48: A wife for Isaac
Lesson 49: Isaac the peace keeper

WHY ELEMENTARY STUDENTS NEED THE TEACHING OF THIS UNIT:

This unit deals with several important aspects of the social and spiritual development of your students (for example: consideration towards others, living in peace with everyone, loving, trusting and being faithful to God).

This unit will help your students understand the relationship between God and the people he chose. All of these stories focus on the importance of the family and how God uses it to bless others.

For your students, the center of their activities and affections revolves around the family nucleus. That is why it is important to teach them biblical principles that reinforce the importance of loving and respecting the members of their family. They will also know that God chooses faithful families to serve in his work.

Lesson 45
God calls Abraham

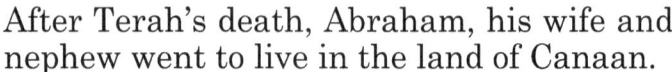

Biblical References: Genesis 12:1-7

Lesson Objective: That your students know that God chooses and calls faithful people to serve Him.

Unit Memory Verse: *And the people said to Joshua, "We will serve the Lord our God and obey him"* (Joshua 24:24).

PREPARE YOURSELF TO TEACH!

In this lesson, your class will learn two fundamental truths:

1. God keeps his promises.
2. God wishes to bless our families.

Your students should feel that they belong to a group, that is, that they can identify with it and feel an important part of it.

God instituted the family to be that group, so that children grow up protected and guided with wisdom. However, many families have lost the essential values and deformed the main purpose.

Your students should understand that God is interested in their families and wants to bless them. Using the life of Abraham and his family as an example, teach them that God wants families to serve and obey him. So He can bless others and spread the gospel through them.

BIBLICAL COMMENTARY

Genesis 12: 1-7. It is interesting to note how many stories of prominent families we find in Genesis. However, it should not surprise us, because one of the purposes of that book is to help God's people know their roots. From the beginning, with Adam and Eve, then Noah and his family, until we reach Abraham, we see examples of God's faithfulness and provision.

God's call to Abraham was not sudden. Stephen's testimony, in Acts 7: 2-4, tells us that God called Abraham when he lived in Mesopotamia, before his father died.

Perhaps Terah, Abraham's father, was the first to receive God's call to leave Ur of the Chaldeans.

Terah and his family, Abraham, Sara and Lot, decided to leave the city where they lived, and traveled through the desert. After Terah's death, Abraham, his wife and nephew went to live in the land of Canaan.

In the time of Abraham, there was a custom that families lived as close as possible. Everyone worked together and helped each other. Typically, large families lived under the same roof. That's why it was difficult for someone to decide to move away from the security, love and collaboration that their relatives offered them.

However, Abraham obeyed God's call and took a step of faith, knowing that the Lord would be with him anywhere.

DEVELOPMENT OF THE LESSON

Home

For this activity you will need a large sheet of paper or four letter-sized pieces of paper taped together, paint, sticks, leaves, and grass.

Draw a horizontal line along the paper and stick it on the wall. Then, divide the class into two teams. One should paint the top of the paper to make the sky, and the other, the bottom, simulating the earth.

Ask them to draw simple houses of different sizes and decorate the roofs, walls, doors, etc., using different materials. Complete the mural with flowers, trees, clouds, the sun, etc.

As they work, talk about the importance of families. Encourage them to tell about some family experiences.

Then, tell them that in today's class we will talk about a very special family which God chose.

A great move

Take the children out of the room for a moment. Have a play time while a volunteer adult helps you put all the chairs in disarray at one end of the room. Then come back and tell them: *Someone moved our chairs! We're going to have to put them where they were before and organize them!*

When the room is ready, give some time to rest, and tell them: *Moving from one place to another is hard work. We got tired just moving the chairs from one place to another, but God asked Abraham to move to a distant land. We're going to learn more about this in today's Bible story.*

BIBLE STORY

Abraham obeys God

Abraham's friends and relatives became very sad when he told them he was moving to another place.

"God told me that I must leave," explained Abraham. "He wants us to live in another land, so I must leave you."

"Are you sure, Abraham?" one of his friends asked him. "It is dangerous for you to leave the city. We will no longer be around to protect you and your family. Why do you want to do it? All your relatives live here!"

"Don't worry. I am obeying God's will. He told me that he will bless all the families of the earth through my family."

"But how is that possible?" they asked. "You are too old to have children. You are almost 75 years old! You and your wife Sara have never had children. So how is God going to bless the world through your family if you don't even have a family?"

Abraham looked at them smiling and said, "I know it's hard to believe, but I trust God. I don't know how he will fulfill his promise, but I know he will."

"You're right, Uncle Abraham," Lot said. "Can I go with you?"

"I don't know where the Lord will take us, but you are welcome if you want to go with us," Abraham replied.

Abraham's friends and relatives helped them prepare everything for the move. They filled baskets with food; then they folded the clothes with great care and put them in sacks; and when they had finished, they put all the luggage on donkeys and camels.

Finally, the day of departure arrived. Abraham, Sara and Lot said goodbye to their relatives and friends, and began a long journey to fulfill God's will.

After many weeks of traveling, they arrived at a place called Canaan. There God spoke again to Abraham.

"This land will be for you and your descendants," God told him.

Abraham believed in God's promise and built an altar to worship and thank him for having taken them safely to the new land.

ACTIVITIES

Pass out the worksheets for Lesson 45. Ask the children to write their name on the line. Provide scissors to cut the figure of the house following the outline. Then, help them trim the windows and doors, as indicated by the solid black lines. Show them how to fold along the dotted lines to open the door and windows.

Give them time to draw pictures of their family in the marked boxes on the next page and decorate their work. When they are finished, tell them to fold the page in half and paste it to finish the activity.

Memorization

Write the memory verse on a piece of poster board or on the board, and repeat it together with your students.

Then, ask them to form a circle and have a volunteer placed in the center. Use a bandana to cover the child's eyes and give him a soft ball. He should throw it to others. The one who receives it must say the verse from memory and take the place of the one in the center.

When most of the children have participated, show the card again and repeat the verse together.

To end

Allow time for your students to mention their prayer requests, and intercede for them. Remind them that God is pleased that we pray for one another, especially for the members of our family.

Encourage them to be punctual in attending the next class to study more about the story of Abraham.

Lesson 46
Abraham lets Lot choose first

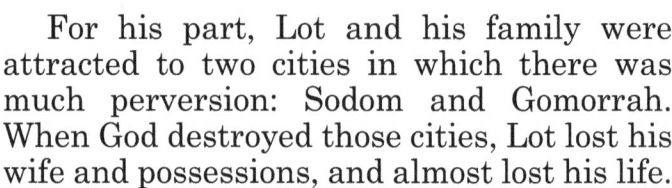

Biblical References: Genesis 13

Lesson Objective: That the students learn to be considerate to others.

Unit Memory Verse: *And the people said to Joshua, "We will serve the Lord our God and obey him"* (Joshua 24:24).

PREPARE YOURSELF TO TEACH!

Elementary students are experts at pointing out when something seems unfair, especially if they think someone is trying to take advantage of them.

At this age, most children are self-centered by nature; they believe that they are the center of all, and always seek to satisfy their needs without taking others into account.

Today's lesson, which shows Abraham's generosity, will help your students recognize that God's provision is for all. They will also learn that He is pleased when they joyfully share what they have with others.

Use this teaching to sow in the hearts of your students the desire to consider the needs of others, and motivate them to share with joy.

BIBLICAL COMMENTARY

Genesis 13:1-18. Abraham and Sarah moved to Canaan, and Lot went with them. After a while, a terrible famine forced them to go to Egypt, where they prospered immensely.

When they returned to Canaan, both Abraham and Lot had many possessions and animals. Their flocks were so large that there wasn't enough food and water for all of their animals, causing fights between the shepherds of both families.

Therefore, they decided to separate and live in different territories. In ancient culture, the older man had the right to choose the place where he wanted to live. However, Abraham allowed his nephew to choose first.

Taking advantage of the opportunity, Lot chose the fertile plain of the Jordan, while Abraham settled in Canaan, the place where God had commanded him to go. There God blessed Abraham for his generous attitude, prospering him even more.

For his part, Lot and his family were attracted to two cities in which there was much perversion: Sodom and Gomorrah. When God destroyed those cities, Lot lost his wife and possessions, and almost lost his life.

This story teaches us that fidelity to God has a reward. When we obey his will, our paths prosper, no matter where we are.

DEVELOPMENT OF THE LESSON

Many animals!

In advance prepare modeling dough (clay) of different colors. Cover the work area with newspapers or plastic bags and distribute the play dough. Ask your students to make various animal figures. They can do as many as the amount of material allows.

As they work, tell them: *What would happen if everyone made so many animals that there was no space left on the table?* (Some would have to take their animals to other tables or to another place.) Explain that today's story is about a problem between Abraham and his nephew Lot, because they had so many animals.

To share!

For this activity you will need a bag of cookies or pieces of fruit (apples, oranges, etc.), paper towels or disposable plates.

While the children watch, spread the cookies or fruit on the napkins or plates, making sure some pieces are larger than others.

Then, ask them to choose the piece they want to eat. When everyone has done so, ask them why they chose the piece they did.

Surely some children chose the larger pieces, and some would have liked the piece that another had already chosen.

Explain: *Many problems arise because people think of themselves first. That is called selfishness. A selfish person does not consider the needs of others, because they are only concerned with their personal well-being.*

In today's class we will talk about a man who was generous and allowed his nephew to choose first.

Distribute the cookies in equal portions, and share them with your students.

BIBLE STORY

Lot chooses where to live

Abraham and Lot had many animals, especially sheep and cattle. Those animals eat grass, and since both had a lot of livestock, there wasn't enough grass for all the animals.

For that reason, the shepherds who worked for Abraham and those who worked for Lot often argued. They were always fighting to get the best places with more grass.

Abraham found out about this situation, so he went to talk to his nephew.

"Lot, you and I are family and there shouldn't be fights between us, nor between our shepherds. There isn't enough land here for everyone, so I think it is time to separate. If you go to the left, I will go to the right; if you go to the right, I'll go to the left."

Lot was surprised when Abraham gave him the opportunity to choose first. According to the custom of those times, the oldest person had the right to choose first. However, Abraham was generous and allowed Lot to choose the land where he wanted to live.

Lot looked around, and saw that the plain of the Jordan River never lacked water. The pastures were always green because it was a very fertile land. In addition, there were two large cities nearby.

"I choose to live in the plain of the Jordan!" said Lot. So he left with his family, his workers and his animals to the land where they would live.

Abraham knew he had done the right thing. Although the land he would stay on wasn't as fertile, he knew that God would take care of him and his family.

Once again the Lord spoke to him, saying, "All the land that you see I will give to you and your offspring forever. I will make your offspring like the dust of the earth, so that if anyone could count the dust, then your offspring could be counted. Go, walk through the length and breadth of the land, for I am giving it to you" (Genesis 13:15-17).

Abraham continued to believe that God would fulfill his promises, so he lived on that land for a long time and God prospered him a lot.

ACTIVITIES

Time to share

Distribute the student worksheets and colored pencils. Ask the children to connect the related figures with a line. Point out that one of the figures represents a problem, while the other represents a solution.

Ask them to tell a brief story about what they think is happening in each situation. Conclude by reviewing what they studied in the Bible story.

Learn to be considerate

Sit with your students and make a list of ways they can show consideration to their peers (For example: sharing toys, lending colored pencils, allowing others to choose first, etc.).

Remind them that God blessed Abraham because he was generous and thought of Lot's well-being rather than his own.

Encourage them to put into practice the ideas they said, and to exercise their generosity during the week.

Memorization

Allow time for your students to fill in the blanks at the bottom of the second page of the worksheet with the letters from the wheel. Thus they will form the memory verse: *"We will serve the Lord our God and obey him"* (Joshua 24:24).

After repeating the text together several times, give some volunteers a chance to say it by heart.

To end

Ask one of the students to pray out loud and intercede for the requests. Conclude by asking the Lord to help your students be considerate to their peers.

Sing a song before saying goodbye, and invite them to the next class to learn more stories about Abraham, the friend of God.

Lesson 47
Abraham believes in God

Biblical References: Genesis 15:1-5; 17:1-5, 15; 18:1-12; 21:1-7
Lesson Objective: That the students learn to trust more in God.
Unit Memory Verse: *And the people said to Joshua, "We will serve the Lord our God and obey him"* (Joshua 24:24).

PREPARE YOURSELF TO TEACH!

In today's complex world, it is often difficult for children to know who to trust.

Your students need to be reassured that God keeps his promises. Unfortunately, perhaps some of them live in homes where promises are never fulfilled. It may be difficult for them to understand that God fulfills what He promises.

Elementary students learn easily to trust and distrust. If someone they love fails, it is often difficult for them to trust again without hesitation. It is therefore important to teach them through this lesson that, despite the circumstances, God is faithful and always keeps his promises.

BIBLICAL COMMENTARY

Genesis 15:1-5; 17:1-5, 15; 18:1-12; 21:1-7.

It is likely that it was difficult for Abraham to trust that God would fulfill his promise, especially after so many years. The religions of that time worshiped false gods that demanded nothing from their followers. They did not require that they be patient, committed, faithful or loyal.

However, Abraham continued to live according to God's will, expecting him to fulfill his promise.

The years passed, and Abraham and Sara still did not have children. Doubt began to seize their hearts and their faith needed to be strengthened. Then Abraham cried out to God, asking for a sign to be sure that everything He had told them would be fulfilled. God, showing him the stars, told him that his offspring would be as numerous as the stars in the sky. God used an element of daily life to remind Abraham of his covenant.

Through time, this man's faith was tested with fire. Many years passed before the birth of Isaac, and during that period, God reminded Abraham that only He is in control of situations, and that His time is perfect. Regardless of Sara's age or the adverse circumstances, God was faithful to His promise and fulfilled it, just as He had said.

Think of a time in your life when God fulfilled one of his promises, and thank him for that. As you teach this lesson, remember and express the joy you felt on that occasion.

DEVELOPMENT OF THE LESSON

Use some of the following activities to reinforce your students' biblical learning.

Stars

For this activity you will need a figure in the form of a star for each student, gold glitter and glue. If you do not have glitter, provide colored pencils.

Get posters or illustrations that show the night sky. Ask your students to identify the moon, stars, constellations, etc.

Then, distribute the stars, glitter and glue so that the students can decorate their stars. As they work, tell them that today they will talk about a covenant (promise/agreement) that God made with Abraham, using the stars of heaven as an example.

When they finish decorating the stars, stick them around the room to represent the sky.

How many stars are there in the sky?

Before class, draw or stick many stars on a piece of cardboard or black paper.

Show your students the paper, and ask them to count the stars.

Tell them: In today's Bible story, God told Abraham to count the stars in heaven to teach him an important lesson.

Guess!

Fill a clear container with seeds or buttons that you have previously counted. Place it on a table, so that all children can see it. Then, ask them: *How many buttons (seeds) do you think there are in this container?*

Ask everyone to write their answer on a piece of paper. Give a small prize to whoever comes closest to the correct amount.

Then, tell them: *God told Abraham that his offspring would be more numerous than the stars of heaven. Do you think Abraham's family was more numerous than the buttons (seeds) in this container? It is hard to imagine such a large family, but God promised Abraham that his family would be a great nation, and God always keeps his promises.*

BIBLE STORY

God keeps his promise

Eleven long years had passed since God promised Abraham that he would make a great nation from him. Could God have forgotten his promise?

Abraham was already starting to get discouraged. But one day God told him, "Don't be afraid. I'll take care of you and give you a wonderful gift."

"But, what can you give me, Lord?" Abraham replied. "I have no children and my servants will inherit everything I have."

Then God took Abraham outside and told him, "Look at the stars of heaven; can you count them?"

"No, Lord, I can't," replied Abraham. "There are too many!"

"Well, so will your descendants be on earth. They will be so numerous that no one will be able to count them," replied God.

Abraham believed in God's promise, but many more years passed, and he and his wife still had no children.

One day it was very hot and Abraham was resting outside his tent. Suddenly, he saw three men approaching him.

"I will bring you water to wash your feet and rest," he said. "I will also bring you something to eat."

Abraham and Sara planned to share a special meal with the visitors, and chose the best foods they had. Sara used the finest flour to prepare bread. Abraham chose one of his best calves for the servant to cook. Then, he brought milk and butter, and attended to the visitors, offering them a delicious meal.

"Where is your wife Sara?" asked one of the visitors.

"She's here in the tent," Abraham replied.

Then the man said to him, "Within one year of this date, your wife will have a child."

Abraham knew that God had sent the visitors to reaffirm His promise.

Sara, who had heard everything from the ten, laughed. "I'm too old to have a baby," she thought. "Abraham is also old. How can something so wonderful happen?"

But after a year, God fulfilled his promise, and Sarah had a beautiful baby whom they named Isaac.

ACTIVITIES

I can also believe in God!

Distribute the student worksheets and the figure of baby Isaac from the Cutout Section (pg. 131). Have the students glue baby Isaac in Abraham's arms.

Then, tell them to fold the page along the dotted line and read the verse together: "Know therefore that the Lord your God is God; he is the faithful God..." (Deuteronomy 7: 9a).

Ask them to trace the dotted word and talk about the importance of believing that God will always keep his promises.

Memorization

Hand out paper and pencils to your students. Ask them to write the memory verse without seeing or copying it. Review their work and help those who need it. Allow time for each to decorate their paper to their liking, and stick them on the wall of the room.

Encourage them to use the Verse of the Month Club card to study the verse at home.

To end

Sing some songs and give thanks to God for being faithful and always keeping his promises. Encourage your students to exercise confidence in God during the week and to tell others what they learned in class.

Remind them that their attendance next week is very important because they will study what happened when the baby Isaac grew up.

Lesson 48
A wife for Isaac

Biblical References: Genesis 24
Lesson Objective: That the students learn to trust in God when they need help.
Unit Memory Verse: *And the people said to Joshua, "We will serve the Lord our God and obey him"* (Joshua 24:24).

PREPARE YOURSELF TO TEACH!

Your students are increasingly independent and have the ability to do many things on their own. In their eagerness to become independent, they may turn their eyes away from authority figures. However, even in this stage of "I can do it myself," they welcome the help of an adult if they have already tried to do something on their own and did not succeed.

They must understand that they can always turn to God when they need help. Also, they should know that you as an adult also depend on God's help. He is much more than a father or a teacher, and is always willing to help us.

Through the story of Abraham's servant Eliezer, teach your class to seek God's help and guidance in their daily lives.

BIBLICAL COMMENTARY

Genesis 24:1-67. The story of the search for a wife for Isaac is the longest chapter of Genesis. This story marks an important transition, for from that point on, it was Isaac who continued God's plans for his people.

God had fulfilled his promise with the birth of Isaac. However, for that promise to continue, Isaac needed a wife who believed in God. Abraham did not want his son to marry a Canaanite woman who followed pagan customs. Therefore, he commissioned his servant Eliezer, who took a solemn oath that he would go to Abraham's land to seek a wife for Isaac. Abraham trusted that God, faithful to his promise, would give the best wife to his son.

Arranged weddings were a common tradition in Biblical times. However, Eliezer prayed asking God to help him in the search, and God answered in an extraordinary way by sending Rebecca to the well.

Abraham believed in God and obeyed him, and taught Isaac to do the same. With Abraham's example, the servant Eliezer also learned to worship and trust Almighty God.

DEVELOPMENT OF THE LESSON

Use the following activities to guide your students' attention to the topic of study.

Isaac grows

For this activity you will need clippings or photographs that illustrate the growth of a person.

Glue them on a poster board, showing the stages of growth, starting with a baby and ending with an elderly person.

Show the illustrations to your students, and explain: *All people go through a process of growth. The same happened with baby Isaac, who we studied last week. After baby Isaac was born, he didn't stay a child forever. He grew up and became an adult. God had fulfilled the promise he had made to Abraham with the birth of this baby. Now he would continue the promise of creating a great nation through Abraham. Isaac also had to have children, and in today's story, we will see what happened to him when he was old enough to get married.*

A wedding!

Show your students pictures of different weddings. Ask them to describe what a wedding is like and what is done in it. Explain that most people now choose for themselves whom they will marry.

However, in the time of Abraham, the parents chose the people with whom their sons and daughters would marry. The father of the man spoke with the lady's parents and they agreed. If everything was favorable, the parents of the bride received gifts from the parents of the groom.

In today's story, we will see what happened when it came time to find a wife for Isaac.

BIBLE STORY

A wife for Isaac

Abraham was sitting under his tent. It had been many years since his son Isaac had been born, and Abraham was already very old and getting tired more and more.

His servant Eliezer took care of him and his belongings. Abraham loved him very much and trusted him as if he were his own son. One day Abraham said to him, "Eliezer, I want you to promise me that you'll help me find a wife for Isaac. I don't want her to be a woman from this country. Go to my land and find a woman from my people."

Eliezer promised Abraham that he would find the right woman for his son. So he began packing special gifts and some food. After putting everything on ten camels, he started the trip. The desert was a very hot place and Eliezer was worried, because he didn't know where to find a good wife for Isaac.

After several days of travel, Eliezer arrived in Nahor. There he found a water well and prayed, "God, I beg you to help me find a wife for Isaac. I ask that the woman who comes to draw water from the well and share it with me and the camels will be the one you have chosen for your servant Isaac."

Before Eliezer finished praying, a beautiful young woman approached the well with a jar to carry water. When Eliezer saw that she had filled the jar with water, he asked for some, and she said, "Drink, sir. I will also get water for your camels to drink."

God had answered Eliezer's prayer, sending the woman he wanted for Isaac to the well!

Eliezer went to Rebekah's house and spoke with her father and her brother Laban. He told them that Abraham had sent him to find a wife for his son Isaac. Then, he handed the gifts to Rebecca's family.

They agreed to the wedding, and preparations began for the return trip. Rebecca said goodbye to her father, her brother Laban and her other relatives, and along with Eliezer, took the road to Canaan.

Isaac and Rebecca soon got married. Eliezer knew that God had helped him find the ideal wife for his master's son. God's promise to Abraham would now continue through his son.

ACTIVITIES

Trust and obey

Hand out the worksheets for Lesson 48. Instruct them to join the points according to the numbering to find the figure of Eliezer. Then, give them time to color the drawing.

As they work, briefly review what they learned in the Bible story.

Psalm 32:8

Going to the next page, ask your students to complete the verse, adding the missing words to the blank lines. Then, read Psalm 32:8 as a class. If you wish, ask them to say their name before reading the verse. Tell them: *This verse is a promise from God. He wants us to trust and obey him always. God wants to instruct us to do the right thing, because he knows what is best for us. When we allow ourselves to be guided by God's hand, we learn to obey Him and our life prospers.*

Memorization

To review the memory verse, write the words of Joshua 24:24 on a piece of poster board or on the board. Read it several times all together. Then, delete a word and read it again; erase a second word and so on, until the board is blank, and they can say the memory verse by heart.

To end

Allow time for your students to pick up and organize the materials they used, and get their belongings. Then pray, asking the Lord to take control of their lives and their decisions. Intercede for the sick and remember those who missed the class.

Sing a song before saying goodbye, and invite them to the next class to study the last lesson of this unit.

Lesson 49
Isaac the peacemaker

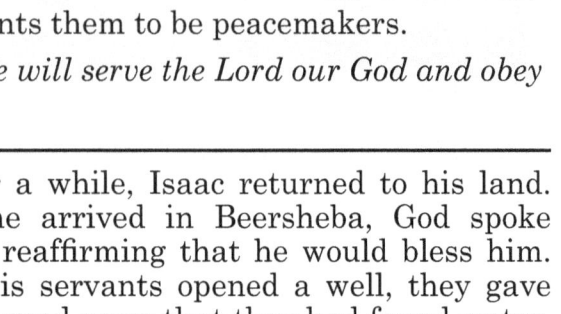

Biblical References: Genesis 26:1-33

Lesson Objective: That the students learn that God wants them to be peacemakers.

Unit Memory Verse: *And the people said to Joshua, "We will serve the Lord our God and obey him"* (Joshua 24:24).

PREPARE YOURSELF TO TEACH!

Unfortunately, it is clear that the environment in which your students develop is increasingly hostile. Just look at the news to see that our society is increasingly corrupt, and the opportunity for a peaceful life is increasingly limited.

Hearing of murders, fights and violence are common for elementary students. However, that is not the way of life that God wants for them. Today's lesson gives us an example of the kind of behavior that God wants us to adopt.

Isaac showed that there is a different way to resolve conflicts. Instead of seeking strife and enmity, he turned away and let God take control of the situation. God blessed Isaac, who tried to maintain a peaceful relationship with his discourteous neighbors.

In a society as conflictive as ours, children need the example of peacemakers.

BIBLICAL COMMENTARY

Genesis 26:1-33. Because of the famine in the land where Isaac lived, the Lord told him to go away for a while to Gerar, land of the Philistines. There people began to feel jealous of him for several reasons: because his wife Rebecca was beautiful; because Isaac prospered; because when Isaac sowed the land God blessed him with an abundant harvest, and his cattle multiplied rapidly.

The Philistines increasingly felt more jealous of Isaac and looked for reasons to fight with him.

When Isaac decided to use the wells that his father Abraham had dug long ago, the Philistines filled them with dirt. So Isaac left Gerar and went to live in a nearby valley. There he found other wells that his father had dug and which the Philistines no longer used, so he reopened them. But when the Philistines realized what he had done, they went to claim the ownership of those wells immediately. Instead of fighting, Isaac decided to leave the place and keep looking.

This happened on numerous occasions, but Isaac remained firm in his desire not to fight and continued to look for water elsewhere.

After a while, Isaac returned to his land. When he arrived in Beersheba, God spoke to him, reaffirming that he would bless him. When his servants opened a well, they gave him the good news that they had found water. After a few days, the Philistines who had caused him trouble went to look for him. They wanted to make peace because they knew that the almighty Lord was with him.

DEVELOPMENT OF THE LESSON

Select some of the following activities to complement the development of today's class.

Families

Provide white paper and colored pencils for your students to draw a picture of their family. Meanwhile, prepare illustrations that represent Abraham's family and Isaac's family. Take as models the drawings in the student worksheet; make them on poster board.

When the children are finished, divide a large piece of poster board into two. On the left side, give the title "Abraham's family", and on the other side, "Families of today."

Glue the pictures of Abraham and Isaac's families where appropriate. Then, have the children glue their drawings on the other side.

Place the mural on a wall, and talk about the similarities and differences that exist between the two types of families. After listening to their answers, explain that although times are different, God remains the same. He wants to bless our families, just as he did with Abraham's.

Peaceful work

For this activity you will need different colors of play-doh or modeling clay, and plastic bags or newspapers to cover the work area.

Depending on the number of students, divide the class into groups of two or three. Give each group play-doh of one color. Then, ask them to create a figure in which they use all the colors. This means that they will have to share the different colors with each other.

Watch the children's behavior closely as they interact, and encourage them to be friendly while they work.

When they finish, gather them and ask them: *What would have happened if one of the groups had refused to share their play-doh color? Do you think you could have finished your project?* Listen to their responses and tell them: *When everyone works together there is peace and harmony. However, when someone decides to fight, the environment is different. In today's Bible story we will study about a man who decided to seek peace, even though his neighbors wanted to fight him.*

BIBLE STORY
Isaac decides not to fight

Isaac was going through a difficult time. There was a great famine in the land where he and his family lived. Soon they would be left without any food. For that reason, he decided to move to Gerar, the land of the Philistines.

Isaac was sure he was doing the right thing because God had told him that he would always be with him.

From the beginning, the Philistines felt a lot of jealousy toward Isaac. First, because his wife Rebecca was a very beautiful woman; and second, because God had prospered him a lot in a short time. When he planted crops, his harvest was so abundant that he earned a lot of money and became rich. He also had many sheep, cows and other types of animals.

The Philistines were so jealous that they prepared a plan to upset Isaac. They knew that Isaac's animals needed water and that he used the wells that his father Abraham had dug. So, when no one was watching, they filled all the wells with dirt.

Abimelech, the king of the region, asked Isaac to leave Gerar, because he was more powerful than them.

Then Isaac went to another valley with his family, his servants and his animals. There, Isaac's servants found other ancient wells and opened them. However, the Philistine shepherds soon arrived to tell them, "The water is ours!"

Isaac didn't want to fight, so he went to another place and dug another well, but the Philistines didn't stay calm. Again they went to fight over the water.

Again, Isaac decided to leave without fighting and reopened another well, but this time Philistines didn't bother him.

After a while, Isaac went to live in Beersheba. One night, God spoke to him saying, "I am the God of your father Abraham, and through him I will bless you and increase your descendants. Don't be afraid because I am with you."

Then Isaac made an altar to worship God and there he put his tent. Then, his servants dug the earth and found another well with fresh and clear water. When King Abimelech heard this, he went to Beersheba to talk to Isaac.

"Why do you come to see me since you treated me very badly and threw me out of your country?" asked Isaac.

"We have seen that God is with you. That's why we want to be your friends and make a deal so you don't hurt us," said King Abimelech.

Isaac was a peaceful man, so he decided to make the deal with the Philistines and prepared a big banquet for them. The next morning they got up very early, and the king and Isaac promised not to hurt each other. After this, the visitors went in peace to their land and God continued to bless and prosper Isaac, the peacemaker.

ACTIVITIES
Who is who?

In this unit your students learned about different characters, and this activity will serve as review.

Hand out the worksheets for Lesson 49. Ask the children to connect the figures with the appropriate description.

Some figures will be related to more than one phrase. Emphasize God's faithfulness to this family. Use this activity to review each lesson in the unit. Point to a character, and ask the children to say what they did and how they showed their obedience to God.

On the next page, ask them to fold the page along the dotted line and emphasize the word "Happy." Discuss how they feel when they get along with others. Listen to their comments and encourage them to put their biblical learning into practice. It is good to avoid fights and be peacemakers.

Memorization

Ask for some volunteers to come forward and quote the memory verse. Prepare simple prizes to recognize the effort of your students.

If you wish, prepare a demonstration of what they studied during these five lessons, and invite their parents to visit the class.

To end

Briefly review the biblical stories they studied. Then form a circle and ask the Lord in prayer to help you all be peacemakers and obey his will, as Abraham and Isaac did.

Make sure everyone takes home the work they did during these five weeks. Invite them to the study of "The Good News of Christmas."

Year 2   Introduction – Unit XII

THE GOOD NEWS OF CHRISTMAS

Biblical References: Luke 1:5-25, 57-80; 1:23-38; Matthew 1:18-25; Luke 2:1-20; 2:21-40.

Unit Memory Verse: *Today in the town of David a Savior has been born to you; he is the Messiah, the Lord* (Luke 2:11).

UNIT OBJECTIVES

This unit will help the students:

- ❖ Celebrate Christmas with joy, thanking God for having sent his Son Jesus.
- ❖ Understand how the Christmas Story shows us that God fulfilled His promises.
- ❖ Trust in God knowing that He fulfills His Word.
- ❖ Learn that Jesus, the Son of God, came to the world as a gift from the Father.

LESSON UNIT A

Lesson 50: Good News for Zechariah and Elizabeth
Lesson 51: Good News for Mary and Joseph
Lesson 52: Good News for the shepherds
Lesson 53: Good News for Simeon and Anna

WHY ELEMENTARY STUDENTS NEED THE TEACHING OF THIS UNIT:

Most elementary children know the story of Christmas. Now they are ready to learn the meaning of this event that changed the history of mankind. They will learn that through this event, God showed us that we can trust him because he always keeps his promises.

Each lesson emphasizes the fulfillment of a promise. In the first place, Zechariah and Elisabeth received the promise of a son who would be responsible for preparing the way of the Messiah. Joseph and Mary received the promise that they would be the earthly parents of Jesus, the Son of God. Also the shepherds received the news of the fulfillment of a promise, since Christ was born in Bethlehem. Finally, Simeon and Anna, who had waited a long time for the promised Savior, could see him with their own eyes.

Through these four lessons, help your students understand that even in a world full of falsehood, we can trust that our God is faithful and always fulfills what He promises.

Lesson 50

Good News for Zechariah and Elizabeth

Biblical References: Luke 1:5-25, 57-80
Lesson Objective: That the students know that God accomplishes what He promises.
Memory Verse: *Today in the town of David a Savior has been born to you; he is the Messiah, the Lord* (Luke 2:11).

PREPARE YOURSELF TO TEACH!

A broken promise can hurt a child's heart. To trust, elementary-aged children need to know that what they are told will come true. As your students experience how God keeps his promises, their trust in him will be strengthened. Trusting that God is faithful to his Word and does not disappoint us will give them greater security and stability.

Christmas is one of the most exciting times for children. Now that the month of December has began, they are likely to be more restless. Therefore, try to channel their energies into productive activities that are related to the lesson. Talk to them about the preparations made by their families before Christmas, but emphasize that the center of this holiday is not gifts or food, but commemorate with joy the birth of Jesus, the Son of God.

BIBLICAL COMMENTARY

Luke 1:5-25, 57-80. Zechariah was a righteous man and faithful priest in the temple of God. His wife, Elisabeth, was also a servant of God. Both were elderly and had never had children.

Zechariah was chosen to offer incense in the sanctuary of the Lord. This was a very great honor for the priest because it was a sacred occasion. The smoke of the incense symbolized the prayers of the people.

While Zechariah offered the incense, the angel Gabriel appeared to him to announce that he would have a son, whom he would call John. He would be great before God and full of the Holy Spirit.

Due to his advanced age, Zechariah doubted the angel's announcement, and because of his disbelief, he remained silent until after the birth of the child.

As the angel promised, after a while the child was born. When he was eight days old, according to the Mosaic Law, they had to take him to the temple to circumcise him. The custom was that the firstborn should have the name of the father, but God had decided that the child would be named John.

For his faithfulness and service, God used Zechariah and Elizabeth to be the parents of the man who would prepare the way for the promised Messiah.

DEVELOPMENT OF THE LESSON

Choose some of the following activities to achieve a more meaningful learning of the study topic in your students.

Without speaking

Ask the children how long they think they could go without speaking. Listen to their responses, and ask how people communicate when they lose their voice (sign language or in writing).

Ask the class to try not to talk while doing the following activities.

Tell them that today's Bible story is about a man who was promised something special by God and could not talk for almost a year.

Christmas decorations

During the week, draw angels and stars on card stock; then cut out the figures. Have glitter, glue and colored pencils on hand.

Give a figure to each child, and ask them to decorate it using the materials provided. Remind them that they should do this activity without speaking. Then, decorate the room with the finished figures.

To prepare the way!

Gather the children and tell them: *When the president of a country is about to visit a city, many preparations are made. There are people who spend many days making arrangements to make the visit as successful as possible. Security officers plan the best route. The maintenance people fix the streets and paint the walls. Gardeners arrange trees and flowers. Why do you think it is important to prepare for the visit of an important person?* Remember that at this time they cannot speak, so they must answer by signing or writing the answers.

Today we will hear the story of the birth of a special person who prepared the way for Jesus.

BIBLE STORY

One answered prayer

"Today I have to offer the incense," thought Zechariah as he entered the temple. He had prepared himself very carefully for that special day. Soon he saw that the smoke of the incense rose gently through the air, reminding him of the prayers of the people.

Suddenly, an angel appeared before him, and Zechariah was frightened.

"Don't be afraid, Zechariah. God has heard your prayer," said the angel. "Your wife Elisabeth will have a son. His name will be John, and many people will rejoice and praise God for his birth. He will be great before God. Because of him, many people will come to God. Your son will go before the Lord with the spirit and power of the prophet Elijah. He will help people return to God and prepare them to receive the Lord."

"But I am very old, and my wife Elisabeth is no longer of child-bearing age. How can I believe what you tell me?" asked Zechariah.

"I am Gabriel," said the angel. "I stand in the presence of God and he has sent me to give you this good news. But since you didn't believe, you won't be able to speak until after the baby is born. Then you will see that everything I have told you is true."

Meanwhile, the people outside the temple asked themselves, "Why is Zechariah taking so long to come out?"

When he finally came out, he tried to tell people what had happened with the angel and the message God had given him. But he couldn't because he couldn't talk.

"Look, Zechariah can't talk! See how he signs with his hands? Surely he had a vision of the Lord!" people said.

Zechariah went home and tried to explain to his wife Elisabeth what had happened, but he couldn't speak.

Soon after, Elisabeth knew she was pregnant. She was going to have a baby. She was so excited!

"God, thank you," Elizabeth prayed. "We wanted a child for so long, and now you have given us one."

"How good God has been in granting Zechariah and Elizabeth a child!" said his friends and neighbors. "They have wanted one for a long time."

"Now Zechariah will have someone who bears his name," they said.

After the required time, the baby was born.

"It's a boy! It's a boy! Zechariah and Elisabeth have a baby boy!" the neighbors said with joy.

When he was eight days old, Elisabeth and Zechariah took the baby to the temple. The Jewish custom was that when families had a new baby, they had to offer a special sacrifice to God, and they named the baby.

Zechariah still couldn't talk. So, when the priests brought the baby to the Lord, they would give him the father's name, but Elizabeth said: 'No! He will be called John!"

"Why?" they asked. None of his relatives is named John. That's very strange; let's ask the father what he wants to call his son.

"What name do you want to give the child?" they asked Zechariah.

Zechariah asked for a tablet and everyone was surprised when he wrote: "John is his name."

At that moment Zechariah recovered his voice and could speak again.

"Praise the Lord!" he exclaimed. "And you, my son will be called prophet of the Most High because you will go before the Lord to prepare his way."

ACTIVITIES

Attendance sheet

Pass out the attendance sheet for Unit XII, as well as the figure of Zechariah and Elisabeth from the Cut-out Section (pg 125). Have them glue the figure in the space that corresponds to it.

As they work, tell them: *During this month we will meet many special people that God chose to be part of his plans. This week we learned that God chose Zechariah and Elizabeth to be the parents of John the Baptist. John was chosen to prepare the way for Jesus, the promised Messiah.*

If you wish, stick the attendance sheets on a poster board to form a mural. This way you will have a visual control of the students who are punctual in their attendance.

The Bethlehem Herald

Distribute the student worksheets, and provide colored pencils or crayons.

Ask the children to imagine what happened in each part of the story, and illustrate the scene below the corresponding titles. They can write the description or draw a picture.

Use this sheet to give an overview of what they learned in the Bible story.

Who can you trust?

Ask the children go to their worksheet titled "Who can I trust?", and provide them with colored pencils.

Ask them to color the figures that represent trustworthy people because they fulfill what they promise.

When they have finished, give time for some volunteers to explain why they decided to color those figures and not others.

Remind them that God is trustworthy. In today's story we learned that he keeps his promises.

Memorization

Divide the class into two groups. Ask one group to say the first part of the verse, and the second group to say the second part. Then, both groups should say the full text together.

Exchange the phrases of the two groups so that everyone studies the full text. Repeat the exercise several times, and then choose some children to say it on their own.

Hand out the Verse of the Month Club cards to take home to review the memory verse of this unit.

To end

Thank your students for attending, and pray for them. Thank God for their faithfulness and for having taught them through this class that He is trustworthy.

Remind them that next week they will continue to study about special people that God chose to carry out his plans, and invite them to come.

Lesson 51
Good News for Mary and Joseph

Biblical References: Luke 1:26-38; Matthew 1:18-25
Lesson Objective: That the students want to be faithful and obedient to God.
Memory Verse: *Today in the town of David a Savior has been born to you; he is the Messiah, the Lord* (Luke 2:11).

PREPARE YOURSELF TO TEACH!

Obedience is a very important subject that is mentioned time and time again in the Word of God. We find many lessons about obedience in the Sunday School curriculum for elementary students. This lesson focuses on "voluntary obedience," which implies a cheerful and willing attitude.

Children usually think that obedience is something they have to do although they would prefer not to. This lesson will help them recognize that when we obey out of love, we feel satisfaction and joy.

God included people willing to obey Him in His plan to send the promised Messiah. Some, like Zechariah, at first showed themselves to be incredulous or reluctant. Others, like Mary, obeyed with pleasure.

With today's story, your students will understand that God wants to use willing and obedient people in his work.

Every day there are fewer days to celebrate Christmas. Therefore, do not be surprised if your students are more distracted than usual, and it is more difficult to focus their attention on learning activities. Use your imagination to lead the class in an environment in which they can express their energy, and at the same time understand the message of the Word of God.

BIBLICAL COMMENTARY

Luke 1: 26-38. Unlike Zechariah, Mary did not doubt for a moment what the angel said to her, but on the contrary, she responded with humility and pleasure. Being a virgin, it was natural that the question should arise: "How will this be?" However, the difference was that she did not doubt the power that God had to make that happen.

When she answered "Behold the handmaid of the Lord," she confirmed her obedience and submission to God's divine will.

Matthew 1: 18-25. Joseph's reaction to knowing that Mary was pregnant was very logical. In those times, the commitment that was made in the courtship was as serious as the marriage itself. That is why he considered leaving Mary in secret, because he did not want to embarrass her in front of everyone.

However, the angel appeared to Joseph to tell him that the baby had been conceived by the Holy Spirit, and that God would use him to bless the nations.

Joseph believed the announcement and decided to move forward with his marriage plans. He and Mary were obedient to the voice of God, even though they did not fully understand what was happening. That is the kind of obedience that God desires of us, without questioning or conditions.

God honored these young people for their obedience, giving them the privilege of being the earthly parents of Jesus, the Redeemer of the world.

DEVELOPMENT OF THE LESSON

Attendance sheet
Welcome the class and give them the Mary and Joseph figure from the Cut-Out section (pg. 125), and have them paste it in the space indicated on the attendance sheet.

Explain: *Last week we heard the story of Elisabeth and Zechariah, the parents of John the Baptist, who would prepare the way for the Lord. In today's lesson we will talk about two special people who were obedient to God's will.*

Angels everywhere
Three of the four lessons in this unit speak of angels who announced God's plan to ordinary people. During the week draw on poster board silhouettes of angels, and cut them out. Prepare a figure as an example.

Distribute the figures, and ask the children to decorate them with glitter or other colorful materials within their reach. They can draw the face, and glue cotton or strips of paper like hair.

Tell them that the angels had a very important role when Jesus was born, because they were in charge of announcing the Good News to many people. Encourage your class to use the angel figures to decorate their home or classroom, reminding them of the Good News of Christmas.

BIBLE STORY
Joseph and Mary listen and obey

"I've been so happy since I found out that my cousin Elisabeth is going to have a baby," Mary thought. "She and Zechariah have wanted to have a child for a long time. It's wonderful that it will finally happen! Maybe one day after Joseph and I get married, we'll have a baby too."

It was only three months before Elizabeth's baby was born and the whole family was excited.

Suddenly, an angel appeared to Mary and said, "The Lord is with you. He has blessed you in a special way among all women."

Mary began trembling. "Who are you?" she asked. "What do you want?"

"Mary, do not be afraid," said the angel Gabriel. "God has chosen you to have a baby. You will name him Jesus. He will be great and they will call him Son of the Most High."

"How can I have a baby?" Mary asked. "I have not married yet."

"Nothing is impossible for God," said the angel.

"I am the servant of the Lord," Mary answered. "I will do what God wants."

Mary was engaged to marry Joseph and did not know how to break the news to him.

"Joseph," said Mary, "I have something important to tell you."

"What is it, Mary?" Joseph asked.

"I'm going to have a baby."

Joseph was surprised, and asked, "How is that possible?"

"Don' fear," Mary answered. "An angel told me that this baby will be special. He'll be the Son of God and we must call him Jesus."

Joseph left Mary's house very confused. "I love Mary, but I don't understand what she said about a baby. Maybe we shouldn't get married," he thought as he walked home.

"I need to sleep," thought Joseph, "I'm going to lie down and rest for a while."

Joseph fell asleep right away. While he was sleeping, an angel of God appeared to him in a dream and said, "Joseph, don't be afraid to marry Mary. The baby she's waiting for is the Son of God. You must call him Jesus. He will save the people from their sins."

Joseph woke up with a start. His dream had been so real! He already knew what he had to do. He would marry Mary and be a father to the promised Son of God.

Joseph obeyed God and took Mary as his wife. They were Jesus' earthly parents. Everything happened just as the angel had said.

ACTIVITIES
What is the difference?

Pass out the student worksheets for Lesson 51. Ask the children to fill in the blanks and find the mysterious word (voluntarily). Then, have them cut through the black lines in the center of the sheet to make two openings.

Give them the figure that corresponds to this lesson from the Cutout Section (pg 127), and explain how to insert it through the openings.

Talk about what is happening in the illustration, and tell them how to move the figure to see what happens when the boy changes his attitude. Remind them that today's story teaches us to be obedient to God's will.

His name will be Jesus

(If you made single-sided copies of the boys for the previous activity, you'll need to make a copy of the angels on page 128 of the Cut out Section. Have the students make similar slits in this worksheet, and insert the angel figure in the same way.) Tell the children to observe the scene in which the angel speaks with Mary. Then slide the figure to simulate that the angel is talking to Joseph. Talk about how these two people obeyed God's voice, and how we can obey when the Lord commands us to do something.

Memorization

On thick cards, copy the words of the memory verse, writing a word on each card. Repeat the verse together twice. Then mix up the cards, and give an opportunity to your students to take turns ordering the words. Repeat the verse each time they order them correctly.

Save the cards to use for the next class.

To end

Thank your students for their attendance, and say something about the next lesson to arouse their interest.

Emphasize that it is important to obey the voice of God, just as Joseph and Mary did. End with a prayer, and sing Christmas songs.

If time and resources allow, prepare a small celebration to remember Jesus' birth in the next class.

Lesson 52
Good News for the Shepherds

Biblical References: Luke 2:1-20

Lesson Objective: That the students express the joy of knowing that Jesus came to save each person.

Memory Verse: *Today in the town of David a Savior has been born to you; he is the Messiah, the Lord* (Luke 2:11).

PREPARE YOURSELF TO TEACH!

During the Christmas season, children receive many messages that encourage selfishness and materialism. Even well-intentioned adults fall into the consumerism of this time by asking, "What do you want for Christmas?" Your students should know that for Christians, Christmas is the time to give and share, not to desire and obtain.

Elementary-aged children identify easily with the shepherds of this story. Often they also feel on the outside, and may not have money to buy gifts for others. However, they will learn that as soon as the shepherds heard the Good News, they went to see the baby Jesus. Then, with great joy, they told everyone about the great gift of God. Help your students understand that, even if they do not have great gifts, the most important thing they can give to others is the Good News of the birth of Jesus Christ, the Savior of the world.

BIBLICAL COMMENTARY

Luke 2:1-20. The Son of the Most High, Jesus the King, began his earthly life wrapped in swaddling clothes and lying in a manger. In contrast to this humble birth, the heavens were full of angels who sang praises and celebrated the arrival of the Messiah.

Those angels, appearing to humble shepherds who cared for their flocks, announced to them the Good News of the birth of Christ.

In the Roman Empire, it was customary for poets and orators to announce peace and prosperity when the emperor's son was born. In the same way, through the heavenly hosts, God announced that his Son, the Savior of the world, had been born in Bethlehem for the rejoicing of humanity.

Shepherds are an important part of this story, not only because through them we relate Jesus to King David, who was also a shepherd (2 Samuel 7:8), but also because they are among the poor, maimed, lame and blind who are invited to the kingdom of God (Luke 14:13-21).

God chose these humble men to be witnesses of the birth of the Messiah, and then they would tell others this Good News. The Bible tells us that "the shepherds returned glorifying and praising God for all the things they had heard and seen, which were just as they had been told" (Luke 2:20).

DEVELOPMENT OF THE LESSON

Use some of the following activities to enrich biblical learning and stimulate your students' participation.

Stars

For this activity you will need stars made of cardboard or poster board, glue and glitter.

Cover the work area with plastic or newspapers, and give a star to each child. Instruct them to write their name in the middle of one of the sides. Then explain that they should put glue, except on their names, and then sprinkle the glitter on it. Eliminate excess by shaking the figure gently. Repeat the operation on the other side, covering the entire star. Let the stars dry for at least 24 hours.

Tell your students that they can take their work home the following week. When the stars dry, make a small hole, and put thread or yarn through it so they can hang.

Attendance sheet

Hand out the figure of the shepherds (Cut-Out Section pg. 125) and have the children paste it in the space for the third Sunday of December. Congratulate those who are about to complete the attendance sheet. Using the figures, briefly review the previous two lessons. Tell them that today's story is about something special that happened to a group of shepherds.

BIBLE STORY

Shepherds receive Good News

"This is terrible!" exclaimed Joseph. "So many people came to Bethlehem to fulfill the order of the governor that there is nowhere to spend the night. All the inns are full!"

Mary sighed. She was so tired from the long trip they had made. Suddenly, she said, "Look, I see a light in that window. Maybe there is a room for us there."

"I doubt it," said Joseph.

"Please, Joseph, try it. I'm very tired and we need a place where we can sleep."

Joseph went to ask, but there was also no rooms available at that inn.

Joseph and Mary walked away slowly.

"They look so tired," the innkeeper thought. "I feel bad for them. Maybe I can find a way to help them."

"Wait a moment!" the innkeeper shouted. "I have a stable in the back. Maybe you could spend the night there, although it's just a barn. There is clean straw where you can rest."

"If it's warm and dry, we'll be fine," Joseph replied. "My wife is very tired and needs a place to sleep."

That night was very special because Jesus was born. Mary wrapped her little baby in cloth and lulled him to sleep. In the stable, there was no cradle for Jesus, but Joseph put clean straw in the manger, the place where they put food for the animals.

On the outskirts of Bethlehem, there was a group of shepherds in the field, taking care of their sheep.

"The sky is clear tonight. How the stars shine!" said a shepherd.

"Look!" exclaimed another, pointing to the sky. "See that bright light there?"

"What could it be?" they asked each other in amazement.

"It's an angel!" the shepherds exclaimed. "He is an angel of God!"

The angel told them, "Don't be afraid. I bring you Good News that will be a great joy to all the people. Today, in the city of David, a Savior has been born, who is Christ the Lord. You will find him lying in a manger, wrapped in swaddling clothes."

Suddenly, the sky was filled with angels who sang: "Glory to God in the highest and on earth peace, good will towards men!"

"Did you hear that?" a shepherd asked.

"Of course!" answered another. "It's the most wonderful news I've ever heard! It's happened as the prophets had announced."

"Then let's go to Bethlehem to see that which God has announced to us," one of them suggested, and the others agreed.

The shepherds went quickly to Bethlehem and there they found the baby in the manger, just as the angel had told them.

"It's true. Everything was fulfilled as the angel announced. He is the Messiah!" they repeated to each other.

The shepherds were very joyful, and they told the Good News of the birth of Jesus, the Son of God, to all the people they met.

ACTIVITIES

Peace to the world!

Hand out the student worksheets, scissors and glue. Allow time for the children to cut out the figures from the bottom of Lesson 52 and paste them in order, based on what they learned in the Bible story.

Ask some volunteers to tell some portion of the story using the figures. Encourage them to tell others the Good News of the birth of the Messiah.

Find the Good News

Ask your class to go to the next page of their worksheets. Tell them to help the biblical characters find the path that leads them to Jesus. Use a different color to trace the path of each character.

Tell them: When the shepherds heard the Good News of the birth of Jesus, they ran to Bethlehem to meet the newborn baby. After seeing Jesus, they told everyone about this event. You can also help others know the Good News, telling them that the reason for Christmas is to celebrate that Jesus, the Son of God, came to earth to save us.

Christmas songs

Lead a time of Christmas carols and let them accompany themselves with homemade instruments. Here we suggest how to prepare some.

You will need: glass bottles or glasses of the same thickness and size, seeds, buttons and plastic containers.

Ask the children to pour different amounts of water into the bottles or glasses; this way they will obtain different tonalities when hitting them with a pencil. Then, put the seeds or buttons inside the plastic containers to use them as rattles.

If there are rhythm instruments in your church, use them also in this time of praise to celebrate the birth of Jesus. Explain to your students that one way to praise God is by singing, as the angels did the night Jesus was born.

Memorization

Ahead of time, hide the cards you used in the previous lesson and ask the children to find them. Then, organize small groups so that in the shortest possible time they put the verse in order and say it out loud.

Repeat the exercise until everyone has participated.

To end

Give thanks to God in prayer for having fulfilled his promises by sending Jesus into the world, and then sing songs of praise. Remind the class that the important thing at Christmas is to celebrate that Jesus came to earth to save mankind from their sins.

notes

Lesson 53
Good News for Simeon and Anna

Biblical References: Luke 2:21-40
Lesson Objective: That the students learn that through Jesus Christ, God fulfilled His promise to send a Savior to the world.
Memory Verse: *Today in the town of David a Savior has been born to you; he is the Messiah, the Lord* (Luke 2:11).

PREPARE YOURSELF TO TEACH!

Today is a special day for your students. Since they have just celebrated Christmas, we suggest that you flexible in class today. Maybe some children want to tell what they did with their family, or maybe mention the gifts they received. After listening carefully, direct the conversation towards the teaching of this unit: the birth of Jesus, the Son of God. Encourage them to imagine the emotion that Simeon and Anna felt when they first saw Jesus, the Messiah. Although he was only a little baby, these servants of God knew that in him, the prophecies had been fulfilled, and that he would be the Savior of the world.

BIBLICAL COMMENTARY

Luke 2: 21-40. Joseph and Mary faithfully fulfilled the laws of God; therefore, when Jesus was eight days old, he was circumcised according to custom. Forty days after his birth, it was time to take him to the Temple to present him before the Lord. The Mosaic Law required that the first-born males be dedicated to God.

Joseph and Mary also brought a pair of turtledoves or two pigeons to be sacrificed in a ceremony that symbolized the purification of Mary after childbirth.

That day in the Temple, they met Simeon and Anna, two faithful servants of God. That day the Holy Spirit guided Simeon to go to the Temple. God had assured him that he would not die before seeing the Messiah.

When he saw Jesus, he knew instantly that He was the chosen one, sent by God to deliver Israel; and he took Him in his arms, blessing God.

Anna, who had been widowed 84 years ago, approached Jesus' parents. She also recognized Jesus the Messiah, and praised God for His faithfulness.

The Holy Spirit had spoken to the hearts of these servants, telling them who the Messiah was.

Do you feel the same joy that Simeon and Anna felt when they saw Jesus? Do you thank God for revealing Jesus to you personally? Your grateful heart and spirit of praise will encourage children to show gratitude to God.

DEVELOPMENT OF THE LESSON

Choose some of the following activities to make the study of biblical truth more relevant and enjoyable.

Simeon and Anna

Write on cards the letters that form the names of Simeon and Anna. Mix them up and place them on a table. Then, ask several children to put them in order to form the names. Give time for everyone to try. When done, tape or glue the letters together and hang the names in a visible place in the room.

Gather your students and tell them: *These are the names of two people who loved God and rejoiced at the birth of Jesus. We'll learn more about them in our Bible story.*

Attendance sheet

Distribute the figure of Simeon and Anna from the Cut-Out Section (pg. 125), and have your students paste it in the correct space on their attendance sheet. Then, ask them to draw a picture of themselves in the last space under Simeon and Anna. As they work, remind them that God chooses special people to help Him carry out His plans.

Review each of the stories they learned. Tell them that just as God worked through all those important biblical characters, He also wants to work through them.

BIBLE STORY

Good News for Simeon and Anna

"When will I see the Messiah that God promised?" Simeon wondered every day. "Will it be today?"

Simeon was a very good man who loved God. He liked to hear the messages of hope that announced the arrival of a Savior. God had told him that he would know the Messiah before he died. But Simeon, being very old, wondered how and when he would see the chosen one of God.

One day the Holy Spirit led Simeon to the Temple, so he walked until he reached the main courtyard. As always, there were a lot of people gathered. People from everywhere were coming to worship God. Some offered sacrifices, while others prayed special prayers. The new parents took their newborns to dedicate them to God.

In the middle of the crowd, Simeon saw a man and a woman who were taking their baby to dedicate him. Somehow he knew that the baby was special, and decided to approach. Although the couple looked poor, and the sacrifice they were going to offer was one of the smallest that the law allowed, there was something different about them.

When Simeon saw the baby, he was sure that it was the child he had expected to see for so long. Then he took him in his arms and exclaimed, "Lord, now I can die in peace because my eyes have seen the salvation you prepared in the presence of all people!"

"This is amazing!" said Joseph and Mary in awe.

At that time, an old woman named Anna also approached them to see the baby Jesus. She was very wise and had devoted her entire life to serving God. When she looked at the baby, she recognized him immediately.

"Thank God!" she exclaimed. "What a wonderful day! We have seen the promised Messiah of God who came into the world to save us from our sins."

ACTIVITIES

Jesus is the promised Messiah

Hand out the worksheets for Lesson 53. Instruct them to cut through the vertical black line at the bottom. Then, fold the page along the dotted lines to create a three-dimensional stage. Give them the figures of Joseph and Marry (Cut-out Section pg. 127)

Encourage them to use their figures and the stage to recreate the story in which Simeon and Ana meet baby Jesus.

Good News for you

Hand out pencils so that the children, can complete the crossword puzzle on the next page, using the keywords provided.

Then, ask them to fill in the blanks of the sentences with the same words of the crossword puzzle. When they finish, they can read the sentences out loud. Encourage them to obey God and trust His promises.

Memorization

This is the last lesson of the unit, and it is very possible that most of your students already know the memory verse. If possible, ask the Sunday School director or pastor if they will give your students the opportunity to tell what they learned in the service.

To end

Since this is the last lesson of the book, prepare a recognition for the students who faithfully worked throughout the year. Remind them that the teachings they learned are biblical truths that God wants them to apply to their daily lives.

Gather them together to pray. Give thanks to God for having fulfilled his promise by sending Jesus as Savior of the world. Also thank them for the year of work in the class, and intercede for the requests that the children have.

If you have time and resources, organize a simple celebration as a way to close the course. Do not stop praying for your students and their spiritual growth, even when they are no longer in your class.

www.ingramcontent.com/pod-product-compliance
Lightning Source LLC
Chambersburg PA
CBHW081346040426
42450CB00015B/3320